OXFORD
UNIVERSITY PRESS

ASPIRE
SUCCEED
PROGRESS

Essential Business Studies
for Cambridge IGCSE®
2nd Edition

Robert Dransfield
Leslie Garrett
Jane King

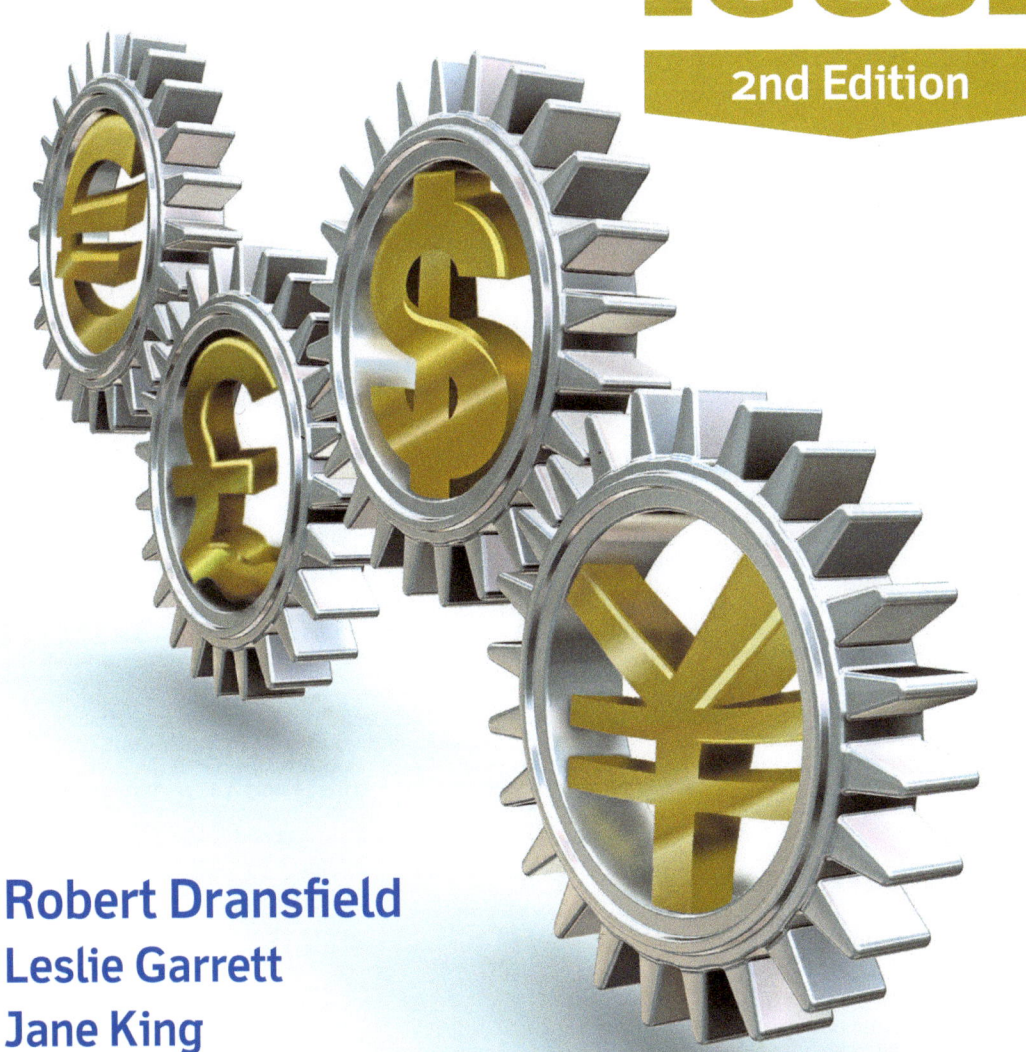

Oxford excellence for Cambridge IGCSE®

OXFORD

OXFORD
UNIVERSITY PRESS

Great Clarendon Street, Oxford, OX2 6DP, United Kingdom

Oxford University Press is a department of the University of Oxford.
It furthers the University's objective of excellence in research, scholarship,
and education by publishing worldwide. Oxford is a registered trade mark of
Oxford University Press in the UK and in certain other countries.

Text © Robert Dransfield 2012, 2014; Leslie Garrett, Jane King 2014
Illustrations © Oxford University Press 2014

The moral rights of the authors have been asserted.

First published in 2012 by Nelson Thornes Ltd

This edition published in 2014

All rights reserved. No part of this publication may be reproduced,
stored in a retrieval system, or transmitted, in any form or by any
means, without the prior permission in writing of Oxford University
Press, or as expressly permitted by law, by licence or under terms
agreed with the appropriate reprographics rights organization.
Enquiries concerning reproduction outside the scope of the above
should be sent to the Rights Department, Oxford University Press,
at the address above.

You must not circulate this work in any other form and you must
impose this same condition on any acquirer.

British Library Cataloguing in Publication Data
Data available

9780198399568

10 9 8 7 6 5 4 3 2 1

Printed in Great Britain by CPI Group (UK) Ltd., Croydon CR0 4YY

® IGCSE is the registered trademark of Cambridge International Examinations.

Acknowledgements

Page make-up: OKS Prepress, India

Illustrations: Bridget Dowty (c/o Graham Cameron Illustration), David Russell Illustration and Fakenham Photosetting

Cover image: © Purestock/Alamy

The publishers would like to thank the following for permission to use their copyright material:

AFP/Getty Images 2.1.2; 2.2.4; 4.3.1; 5.3.2; 6.1.1; © age fotostock/Alamy 5.3.2; Art Directors & Trip 1.4.4; 4.3.1; 6.3.2; AP/Press Association Images 1.5.2; Bonux 3.1.1b; Centennial Coal 5.5.4; Charles Bowman/Photolibrary/Getty Images 4.1.2; 2009 ChinaFotoPress/Getty Images 3.3.4; Construction Photography/Corbis 2.3.5; Chris Howes/Wild Places Photography/Alamy 4.2.3; dbimages/Alamy 1.4.3; DBURK/Alamy 4.1.1; Dyson 1.3.1; Elaine Gilligan/FoF EWNI. 6.2.4; Ford 3.4.1; © 2014 THE FORD MOTOR COMPANY 2.1.3; Fotolia 1.1.1; 1.2.2; 3.1.4; 5.1.1; 6.3.3; Getty Images 3.1.2; 3.2.1; Getty Images/John Burke 1.4.1c; H.J.Heinz Co. Ltd 3.4.3; Images of Africa Photobank/Alamy 3.3.5; iStockphoto 1.2.1; 1.3.4; 1.4.1b; 2.2.3; 5.5.3; Jagadeesh/Reuters/Corbis 4.4.1; Jeff Greenberg/Alamy 4.1.4; JOHN COGILL/AP/Press Association Images 2.1.1; Juice Images/Alamy 1.3.2; KEITH BEDFORD/LANDOV;

Press Association Images 3.3.1; 5.1.3; Kenya Airways Europe 2.4.3; MB /Alamy 3.1.3; Mitchell Kanashkevich/Getty Images 6.2.3; mohammad asad/Demotix/Press Association Images 5.1.2b; PAWAN KUMAR/Reuters/Corbis 1.5.3; PhotosIndia.com LLC/Alamy 1.3.3; Rafiqur Rahman/Reuters/Corbis 6.2.1; REX/Image Broker 2.1.4; REX/Pat McEnery 2.3.4; REX/Sipa Press 2.3.3; REX/Top Photo Group 6.1.4; Richard Drew/AP/Press Association Images 1.5.1; RubberBall/Alamy 1.4.1a; Photograph courtesy of Singapore Airlines 1.1.2; Still Pictures/Robert Harding World Imagery 4.2.2; Stock Connection/Rex Features 5.1.2a; Suzy Oakes (www.mill-road.com) 6.1.2; Toyota PLC 4.1.3; 5.1.4; Triangle Images/Getty Images 2.4.2; UIG via Getty Images 2.1.5.

Although we have made every effort to trace and contact all
copyright holders before publication, this has not been possible in all
cases. If notified, the publisher will rectify any errors or omissions at
the earliest opportunity.

Links to third party websites are provided by Oxford in good faith
and for information only. Oxford disclaims any responsibility for
the materials contained in any third party website referenced in
this work.

Contents

	Introduction	v
	How to use the practice questions, and Command words explained	1

Unit 1 Understanding business activity

1.1	Business activity	2
1.1.1	The purpose and nature of business activity	2
1.1.2	The importance of specialisation	4
1.2	Classification of businesses	6
1.2.1	Types of business activity	6
1.2.2	Private and public sector businesses	8
1.3	Enterprise, business growth and size	10
1.3.1	Characteristics of successful entrepreneurs	10
1.3.2	Contents of a business plan and how business plans assist entrepreneurs	12
1.3.3	Why and how government supports business start-ups	14
1.3.4	Business growth and measurement of size	16
1.3.5	Why businesses fail	18
1.4	Types of business organisation	20
1.4.1	Sole traders and partnerships	20
1.4.2	Other types of business organisation	22
1.4.3	Objectives, growth and business organisation	24
1.4.4	Limited and unlimited liability	26
1.4.5	Business organisations in the public sector	28
1.5	Business objectives and stakeholder objectives	30
1.5.1	Business objectives	30
1.5.2	Stakeholders and their different objectives	32
1.5.3	Aims of the private and public sectors	34
	Practice questions	36

Unit 2 People in business

2.1	Motivating workers	38
2.1.1	Motivation	38
2.1.2	Why people work	40
2.1.3	Key motivational theories	42
2.1.4	Financial rewards	44
2.1.5	Non-financial rewards	46
2.2	Organisation and management	48
2.2.1	Roles and responsibilities	48
2.2.2	The role of management	50
2.2.3	Leadership styles	52
2.2.4	Trade unions	54
2.3	The workforce	56
2.3.1	The recruitment and selection process	56
2.3.2	Recruiting and selecting in practice	58
2.3.3	Training	60
2.3.4	Dismissal and redundancy	62
2.3.5	Employment legislation	64
2.4	Internal and external communication	66
2.4.1	Communication	66
2.4.2	Internal communication	68
2.4.3	External communication	70
	Practice questions	72

Unit 3 Marketing

3.1	Marketing, competition and the customer	74
3.1.1	The role of marketing in a business	74
3.1.2	Market changes	76
3.1.3	Market segmentation	78
3.1.4	Mass markets and niche markets	80
3.2	Market research	82
3.2.1	Primary and secondary market research	82
3.2.2	Presentation and use of results	84
3.3	The marketing mix	86
3.3.1	The four Ps	86
3.3.2	The product	88
3.3.3	The price	90
3.3.4	Place – distribution channels	92
3.3.5	Promotion	94
3.3.6	Technology and the marketing mix	96
3.4	Marketing strategy	98
3.4.1	Elements of a marketing strategy	98
3.4.2	Legal controls related to marketing	100
3.4.3	Problems of entering new markets abroad	102
	Practice questions	104

Contents

Unit 4	**Operations management**	
4.1	Production of goods and services	106
4.1.1	The meaning of production	106
4.1.2	Methods of production	108
4.1.3	Lean production	110
4.1.4	How technology has changed production methods	112
4.2	Costs, scale of production and break-even analysis	114
4.2.1	Costs and classification of costs	114
4.2.2	Scale of production	116
4.2.3	Break-even analysis and cost-based decision making	118
4.3	Achieving quality production	120
4.3.1	Quality	120
4.4	Choosing locations	122
4.4.1	Factors influencing location and relocation	122
	Practice questions	124

Unit 5	**Financing business activity**	
5.1	Business finance: needs and sources	126
5.1.1	The need for finance	126
5.1.2	Major sources of finance	128
5.1.3	Sources of internal and external finance	130
5.1.4	How to choose finance	132
5.2	Financial information and decision making	134
5.2.1	Cash and cash-flow forecasts	134
5.3	Income statements	136
5.3.1	Profit	136
5.3.2	The function of profit	138
5.3.3	Income statements	140
5.4	Balance sheets	142
5.4.1	Main elements of the balance sheet	142
5.5	Analysis of accounts	144
5.5.1	Financial statements	144
5.5.2	Financial statements (continued)	146
5.5.3	Working capital	148
5.5.4	Users of accounts	150
	Practice questions	152

Unit 6	**External influences on business activity**	
6.1	Government economic objectives and policies	154
6.1.1	Government intervention	154
6.1.2	The business cycle	156
6.1.3	Government economic control and business activity	158
6.1.4	Tax and interest rates	160
6.2	Environmental and ethical issues	162
6.2.1	The impact of business activity on the environment	162
6.2.2	External costs and benefits	164
6.2.3	Ethics in business	166
6.2.4	Legal controls over business activity	168
6.3	Business and the international economy	170
6.3.1	Globalisation	170
6.3.2	Multinational companies	172
6.3.3	Exchange rates	174
	Practice questions	176
	Glossary of key terms	178
	Index	183

Additional resources are available online at: www.oxfordsecondary.com/9780198399568

Introduction

This book is designed specifically for Cambridge International Examinations (Cambridge) IGCSE® Business Studies (syllabus 0450). Experienced examiners have been involved in all aspects of the book, including detailed planning to ensure that the content adheres to the syllabus as closely as possible.

Using this book will ensure that you are well prepared for the exam at this level, and also studies beyond the IGCSE level in Business Studies. The features below are designed to make learning as interesting and effective as possible:

STUDY TIP

These give you hints on how to avoid common errors or provide useful advice on how to tackle questions.

TOPIC AIMS

These are at the start of each spread and will tell you what you should be able to do at the end of the spread.

SUMMARY QUESTIONS

These questions are at the end of each spread and allow you to test your understanding of the work covered in the spread.

CASE STUDY | Subject

These are real-life examples to illustrate the subject matter within the unit, and are accompanied by questions to test your understanding.

KEY POINTS

These summarise the most important things to learn from the spread.

DID YOU KNOW?

These are interesting facts chosen to stimulate your interest in business studies. Make sure you read them all, as some "Did you know?" facts are needed for the examination.

At the end of each chapter, there is a double page of examination-style practice questions. These include both short-answer summary questions to test your understanding and learning of the unit just covered, and longer-answer questions preceded by a short scenario.

All the questions feature the command words that you will find in the exam. Explanatory notes on these, along with some guidance on answering the questions, are provided here.

The questions, example answers, marks awarded and/or comments that appear in this book and on our website were written by the authors. In examination, the way marks would be awarded to answers like these may be different

At the end of the book, you will find a glossary of the key terms highlighted in bold in the text.

v

How to use the practice questions and Command words explained

The questions at the end of each unit in the book are to help you practise your exam technique after completing all the work in the unit. You should answer them without referring to the information in the book or your notes.

The short-answer questions test your knowledge and understanding of what you have learnt. Generally, these will ask you to state, identify, define and explain one or a number of factors, differences or meanings. Your answers will be fairly brief, perhaps bullet points, but avoid single-word 'lists', especially where an explanation is required. Do not spend too long or write too much – 2–4 lines is sufficient for these answers. Where an example is required, give one from your own experience, either as a consumer or as an observer of your local business environment.

The longer-answer questions introduce you to the 'case study' approach, in which questions are based on a specific business scenario. Read the material carefully, because this will help you to give an answer that is appropriate to the business concerned. So, for example, do not recommend TV advertising for a small business; do not suggest 'access to raw materials' as a location factor for a retail business, as this is only really applicable to a production business. Read the case study carefully and try to put yourself in the role of the business person in the text.

Make sure you can answer the following:

- Is this business large or small?
- What are they selling – a product or a service?
- Is the business objective profit or another, such as public service?
- Who are the customers?
- What challenges does the business face (e.g. competition)?

Make sure you refer to the circumstances of the business, rather than just mentioning the company by name. Consider both sides of an issue and come to a supported conclusion.

The instruction in the question is given by the command word: as the term suggests, this tells you what is required. The following is a list of the command words you are likely to see in your examination.

Calculate, e.g. 'Calculate the gross profit margin of a business.' You need to do some mathematics to produce an answer. Always show your workings.

Consider, e.g. 'Consider the two options given in the case study.' You need to weigh up the merits of a situation or decision and give the opposing view as well.

Define, e.g. 'Define market research.' State the exact meaning of the term; this will be a short answer, sometimes including an example to illustrate it.

Explain, e.g. 'Explain what is meant by a price elastic demand.' This term enables you to show your understanding of a term or topic. You can do this by including an example or a descriptive development.

Give, e.g. 'Give an example of a fixed cost.' This is a short-answer command, requiring you to state a fact or provide an example to demonstrate your understanding.

Identify, e.g. 'Identify two factors a company should consider before deciding to issue more shares.' 'Identify' (or 'State') requires you to select from a number of possibilities. Only a brief answer is necessary, so a list may be fine, but if you are unsure, include a sentence of clarification or an example.

Justify, e.g. 'Should company X buy more machinery? Justify your answer.' This is a longer answer in which you should support your answer with reasons.

Outline, e.g. 'Outline the main features of a business partnership.' You should give a short description (in this example, of the main features of the partnership).

Recommend, e.g. 'Recommend which option the company should take.' You should make a positive suggestion, usually with reasons that support your ideas.

State, e.g. 'State two features of a sole-trader business.' Provide a short answer; this is usually intended for you to show your knowledge. (See also the notes for 'Identify' above.)

Why, e.g. 'Why has the market share of the company fallen?' You should give reasons for an event or outcome and provide some development of the points you make in your answer.

1 Understanding business activity

1.1 Business activity

1.1.1 The purpose and nature of business activity

TOPIC AIMS

Students should be able to:

- understand the purpose of business activity
- understand the concept of adding value and how value can be increased
- understand the concepts of needs, wants and scarcity and opportunity cost.

ACTIVITY

Which of the following would you describe as your needs and which would you describe as additional wants? Justify the choices you make.

A midday or evening meal / a bed to sleep in / a bar of soap / a visit to the cinema / a blanket / a roof over your head at night / a toothbrush / a computer / a bottle of water / new clothes / a book to read.

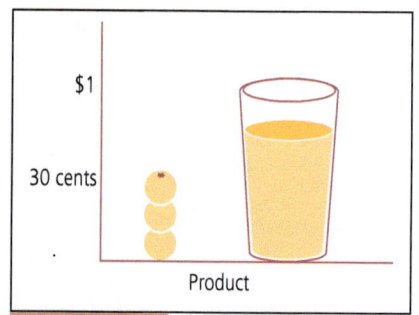

Figure 1.1.1.1 Value adding. Increasing the worth of 3 oranges bought for 30 cents to a glass of orange juice sold for $1

Satisfying wants and needs

Businesses are usually set up to satisfy the wants and needs of customers. Everybody has wants and needs. We *need* food, drink, clothing, shelter and other essentials to stay alive. Other things are not quite so essential, but we still *want* them so our life can be enjoyable.

Business activity is concerned with satisfying these wants and needs. The act of preparing a good or service for sale is called production.

Businesses are set up to satisfy our needs by providing physical goods (manufacturing) and services. When you visit a restaurant not only are you provided with a physical product, the food, but you also receive a service in the form of a member of the restaurant staff bringing the food to the table and making sure that you have everything that you want to enjoy the meal.

Adding value

Businesses aim to provide products and services to customers that are more attractive than those of their competitors. Everything that a business does to make a good more desirable is **adding value**.

For example, cold fresh orange juice is enjoyed across the globe. Oranges are grown in temperate climates such as California (United States), Libya (North Africa) and Italy (Southern Europe). The oranges are transported in lorries, freight trains and ships across the globe. Hotels and restaurants buy and squeeze the oranges to make a fresh drink for the end customer. Ice may be added to cool the juice.

A restaurant selling fresh squeezed orange juice might buy three oranges at 10 cents each (totalling 30 cents) to make a glass of fresh orange juice which it sells to a customer for $1. The value added by the restaurant is therefore 70 cents. $1 – 30 cents = 70 cents.

Scarcity

We cannot have everything we want: we have to make *choices*. This is because resources are scarce: there are not enough for all the things that we would like to do. If we turn a field or park into a car park, then we lose the green space. Choices have to be made all the time.

In the same way, a business makes choices. Farmers make choices about when and how to improve their land. Farmers in Jamaica can decide to grow sugar cane or coffee. They sometimes make choices about who to sell their produce to (e.g. at a local market or to an agent of a food company).

Stage of production:	How value is added
1 Growing the oranges	Farmers look after the orange trees for several years before they give fruit. Each year they must be treated against pests.
2 Transporting the oranges	Fresh ripe oranges are transported closer to market.
3 Preparing the oranges	The juice is squeezed from the oranges and ice added.
4 Serving the customer	The juice is presented to the end consumer in a polite and friendly way.

Figure 1.1.1.2 Adding value to a product: the customer benefits from value being added at each stage of production

Enjoying fresh, cold orange juice – value is added in growing the oranges and also in serving the juice to the end consumer.

STUDY TIP

One way of making a product more desirable, and so adding value, is by branding. A brand is any distinguishing mark that is associated with a product. Consumers are often attracted by brand names and many people will pay more for branded products.

DID YOU KNOW?

Opportunity cost is the term used to describe the cost of a choice made in terms of the next best alternative. For instance, the opportunity cost of the choice made by a business to buy a new computer may be the building repairs that can no longer be afforded.

SUMMARY QUESTIONS

1. In your own words, write definitions for: needs, wants, scarcity, choice, opportunity cost, adding value.
2. How might packaging of a product add value to it? Explain your answers.
3. How would you explain the difference between wants and needs? Give further examples to show the difference.

KEY POINTS

1. Everyone has basic needs for food, shelter and clothing in order to survive. On top of these we have additional wants.
2. Businesses are set up to meet the needs of consumers.
3. Businesses produce goods to help consumers satisfy their wants and needs.
4. Businesses add value, to make products more desirable and suitable for customers.

3

1.1.2 The importance of specialisation

TOPIC AIMS

Students should be able to:
- explain the importance of specialisation
- outline the advantages and disadvantages of specialisation.

To specialise is to concentrate on a particular task. Specialisation in business takes a number of forms:

- Firms specialise in particular activities and products.
- Factors of production specialise in particular areas of production.
- Countries specialise on certain lines of economic activity.

Specialisation by businesses

Firms concentrate on particular areas of activity in which they have built up a competitive advantage over rivals. Competitive advantage involves superiority in terms of having a better product, better marketing of a product, cheaper prices or some other advantage. For example, Shell the oil company concentrates on the oil and gas sector, Singapore Airlines focuses on luxury long-distance air travel, and Intel concentrates on producing computer chips. There are two important aspects of specialisation by firms:

- Firms concentrate on doing things that they do better than rivals.
- Firms concentrate on doing those things that involve the best use of resources by that company. For example, Shell could potentially focus on another industry, e.g. retailing. However, over time Shell has built up a skilled workforce, strong products, and research and development into new products – so that today it is a really efficient operator in the oil and gas industry. Shell's most efficient use of its existing resources is therefore in oil and gas extraction, refining and distribution to the end consumer. Shell therefore specialises in what it does best. Shell can be said to have a comparative advantage in using its resources in oil and gas production. Compared with all the other ways that the company can use its resources the greatest advantages can be gained through specialising in oil and gas.

Singapore Airlines focuses on its comparative advantage in producing high-quality, long-haul air travel.

Specialisation by factors of production

Factors of production are the resources that go into making products. There are four categories of factors of production – land, labour, capital and enterprise. Land not only includes physical land but also other natural resources, e.g. rivers and seas providing fish stocks. Labour consists of the physical and mental effort of workers. Capital includes all those items that go into producing other things, e.g. machines and tools. Enterprise is the factor that brings other factors together to produce goods. Entrepreneurs are people who take risks by running businesses. Each of these factors will specialise on particular activities and lines of production depending on the areas in which they have greatest comparative advantage.

The division of labour is one example of specialisation. Division of labour involves breaking down a production process into a number of clearly defined specialist tasks. The reason for doing this is that the total output of a group can be increased if, instead of each person trying to do everything, each one specialises in a particular skill or activity (i.e. the activity in which they have the greatest comparative

STUDY TIP

Specialisation in individual businesses, linked with division of labour, is usually applicable in larger businesses that have enough staff to split into functional areas.

advantage). Similarly, a piece of land will normally be used for the purpose that yields the highest return, e.g. a site for an office block, or for growing potatoes, or a swimming pool. Machinery can be used for producing particular components or products. Entrepreneurs will concentrate on enterprises in which they have the greatest ability.

Specialisation by region or country

Regions and countries focus on those products where they have the greatest comparative advantage – for example, today Scotland concentrates on alternative energy (e.g. wave and wind power), whisky and water, whereas China concentrates on textiles and a range of manufactured goods.

Advantages of specialisation	Disadvantages of specialisation
Resources can be focused on their most productive lines.	Specialisation can lead to over-reliance on a set task or product. When the product or task is no longer required the specialist becomes redundant.
Focusing on a set task enables an individual, company, region or country to become more productive in that task.	Focusing on set tasks means that specialists spend all their time doing the same or similar things with little opportunity for variety.
Larger outputs can be produced at lower unit costs.	Narrow specialism might make it difficult for businesses, individuals, regions and countries to respond to change because they lack flexibility.
Concentration of specialists enables the sharing of knowledge and skills between specialists.	Where tasks are closely linked, delays or hold-ups in one area can slow down the whole process.

CASE STUDY: Prawn hatcheries in Bangladesh

The development of freshwater prawn hatcheries in Bangladesh illustrates the benefits and drawbacks of specialisation. In recent years the number of freshwater prawn hatcheries has increased substantially as these hatcheries supply the large global export trade. Today there are estimated to be 120 000 farmers operating in this field in Bangladesh. Hatcheries have replaced traditional agriculture in which farmers produced many different crops for their own consumption and for sale to others. Prawn farming is labour-intensive work. Prawns command good prices on international markets, but the product is notoriously susceptible to health issues which can lead to import bans in some countries when health standards fall below expected requirements.

Questions

1. How can Bangladeshi farmers and Bangladesh as a country benefit from the freshwater prawn industry?
2. How can Bangladeshi farmers and Bangladesh as a country lose out from specialisation in the prawn industry?

DID YOU KNOW?

Comparative advantage is a situation in which an individual, company, region or country can produce a good at a lower opportunity cost than a competitor.

KEY POINTS

1. Specialisation is the focus on specific tasks and activities.
2. Specialisation can lead to increased production levels.
3. Specialisation can result in over-concentration on particular activities and products.

SUMMARY QUESTIONS

1. Identify a business that you consider to be a specialist business. How can this firm be said to have a comparative advantage in its main line of production?
2. Give two examples of specialist workers and specialist machinery in (a) agriculture, (b) manufacturing and (c) service industries.

1.2 Classification of businesses

1.2.1 Types of business activity

TOPIC AIMS

Students should be able to:
- describe and classify business activity in terms of primary, secondary and tertiary sectors:
  - understand the basis of classification
  - use examples to demonstrate understanding
- demonstrate an understanding of changes that have taken place in these sectors within your own country:
  - identify the key features of the structure of your own national economy.

A haircut is a service provided by a skilled hairdresser.

STUDY TIP

The process of shifting resources from primary to secondary activities is industrialisation. More recent changes involving shifting more resources into tertiary activities is deindustrialisation.

Business activity is often broken down into three types:
- extractive (**primary industry**)
- manufacturing and construction (**secondary industry**)
- services (**tertiary sector**).

Brazil is the world's second-largest ethanol supplier after the United States. The following table shows the three stages involved in providing ethanol fuel for cars in Brazil.

Extractive industries

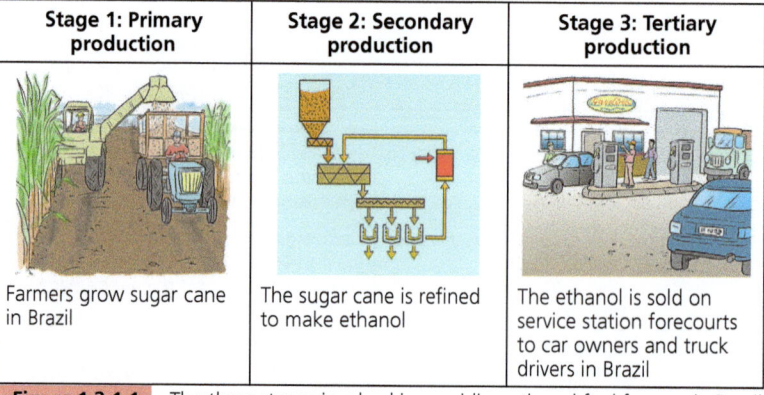

Stage 1: Primary production	Stage 2: Secondary production	Stage 3: Tertiary production
Farmers grow sugar cane in Brazil	The sugar cane is refined to make ethanol	The ethanol is sold on service station forecourts to car owners and truck drivers in Brazil

Figure 1.2.1.1 The three stages involved in providing ethanol fuel for cars in Brazil

Extractive, or primary, industries are concerned with using natural resources. They include farming, mining and oil drilling. Farmers grow and harvest crops and farm livestock, while miners take out fuel and minerals from the ground. Primary industries sometimes produce raw materials like iron ore (for making steel) and oil (for making petrol, plastics, fibres, etc.). They also produce finished products like fish and oranges.

Manufacturing and construction industries

Manufacturing and construction industries are concerned with making and assembling products. Manufacturers use raw materials and parts from other industries. Most products go through several stages of production: when the good is only partly made, it is a semi-manufactured good. Examples of manufactured products are furniture, cars, chocolate and oil rigs. An example of a semi-manufactured good would be the shell of an aeroplane that has not yet had the engine and inside furnishings (seats, etc.) added.

Service industries

Service, or tertiary, industries give something of value to people, but are not physical goods. You can physically touch or see a packet of biscuits, a bicycle or a computer. You cannot touch or hold a visit to the cinema or a lesson given to you in school: these are both services.

Other services include banks keeping your money safe, public transport carrying people around or hairdressers cutting your hair.

| CASE STUDY | Employment by major industry sector in different countries |

Employment is classified into different industries by a national classification system such as the Standard Industrial Classification (SIC) in the UK or the North American Industrial Classification System (NAICS) in North America. This identifies and classifies specific sectors, e.g. 11 Agriculture, Forestry, Fishing and Hunting, which is then broken down into further sectors, e.g. 111 Crop production, and then into types of crop production, e.g. 1111 Oilseed and grain farming. The latest forecast figures for the US for 2016 are that 1.6 per cent of the population will be employed in primary industry, 12.7 per cent in secondary industry, and the vast majority (85.7 per cent) in the tertiary sector. This data for the US contrasts with that of newly industrialised countries (NICs) such as Brazil. In Brazil, roughly 20 per cent of the population is still engaged in agriculture and other primary industries, and a further 14 per cent in manufacturing, with the remainder working in services.

Questions

1 In your country which is the largest sector of the economy: primary, secondary or tertiary?

2 What are the main types of industries involved in your largest sector?

3 What industrial classification system is used in your country? What industries are recognised in this classification?

SUMMARY QUESTIONS

1 The following statistics relate to employment by the industrial sector in China. (Source: *China Statistical Yearbook, 2012*)

	Primary (%)	Secondary (%)	Tertiary (%)
1978	70	18	12
1988	58	22	20
1998	50	23	27
2009	40	27	33

Describe the key trends that you see in the data. Explain why these changes might have occurred. Do you expect these trends to continue?

2 What are service industries? Give five examples of jobs in service industries.

3 State whether you would classify the following industries as primary, secondary or tertiary. Give reasons for your choices.

Construction / transportation and warehousing / retail trade / financial activities / manufacturing / mining / farming / educational services / leisure and hospitality / fishing.

DID YOU KNOW?

The process of development has involved the transformation of society over time. In the first wave of development the focus was on primary activity – particularly agriculture and fishing. In the second wave societies experienced an industrial revolution with the growth of manufacturing industry to become the main form of economic activity. In the (most recent) third wave, developed societies principally focus on tertiary (service sector) activity.

ACTIVITY

Group the following activities under the headings of Primary, Secondary and Tertiary Industry.

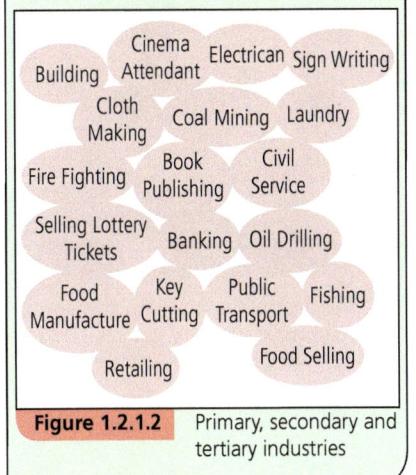

Cinema Attendant, Electrican, Sign Writing, Building, Cloth Making, Coal Mining, Laundry, Fire Fighting, Book Publishing, Civil Service, Selling Lottery Tickets, Banking, Oil Drilling, Food Manufacture, Key Cutting, Public Transport, Fishing, Retailing, Food Selling

Figure 1.2.1.2 Primary, secondary and tertiary industries

KEY POINTS

1 It is helpful to classify business activity into primary, secondary and tertiary sectors.

2 There has been a global increase in the tertiary sector.

1.2.2 Private and public sector businesses

TOPIC AIMS

Students should be able to:

- explain the purpose of business activity in terms of the objectives of non-profit-making activity, private enterprise and public enterprise
- classify business enterprises between private sector and public sector in a mixed economy.

The private and public sector

Another major classification is into the public and private sectors. The private sector consists of businesses that are owned by private individuals, e.g. people that own and run businesses directly themselves, and businesses that are owned by shareholders, i.e. people who have bought a share in a company (they have the right to share in the profits of the company and to appoint directors to run the business on their behalf).

Private enterprise organisations
Goals include
Making a profit
Other secondary goals

Public enterprise organisations
Goals include
Running public services well
Providing ferry and postal services to rural communities
Providing street lighting, police service

Figure 1.2.2.1 Goals of businesses in the public and private sector

In China many of the largest companies such as China Mobile are in the public sector, i.e. they are owned by the government.

Most economies in the world today consist of a mix of private sector and public sector enterprises and are hence called 'mixed economies'.

In some economies the majority of production is carried out by state-owned (i.e. government-owned) enterprises. For example, in China and Cuba government-owned enterprises (the public sector) are responsible for the majority of production. In contrast, in the US, Canada, Mexico, Japan and the EU countries the majority of production is carried out by private businesses in the private sector.

Over the last 20 years the size of the private sector has increased. For example, in countries such as China and Cuba, where in the past business activity was almost exclusively in government hands, the government has allowed an increasing number of private sector businesses to set up particularly in the small business sector, e.g. hairdressers, taxi firms, photocopying companies, etc. Increasingly the government in the People's Republic of China has encouraged the set up of large private sector businesses that can be competitive on the world stage, such as the computer company Lenovo.

You will see in Unit 2, however, that private enterprises may have additional, or secondary **objectives**. India's Tata Group of companies created India's first steel plant, hydroelectric plant and inorganic chemistry plant. Today the group has operations in six continents and produces many different goods. The group is not concerned solely with profits; however, in 1941 it created the Tata Memorial Hospital, India's first hospital for the treatment of cancer.

Setting up and running a private enterprise involves risk. The person who takes this risk is an **entrepreneur**. If the business succeeds, the entrepreneur makes a profit. Should it fail, he or she will be

STUDY TIP

The process of taking an activity into the public sector is nationalisation. Sometimes activities are denationalised or privatised. Think about why such changes might be necessary.

responsible for the losses. The loss could involve having to sell personal possessions, in order to meet the business debts.

Public enterprise

In many countries, the government is a major employer. Governments employ public sector workers to carry out work on their behalf, such as providing a police force, education and a health service. The size of the public sector varies from country to country. Figure 1.2.2.2 shows some of these differences.

The goal of a public sector enterprise such as Indian Railways is to provide an essential economic service for the nation. Hundreds of millions of people in India rely on the railway service to get around the country and to transport goods.

Public sector enterprises need to be carefully run. They are often funded by taxpayers' money, so they need to look after the taxpayers' interests by providing the best possible value for money.

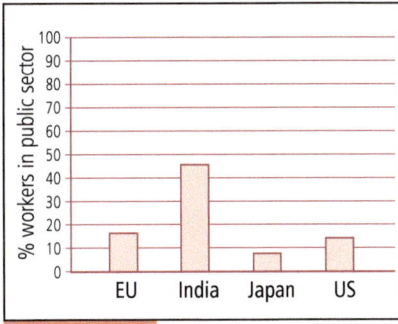

Figure 1.2.2.2 Public sector workers in four regions in 2013

> **DID YOU KNOW?**
>
> In India, large numbers of people work for government-owned businesses, including India's largest employer, Indian Railways. The energy companies are also state-owned, as is Indian Airlines.
>
> Indian Airlines is currently facing major competition from the new privately owned low-cost airlines, especially Indigo Airlines, India's fastest-growing business.

> **ACTIVITY**
>
> Identify a public sector company that operates in your country. When did this company become part of the public sector? What are the main activities of this company?

> **SUMMARY QUESTIONS**
>
> 1. Explain how goals of public sector organisations may differ from those in the private sector.
> 2. Read the following statements and then suggest whether the organisation is more likely to be in the private or public sector.
>   - Our goal is to make a profit for our owners. We will achieve this by providing excellent customer service.
>   - Our goal is to provide an efficient postal service to every single household in the country. This includes providing deliveries every day to out-of-the-way locations.
>   - Our goal has always been to make a profit. If we provide additional benefits to the wider community, this is a bonus.
> 3. Classify the following according to whether they are primary, secondary or tertiary and private or public sector.
>   - a A state-run mining company
>   - b A telecoms company owned by shareholders
>   - c A small family-run hotel company
>   - d A government-owned steel manufacturer
>   - e A joint venture between a family business in China operating in insurance and a foreign company.

> **KEY POINTS**
>
> 1. The private sector of the economy consists of firms that are owned by private individuals including shareholders.
> 2. The public sector of the economy is the state-run sector.
> 3. In recent years there has been a tendency in many economies for a reduction in the number of state-run enterprises.

1.3 Enterprise, business growth and size

1.3.1 Characteristics of successful entrepreneurs

TOPIC AIMS

Students should be able to:
- identify the characteristics of successful entrepreneurs.

Being enterprising

An entrepreneur is someone who not only comes up with a great new idea but is also able to put this idea into practice.

CASE STUDY — James Dyson and the Dyson Dual Cyclone

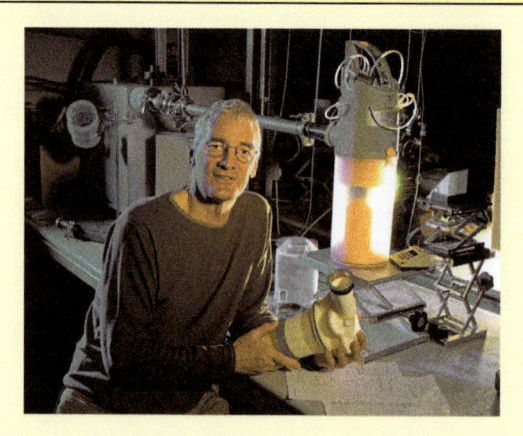

James Dyson was doing some housework in 1979. His first job was to vacuum the living room using a Hoover Junior machine. The vacuum cleaner that he was using employed the standard technology of the time – the air being sucked through the nozzle and the dirt and dust trapped in a cloth bag between the intake and the exhaust.

James felt that the system was very inefficient because there was so much dirt and dust that was not being sucked up. As a consumer he felt that the existing method did not fully meet his needs. He felt that given time he could add value to the machine to make it better.

James was already a well-known designer, having invented (among other things) the 'ballbarrow' (a wheelbarrow with a ball rather than a wheel). As chance would have it, his business was installing a powder coating plant for the ballbarrows. To capture dust that was not being sprayed into the barrows, they were using an industrial cyclone made of steel and about 6 m tall. Cyclone towers are a well-known industrial filtering system, with air being dragged into a tower and whirled around, at very fast speeds, forcing the dust against the outer wall of the cyclone. James realised that the cyclone system could be applied to vacuum cleaners to enable them to work more efficiently. He started to work on the task, which took him four years and 5 127 prototypes (i.e. trial models). He realised that for household vacuuming you need a dual cyclone – one to separate out larger items like cigarette ends and dog hairs and the second to catch the smaller particles. Unlike traditional vacuum cleaners, the Dyson Dual Cyclone does not use bags. The product has proved to be a great success story, revolutionising the industry and turning the Dyson company into a large and successful international business manufacturing and exporting the product across the globe.

Questions

1 How did James Dyson turn an idea into an effective product?

2 What does this case study tell you about the qualities of an effective entrepreneur?

Starting an enterprise

People like James Dyson start their own enterprise for a variety of reasons. Some have a bright idea that they think will make them rich (e.g. a ballbarrow or dual cyclone). Others find themselves unemployed and start their own business to survive. Some can only be themselves when they are their own boss. Others want to give something to the community and can see no other way of doing it except by setting up on their own. However, setting up an enterprise is not for everyone. It requires a lot of hard work and long hours to make an enterprise a success. It also requires a lot of attention to detail, not just the creation of exciting ideas. Often someone who is creative and imaginative (important qualities for an entrepreneur) will need a business partner with greater attention to detail and who can set firm commercial foundations in place (other qualities of an entrepreneur).

Characteristics of entrepreneurs

Generally speaking it is possible to identify a number of characteristics of entrepreneurs. As you work through the list consider whether the points apply to you.

Characteristics	Do you have these characteristics?
Logical, perceptive, organised, realistic, responsible – good at getting things done.	
Outgoing, confident.	
Good communicator – able to get a point across.	
Sociable, good leader – can win people over instead of irritating them.	
Single-minded, decisive, independent.	
Open-minded, able to take advice.	
Flexible, adaptable.	
Opportunist, risk taker, ambitious.	
Hard-working, committed, determined, 'get up and go' type.	
Tough – often the best test of a successful entrepreneur is their ability to deal with failure.	
Individual – not afraid to stand out from a crowd, or of what others think.	

STUDY TIP

Being enterprising does not always involve inventing a totally new product. An entrepreneur may find a new variation or style on an existing product, or a new process of production or selling.

KEY POINTS

The key characteristics of successful entrepreneurs include:
- the willingness to work long hours and to work hard
- willingness to take risks in order to establish a successful enterprise
- ability to take tough decisions and not to be put off by failure
- ability to spot new opportunities
- good communication skills and the ability to get on with people.

SUMMARY QUESTIONS

1 Identify a celebrated local entrepreneur in your country. To what extent does he or she have the characteristics that have been outlined in this unit?

2 How could you go about developing the characteristics required to be a successful entrepreneur?

3 What enterprising ideas do you have? What would you need to turn these ideas into a successful enterprise?

1.3.2 Contents of a business plan and how business plans assist entrepreneurs

TOPIC AIMS

Students should be able to:
- identify the contents of a business plan
- show how a business plan assists entrepreneurs.

How a business plan assists entrepreneurs

A good business idea on its own does not create a good business. What is required in addition is the ability to organise and plan.

A business plan is one of the key ingredients of any successful business, no matter how big or well established. If you want to start a business, it is vital. It helps you to anticipate problems and work out how to deal with them. It also gives essential information to the people whose support you need – particularly anyone lending you money.

A business plan is a complete description of a business and its plans for the next one to three years. It explains what the business does (or will do if it is a new business). It suggests who will buy the product or service and why. It provides financial forecasts demonstrating overall viability, and it indicates the finance available and explains the financial requirements.

The business plan should be presented in a form that can be quickly and easily understood. The main part of a business plan normally needs no more than 8–10 pages supported, if necessary, with more detailed appendices.

Contents of a business plan

A simple business plan should be clearly set out under the following headings:

1. Executive summary. A very brief summary of the key features of the business and the business plan.
2. The owner. This section should give some information about the owner (or owners) including their educational background and what they have done (previous work experience). It should contain the names and addresses of two referees.
3. The business. This should first contain the name and address of the business and then go on to give a detailed description of the product or service being offered, how and where it will be produced, who is likely to buy it, and in what quantities.
4. The market. This section will describe the market research that has been carried out, what it has revealed, and it should give details of prospective customers – how many there are, and how much they would be prepared to pay. It should also give details of the competition.
5. Advertising and promotion. This should give information about how the business will be publicised to potential customers. It should give details of likely costs.
6. Premises and equipment. This section should show that the business has considered a range of locations and then chosen the best site. It should also give details of planning regulations (if appropriate). Costs of premises and the need for equipment should be included.
7. Business organisation. State whether the enterprise will take the form of sole trader, partnership, company or cooperative.

Securing finance for a great idea requires the presentation of a business plan showing that the idea is a viable business proposition.

STUDY TIP

Remember that a business plan is a 'working document', against which targets may be monitored. A good business plan develops with the business and thus can change over time.

8 **Costings.** The business should give some indication of the cost of producing the product or service, and the prices it proposes to charge. It is then possible to make profit calculations.

9 **The finance.** This should give details of how the finance for the business is going to be raised. How much will come from savings? How much will need to be borrowed?

10 **Cash flow.** This should list all expected income and outgoings over the first year. Cash-flow calculations are important, but at this stage they can only be approximate.

11 **Expansion.** Finally, the business should given an indication of future plans. Does it want to keep on producing a steady output or is a dramatic expansion possible? Does it intend to add to its product range? What kind of new competition is likely to emerge, and how will the business deal with it?

DID YOU KNOW?

Presentation is crucial in setting out your business plan. Make sure that your plan is well set out, clear and well written. Photographs and illustrations may be useful in giving a clear indication of what you propose to make and/or sell.

CASE STUDY | An effective business plan

In 1.3.1 we saw how James Dyson was able to convert a great idea into a successful business. In order to secure finance for his ideas he would need to show his plans to outside investors and to lenders such as banks. The following things would help to convince them to finance the business:

1 The detailed research that had gone into perfecting the product (e.g. over 5000 prototypes) to come up with a working model.

2 They would have also wanted to see a demonstration of the final model of the product.

3 They would have wanted to check on the manufacturing costs to see how these compared with the price of the product.

4 They would want to know about the advertising and promotion of the model.

5 In particular they would want to know that there was a sufficiently large market for the product to make it worthwhile.

6 They would want to know about Dyson's track record as an entrepreneur and running a successful business.

7 They would want to know about the timing of inflows and outflows of cash to and from Dyson's business to make sure that he always had enough cash to pay his bills.

8 They would also want to know about ideas for future expansion of the business and what the financial implications of this would be.

Questions

1 Identify a business idea of your own. What does it entail? How would you be able to persuade potential investors that your idea is a good one?

2 What details would you need to include in a business plan if you were going to be able to convince investors to invest in you and your idea?

SUMMARY QUESTIONS

1 What are the most important details that should go into a business plan in relation to the following?

  a who the owner is

  b who makes up the market and market characteristics

  c finance of the business

  d potential profitability of the business.

2 When should you make out a business plan and how long should it be?

KEY POINTS

1 A business plan helps the entrepreneur to decide whether to proceed.

2 The plan can be presented to providers of finance.

3 The plan should give details of the owner, the idea, the market, the advertising and promotion, costs, cash flow and likely profits.

1.3.3 Why and how government supports business start-ups

TOPIC AIMS

Students should be able to:
- outline the reasons why government supports business start-ups
- explain how a government supports business.

Why government supports business start-ups

Small and medium-sized businesses (see 1.3.4) provide the engine of growth of economies across the globe. These relatively small companies provide about 90 per cent of all employment opportunities in many newly industrialising economies such as India. Business start-ups provide real opportunities for employment, not just among the people that set up these enterprises but among those that work for the enterprises. The Ministry of Micro, Small & Medium Enterprises in India has estimated that about 45 per cent of all manufacturing jobs are in this sector, as well as accounting for 40 per cent of all exports. There are about 30 million small enterprises in India.

Therefore, it is not surprising that governments across the globe support the set-up of new businesses as they:

- employ large numbers of people
- account for a large component of employment growth in countries
- account for a substantial component of the production of goods and services in economies
- enable equitable growth – in other words they provide good opportunities often for the poorer members of society
- account for a substantial proportion of the exports of a country
- encourage new ideas and new technologies that help a country to develop new opportunities.

Small enterprises also tend to be much more labour intensive than larger enterprises because they use less capital (e.g. machinery) and more physical labour (thus acting as major employers).

Government also recognises that the small firms of today will become the large firms of tomorrow.

Figure 1.3.3.1 In India the MSME provides a variety of support to start-up enterprises.

STUDY TIP

Governments may be keen to support small businesses, but they will usually only provide funding such as grants to an entrepreneur with a well thought through business plan and some funding of their own to contribute.

How government supports start-up enterprises

The three main ways in which government supports start-up enterprises are:

- by providing support with the start-up process. This includes providing help with advisers (e.g. showing how a business owner can create a business plan or acquire finance)
- by providing direct financial and other forms of help. Specific government grants and loans (e.g. related to the acquisition of capital/machinery/premises etc.; technical help through research and product development centres)
- by removing obstacles to the setting up of businesses (e.g. simplifying paperwork to set up a company, low business taxes, simplification of laws to increase the ease of doing business).

Grants and loans

Two of the main ways that a government supports start-ups is through grants and loans. Typically a grant does not need to be paid back, whereas a loan would need to be paid back with interest (although this may be relatively low for a start-up).

Grants are normally given where the start-up helps the government achieve objectives, e.g. to reduce unemployment, or to focus on high-growth sectors of the economy.

Government institutions to support start-ups

Many governments provide a range of support mechanisms for new businesses. For example, in India the Ministry of Micro, Small & Medium Enterprises (Sukshma Laghu Aur Madhyam Udyam Mantralaya) provides grants (funds) to support small businesses to meet capital costs, as well as funds for working capital. The government provides low-cost loans to encourage the development of modern companies. There are specific government institutions that help directly, such as the Small Industries Development Bank of India (SIDBI) providing loans and grants to start-ups in important industries. The National Bank for Agricultural and Rural Development (NABARD) supports farmers and others in rural areas. The Ministry has also set up cluster centres across India. These consist of a cluster of useful services such as design centres, testing laboratories and skill development centres. They support small businesses to engage in research and development, technology upgrades, the standardisation of products, quality testing, marketing and branding activities.

KEY POINTS

1 The government supports start-ups because they create jobs and output as well as contributing to exports of a country.

2 The government offers grants and loans, help in business planning, other advice, tax breaks for start-ups and less regulation of business activity than for larger companies.

CASE STUDY | Backing small business in the UK

In 2010 the UK government produced a report ('Backing Small Business') setting out its support for small businesses. The report showed that 60 per cent of jobs are in this sector and 50 per cent of the value of all goods produced is in the small-business sector. The report showed how the government would make more funding available for this sector, and that the government is investing in Technology and Investment Centres to support small businesses. Regulations and laws were also being changed to support this sector. Key aspects included:

- reducing taxes on small profits (to 20 per cent)
- simplifying taxes for small businesses
- promising to introduce the One-in, One-out rule so that new regulations on small business would only be introduced if existing rules were removed, benefiting small businesses
- making it easier for small firms to acquire finance (setting up a fund to be available to small businesses) particularly for firms with high growth potential and those focusing on exporting
- making it easier for small firms to win government contracts and arranging rapid payment for providing supplies to government
- reducing the paperwork to set up a business
- providing access to mentors (advisers) and small loans to help the unemployed to set up their own enterprise.

Questions

1 What similarities can you see between the ways in which the Indian and UK governments are supporting small enterprises?

2 What other approaches can you think of that might support the development of new enterprises?

SUMMARY QUESTIONS

1 A country is seeking to develop alternative energy sources, e.g. solar power. What would be the relative merits of offering start-up companies in this sector (a) government grants and (b) government loans?

2 In which sectors of your economy do you mainly find start-up enterprises?

1.3.4 Business growth and measurement of size

TOPIC AIMS

Students should be able to:

- show understanding of the different methods of measuring the size of business units (e.g. numbers of employees, capital employed)
- show awareness of the problems of using the different methods
- understand the different ways by which a business can grow
- explain reasons why businesses seek to grow
- describe the problems connected with the growth of a business.

DID YOU KNOW?

If a business wishes to take over another business, it will set out to purchase more than 50 per cent of the shares. As soon as the investing business has one share over 50 per cent of the shares, it is in control of the company it has taken over. It can make all the decisions as it cannot be outvoted by other shareholders. The business that has acquired over 50 per cent of the shares in another is known as the holding company. The business whose shares have been bought up is known as the subsidiary.

How do you measure the size of a farm? This huge farm owns a lot of capital, and has a very high sales turnover, yet it only employs a small number of employees.

Measuring the size of a business unit

You will often come across the terms small, medium and large businesses. However, it is not always clear what the difference is. In different industries, size is measured in different ways. Also, the definitions used will vary from country to country. The following table shows how the size of a business is measured.

Method	How is it done?
The **number of employees**	A small business might be one employing fewer than 50 employees.
The **value of output**	Determined by the value of sales in a year: a small business might be one selling up to $6.5m worth of goods.
The **market share of the business**	Determined by the share of the market that the business is responsible for: a small firm might supply less than 5% of the market.
The **value of the capital employed** by the business	Determined by the value of what the business owns.

The number of employees is a straightforward method. However, it is difficult to compare businesses in different industries. For example, a huge modern farm, working with the latest machinery, may employ just a few people. In contrast, a local supermarket may employ a hundred or more people.

The following table shows how the definition of small business in South Africa varies from industry to industry.

Sector (broad group of industries)	Size	Employees (less than)	Annual sales turnover (less than)	Capital employed (less than)
Agriculture	Medium Small Very small Micro	120 50 10 5	R4.00m R2.00m R0.40m R0.15m	R4.00m R2.00m R0.40m R0.10m
Manufacturing	Medium Small Very small Micro	120 50 10 5	R40.00m R10.00m R4.00m R0.15m	R15.00m R3.75m R1.50m R0.10m

Business growth

Businesses may be able to gain advantages over competitors by growing: they may be able to cut costs and win a greater share of the market. By growing they may also be able to develop new products or sell to new markets. Growth may be internal (inside the business) or external (joining together with existing businesses).

Internal growth

'Organic' growth takes place within a business. Money to finance the expansion can come from ploughing back profits or asking the owners to put in more 'capital'. Many small businesses grow organically in their early years. This is because the owners will not want to risk borrowing money from outside the business. However, it is quite a slow way of growing a business. Internal growth can then take place by investing in new products or selling more of existing products.

External growth

External growth involves the takeover of another business, or merger with another business.

An important way of raising finance in a large company is to sell shares. One **share** represents one unit of ownership in the business. (A **shareholder** is someone who is a part-owner of the business; they will typically have many shares.)

A merger occurs when two businesses combine to form a single company. The existing shareholders of both businesses retain a shared interest in the new business.

An acquisition occurs when one business gains control of part of another business. A business may be prepared to sell off one of its divisions that it no longer wishes to keep.

Businesses carry out external growth in order to:

- buy new and exciting brands where sales are likely to be high
- acquire new inventions and new technologies
- break into new markets, perhaps in other countries.

DID YOU KNOW?

Classifying business size according to value of output of goods produced brings similar results to an approach based on classification according to the size of sales revenues of companies.

KEY POINTS

1 There are a number of ways of measuring the size of a business.

2 Businesses can grow 'organically' from within (e.g. ploughing back profits into the business, raising money from owners), or externally (e.g. by merger, takeover or acquisition).

SUMMARY QUESTIONS

1 Compare the merits of the following methods for classifying the size of retail units.
   - Capital employed in the business
   - Size of sales revenues
   - Number of employees
   - % market share

2 The following are methods for defining a business: the number of employees / sales turnover / market share / capital employed.

   Which method/s do you think would be the most useful for classifying whether a business is small, medium or large? Explain your answer.

3 What methods of growth would you suggest to the owner of a small successful family hotel that has accumulated profits for several years?

1.3.5 Why businesses fail

TOPIC AIMS

Students should be able to:
- analyse the causes of business failure
- identify reasons why new businesses are at greater risk
- explain why some businesses remain small.

STUDY TIP

Remember, it is possible for even a profitable business to fail if it runs out of cash. Lack of cash flow to pay bills is a major reason that businesses stop trading.

The causes of business failure

You will often see statistics which show that a large number of businesses close down within 12 months or two years of start-up. However, it is important to differentiate between business failure and business closure. A study carried out in the US by Brian Headd showed that in fact one-third of businesses that close down are actually successful in terms of trading profitably, but the owner has decided to close them down for one reason or another, e.g. moving on to something else. The study (Redefining Business Success) showed that in the US about two-thirds of businesses survive two years or more and a half survive four years or more. However, many do fail and it is important to know why.

Common causes of business failure are as follows:

- Not having enough cash to pay outstanding bills. The business may be profitable, but it has managed badly the timing of receipts from people that owe the company money (trade receivables) and payments to those that the company owes money to (trade payables). Running out of cash (and not being able to borrow more) is a common cause of business failure.
- Operating in a line of business where profit margins are low. In some industries (often because of competition) profit margins are low. A poorly run business in such an industry has a much higher chance of failing.
- Failure to meet the requirements of customers. A successful company understands its customers and their requirements. Lack of such understanding can lead to failure.
- Changes in the external environment. The external environment consists of all of those factors outside the business over which the business has little control. These factors include:
  - the level of competition – increased competition can slash profit margins
  - changes in laws and regulations – rules governing business activity can substantially increase the cost of doing business, e.g. a law governing how a business disposes of its waste
  - changes in consumer preferences and tastes. Businesses that continue to produce products that become outdated fall behind the times and their sales will reduce.
- Poor selling of products. It is not enough to have the right products. A business also needs to make sure that customers know about these products and understand what they are offering.
- Relying too much on a single customer. Relying on a single customer is like putting all of your eggs in the same basket. If the customer gets into financial difficulties and has to close down then the market will disappear overnight. The customer may fail to pay what they owe to the business and it will be unable to retrieve this.

- Poor management is another cause of business failure.
- Lack of planning. Lack of a plan for the future means that a business has poor direction.
- Trying to grow too quickly. Successful early start-ups can often result in the owners overstretching themselves in order to secure even more profit. A business will often borrow in order to grow. Where sales prove to be lower than anticipated, the business will be faced with a lack of finances, while interest payments on borrowed money still have to be made.

Why small businesses are at greater risk

The reasons why new businesses are at greater risk of failing are very similar to the reasons listed above:

- A larger proportion of start-ups than existing businesses are set up by younger people who have less business and management experience.
- Start-ups typically need to borrow funds in order to get the business off the ground. Right from the start repayments on these loans have to be made, yet it may take the business a while to generate cash.
- Start-ups have less experience of the market than existing businesses, which have already learned important information about the market.
- Start-ups may not fully anticipate the strength of existing competition, the cost of setting up, the importance of careful planning and other important factors associated with setting up.
- New entrepreneurs are typically more optimistic about sales and market trends than existing entrepreneurs who may have a more realistic picture of the market.
- Start-up entrepreneurs may focus on a small snapshot of their success as an entrepreneur. Business tends to go through a cycle of growth and slow down in business activity. A new start-up may just focus their planning on the growth part of the cycle and underestimate the way in which the market for their product (and the whole economy) may contract in future periods.

Why some businesses remain small

While many businesses benefit from growth (e.g. being able to draw on larger profits and to raise capital from lenders more easily) others prefer to remain small. Reasons for remaining small include:

- the flexibility of the business, including the ease with which owners can make quick decisions
- the benefits of not having to raise large sums of capital that increase the debt of a business
- the greater control that the owners retain over their business
- the direct interface that owners and managers can have with customers
- the benefits of understanding your market more fully because its scale is limited
- the reduced level of complexity of decision-making resulting in a less-stressful life for the owners.

KEY POINTS

1. There are a number of reasons why businesses fail. Factors in the external environment include increasing competition and changing consumer buying patterns.
2. Causes of failure from within the business include lack of management experience and lack of cash to finance business activity.
3. Some businesses remain small because the owners prefer to operate at this scale as they have more interaction with customers, as well as greater personal control and flexibility over how they run the business.

SUMMARY QUESTIONS

1. A number of businesses in your neighbourhood will have closed down in recent times. Which of the factors listed in this unit appear to have resulted in them closing down?
2. If you were the owner of a small local business why might you want to continue to operate on a small scale rather than to expand?

1.4 Types of business organisation

1.4.1 Sole traders and partnerships

TOPIC AIMS

Students should be able to:
- describe the main features of sole traders and partnerships
- understand the differences between sole traders and partnerships.

When setting up a business, one of the first decisions is 'what type of business to form'. The type of business chosen determines the legal status of the business and how easy it is to raise capital.

The sole trader

This section looks at privately owned businesses – that is, ones that are owned by individuals or groups of owners rather than by the government.

Private businesses (private sector)
Sole traders
Partnership
Companies (including multinationals)

Public businesses (public sector)
Government-owned businesses

A **sole trader** is the most common form of business ownership and the easiest to set up. Examples include street-corner flowers or drinks sellers in cities, tailors and operators of shoeshine services. A sole trader is a business owned by one person – though it may still employ a large number of people.

The table below shows some of the advantages and disadvantages of setting up as a sole trader rather than as a larger business.

Advantages	Disadvantages
Easy to set up; no special paperwork is required	Having unlimited liability endangers personal possessions
Usually a small business; less capital is required	Finance can be difficult to raise
Speedy decisions can be made by the owner – few people involved	Small scale limits discounts and other benefits of large-scale production
Personal attention given to business affairs	Prices often higher than those of larger organisations
Special services can be offered to customers	Ill health, holidays, etc. may affect the running of the business
Can cater for the needs of local people; because the business is small, the owner comes into contact with the customers	Only one owner may mean narrow range of skills
Profits do not have to be shared	Mistakes possible, because no colleagues to consult for advice
Business affairs can be kept private	

Unlimited liability

When you set up a business you will need capital to run it. Sole traders have only their own resources to draw on. They will finance their business through savings, and borrowing from banks and on their credit card.

STUDY TIP

It is a common mistake to assume that a sole trader is a business that employs one person. Remember that the term refers to the number of owners, not the number of employees.

Any debt that a sole trader builds up has to be paid by the owner. They are personally responsible for all the debts of the business. This situation can be contrasted with larger companies. Owners of a company have legal protection known as **limited liability**: this limits the debts owed by an individual owner of a company to the sum of money they have put into their business. In contrast, sole traders' debts are unlimited. If sole traders find themselves in debt, they may have to sell off their house, car and other possessions in order to pay what they owe.

Partnerships

A **partnership** is a business association between two or more owners of an enterprise. Setting up a partnership usually involves creating a legal agreement between the partners. Partnerships usually have between 2 and 20 members, though this varies between countries. In some countries, legal restrictions allow a maximum of 20 partners.

Partnerships are common in many types of business – small shops as well as professional practices like vets, doctors, solicitors and dentists.

The table shows the advantages and disadvantages of setting up a partnership.

Advantages	Disadvantages
Capital from partners, so more capital available	Unlimited liability (except for 'sleeping partners', who put money into the business but do not get involved in its running)
Larger scale than sole trader	Disagreements between partners
Members of family can join	Limitation of number of partners (in many countries restricted by law to maximum of 20)
Affairs can be kept private	If partnership was set up by legal agreement, it will need to be re-formed if one partner dies
Risks and responsibilities spread among partners	

Most partnerships are not protected by limited liability.

SUMMARY QUESTIONS

1 Abdul is considering setting up a small business repairing broken windows and is not sure whether to set up as a partnership or a sole trader. What would be the benefits of forming a partnership in terms of the following?

Access to capital / liability / ease of setting up the business / access to skills

What other advantages might there be to setting up a partnership?

2 What is limited liability? How does not having limited liability disadvantage many sole traders and partnerships?

3 Set out a table showing the main differences between partnerships and sole traders.

ACTIVITY

Choose a business and decide on its purpose. Set out a partnership agreement between yourself and a friend for a small enterprise that you could set up.

The agreement should cover these topics:

- Who will provide the capital, and how much.
- How the profits or losses will be shared.
- The duties of the partners.
- When profits will be taken from the business (e.g. monthly).
- Procedures for bringing in other partners and for settling disputes.

DID YOU KNOW?

In limited partnerships, one or more of the partners can have limited liability: if a partnership runs into debt, the maximum amount in law that they are expected to lose is what they put into the business. Limited partners would not have to sell off private possessions to pay off the debts of the partnership.

KEY POINTS

1 A sole trader enterprise is run by one person. A partnership is owned and run by two or more people.
2 Sole traders and partners typically do not have limited liability. Capital raised is restricted to the owner's own savings, borrowing and any profits made.
3 A sole trader has control over their own business and takes all the profits.
4 Partners can share skills and spread the workload of running the business.

1.4.2 Other types of business organisation

TOPIC AIMS

Students should be able to:

- describe the main features of limited companies, franchises and joint ventures
- understand the difference between unincorporated businesses and limited companies.

A company

'**Company**' suggests a group of companions who have come together to set up a business. The business they set up becomes a legal body, separate in law from the owners. To become a company, a business needs to become legally incorporated. This involves registering the company with the Registrar of Companies in the country in which the company has its head office.

The owners of a company are its shareholders. They appoint a **board of directors** to make the **strategic decisions**. The decisions they make include how much profit to distribute to shareholders, and what direction the business should take. The managing director is the senior director, with the lead role for managing the business.

The reasons for **incorporating** a business include:

- If the business gets into financial difficulty, shareholders risk losing only the value of their shareholding in the business. Their private possessions are protected by limited liability and only the assets of the business are at risk.
- An incorporated business is easier to sell than an unincorporated one, because all the complicated arrangements of setting up the business have already been done. Companies are expected to keep detailed accounts so that buyers can immediately see how the company is doing financially when they buy it.

The main disadvantages of a company concern the administration needed to register the company and the requirement to produce annual reports. Detailed accounts have to be kept.

The table shows the two types of **limited companies**.

```
Shareholders
(own company)
    │
  choose
    ↓
Board of Directors
(make the key decisions of the business)
    │
  led by
    ↓
Managing Director
```

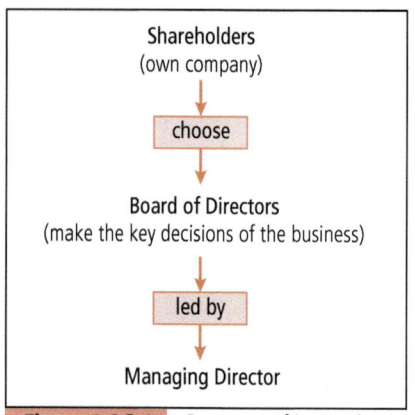

Figure 1.4.2.1 Purposes of internal communication

Private companies (ltd)	Public companies (plc)
1 Shares can only be bought direct from the company with the permission of the board of directors.	1 Shares can be bought and sold on a stock exchange. Anyone can buy them.
2 Usually has quite a small number of shareholders. May be a family-run business.	2 Can have a large number of shareholders (may be millions) all over the world.
3 Has access to less capital than a public company.	3 Has access to more capital.

The main advantage of being a **private company** is that the original owners can stop outsiders from buying up their company. Having a smaller number of people from whom to draw funds, however, may restrict growth. The main advantage of being a public company is access to large amounts of capital, which enables growth.

DID YOU KNOW?

Shareholders appoint directors to manage the day-to-day running of a limited company. Every year directors report to shareholders at an annual general meeting (AGM). At the AGM, shareholders have an opportunity to question directors on company policies and decisions, e.g. bonus payments and dividend distribution.

Franchises

A **franchise** business is made up of a franchisor and franchisees. The franchisor is an established enterprise (often a public limited company) with a well-known name and products or services. The franchisor grants a licence to a franchisee to produce a product, sell products or provide services in a given area. Examples of franchises include food franchises (e.g. a McDonald's franchise), a coffee shop franchise (e.g. Costa Coffee or Starbucks), and retail franchises such as United Colors of Benetton, operating in over 120 countries.

The franchisee pays for the franchise to trade in a given area, but will receive training and equipment from the franchisor. They will be expected to share the profit with the franchisor.

The main advantage to the franchisor is that they only have to invest a limited amount of capital in each franchise, but they take profits from the franchisee. The franchisee will work hard to make a success of the business, but in turn benefits from working with a proven business idea, trading under a well-known name and getting support and materials from the franchisor.

> **DID YOU KNOW?**
>
> Stock exchanges exist across the world where traders buy and sell shares in public companies on behalf of clients. Examples are the South African Stock Exchange in Johannesburg, the New Zealand Stock Exchange in Wellington, and the Jamaican Stock Exchange in Kingston. Companies whose stocks are listed on these exchanges can raise funds both within the home market and internationally.

> **ACTIVITY**
>
> Speak to a franchisee in your own country. Find out how they came to be in the business. What is the relationship with the franchisor? Share your findings with the class.

Joint ventures

A joint venture (JV) is formed when two independent businesses set up a new enterprise in which they jointly own a stake. It can take the form of an incorporated business or a partnership.

Joint ventures are commonly used when a business from one country wants to enter a new country, but prefers to do so with a local partner. The local partner will have a lot of contacts and know how to conduct business in that market. A lot of oil companies create joint ventures to search for and then exploit oil reserves. Many Western companies have created joint ventures when entering the Chinese, Indian and other South East Asian markets.

> **STUDY TIP**
>
> Joint ventures are often used as a means of avoiding tariff barriers and so gaining access to new markets. They reduce the amount of capital that a company needs, but they can also cause difficulties for that company, such as controlling the quality of the products or services provided.

> **SUMMARY QUESTIONS**
>
> 1 Why might a group of friends setting up in business for the first time prefer to create an incorporated rather than an unincorporated business?
>
> 2 What benefits might a Western European manufacturer of chocolate and confectionery products gain from setting up a joint venture with an existing Chinese manufacturer rather than setting up its own independent plant there?
>
> 3 Fast-food franchises such as McDonald's are found in many countries. What would be the advantages to a local franchisee of working with McDonald's rather than setting up their own food business?

> **KEY POINTS**
>
> 1 A company is owned by shareholders who are able to bring capital into a business.
>
> 2 Shareholders are protected by limited liability. The financial risk is limited to the value of the shares they hold.
>
> 3 Another way for a business to grow with less risk to its own capital is to sell franchises.
>
> 4 A good way of entering a foreign market is to create a joint venture with a local company.

1.4.3 Objectives, growth and business organisation

TOPIC AIMS

Students should be able to:

- discuss the appropriateness of a given form of organisation (e.g. sole trader, partnership, company or franchise) in enabling a business to achieve its objectives
- recommend and justify suitable forms of business organisation to the owners and management in a given situation.

Business objectives

We have seen that a key objective of businesses is to make a profit. However, how they make a profit varies with the type of business. Every big company began as a small company, often with just one or two enterprising individuals at its head. The person starting up the business may simply seek to earn a living and to support their family. They may prefer to work for themselves rather than for someone else.

A business that wants to remain small and to maintain control within a small group of owners will best operate as an unincorporated business. However, when businesses want to grow and purchase expensive capital, it makes sense to become incorporated and raise money from a large number of shareholders.

The table shows the key differences between various business forms.

CASE STUDY — Hero Cycles

The Hero Group in India provides an excellent example of business growth. In the 1940s, Brij Mohan Munjal, in partnership with his three brothers, started supplying components to local bicycle businesses in Amritsar. In 1947, the family had to move to Ludhiana, which was a major centre for Indian bicycle manufacture. The Munjals expanded their business to become a major supplier of bicycle parts in India.

They then moved from just supplying parts to manufacturing them. They produced handlebars, front forks and bicycle chains. In the mid 1950s, the government in the Punjab was keen to encourage bicycle manufacture. The Munjals set up a company, Hero Cycles, and started to manufacture 7 500 bicycles a year.

Since then, the bicycles have become renowned throughout the world, offering sturdy, value-for-money cycles.

In the mid 1980s, the company joined together with Honda to manufacture motorcycles. Today, Hero is the largest producer of motorcycles in the world.

1940s	1950s	1980s	2000s
Partnership of four brothers – bicycle supplies	Company making bicycles – one of the largest in India	International venture producing motorcycles as well as bicycles	Global leader in bicycles and motorcycles

Questions

1. What objectives do you think the Munjal brothers would have had in the early days?
2. What would have been the advantages of running the business as a partnership?
3. What objectives do you think Hero Cycles is likely to have today? How will these have changed from the early objectives?
4. How does the business benefit today from being a public company?

Hero Cycles were able to profit from the popularity of bicycles in India.

The partnership would have been appropriate when the brothers first set up because they only needed a little capital and they had enough skills to run a family business. However, when the company wanted to grow into a national, and then international, business, it was essential to become an incorporated business.

Organisation	Objectives	Control	Sources of finance	Distribution of profits
Sole trader	To provide a living for the owner, profit, growth	By the one owner	Owner's capital, overdraft, credit card, loans, grants, mortgage, profit	All to the owner
Partnership	To provide a living for the owner, to run a professional service, profit, growth, increased market share	By the partners	Partner's capital, credit card, overdraft, loans, grants, mortgage, profit	Between partners
Incorporated business	Profit, growth, increased market share	By the board of directors, and managers working on their behalf	Share capital, overdraft, loans, mortgage, debentures, profits	Between shareholders
Franchise	For the franchisor – to expand business over a wider area and increase profits; for the franchisee – to set up a profitable enterprise using the support of the franchising organisation	By the franchisee, subject to limitations established when forming the franchise	Franchisees have to pay a fee to the franchisor to buy the franchise rights; they can then access other sources of finance, such as bank loans, to keep the business running	Franchisees pay a set percentage of their profits to the franchisor
Joint venture	To create a new venture based on an agreement between two existing companies; to make a profit in a new area of operations	The new venture becomes a distinct entity, with responsibility for running the venture	Funds provided by the companies that create the joint venture; the JV can then access other sources of funds	The joint venture distributes the profits to the companies that set it up

Business owners can also grow their business through setting up franchise outlets, which they can do when the business is sufficiently well known.

Creating a joint venture is particularly helpful in moving into overseas markets. Often there are restrictions involved in moving into new countries. Setting up a joint venture enables a business to make contacts and to take advantage of the local knowledge provided by a local partner.

ACTIVITY

Interview a local business owner in your area. This might be a member of your family or a close family friend. Your teacher may help with the arrangements. What type of business organisation have they set up? What are the advantages of the form of business organisation they have chosen?

SUMMARY QUESTIONS

1 What type of business would you form if you wanted to do each of the following? In each case, justify your choice.
 - Keep control of the business as the original owner.
 - Access a foreign market where there are many legal and cultural differences from your own country.
 - Expand quickly without risking your own capital.
 - Raise a lot of finance from a range of owners.

2 Identify a small business in your local area. How could this business change its form if it wanted to expand? What would be the advantages of doing so?

3 Who makes the decisions in a:
 - partnership?   • franchise?   • company?

KEY POINTS

1 Business objectives are best met when there is a suitable form of business organisation.

2 Sole traders and partnerships are a good way of setting up a small independent business.

3 If a firm wants to expand and grow, it may need to become a company, or it may set up a franchise.

4 Forming a joint venture can help a company expand into a new market.

1.4.4 Limited and unlimited liability

TOPIC AIMS

Students should be able to:
- understand the role and function of entrepreneurship
- understand the concept of risk and ownership
- understand the concept of limited liability.

Nestlé produces many of the world's best-known food brands. It is a Swiss company with over 250,000 shareholders. The shareholders share in the profits made, but also take a risk that the company will not make a profit. Each shareholder has limited liability.

Risk and ownership

One of the words most commonly associated with business is **risk**. The owners of a business risk the capital that they put into it. The capital may come from their life savings, from money they have received in redundancy pay, or even a loan secured against their house or other valuable possessions. More businesses fail than succeed, and the casualty rate of new businesses is particularly high in the first year of trading.

This principle of risking capital is the same for sole traders, partners, shareholders in a company, franchise operators and owners of joint ventures.

The owners of a business are liable for its debts. The amount of liability that sole traders and most partners are accountable for is not restricted to the sums that they have put into the company. They are required by law to meet all the liabilities of their business. As we have seen, this could mean having to sell their car, their house and other possessions to meet business debts (see 1.4).

Limited liability

In the 1850s, the British and French governments passed laws that would allow individuals and groups to invest in companies. This was the principle of limited liability (see 1.4). It limits the risk for a shareholder to the sum they have invested in a company.

Most large businesses are set up as limited companies (incorporated businesses). These companies have shareholders. A shareholder might

DID YOU KNOW?

Figures for the United Kingdom suggest that four out of five new businesses fail. However, a study carried out in Australia showed that although two out of three businesses closed down within 10 years of starting, the most common reason for this was that the existing owner sold out to a new owner, who changed the name.

ACTIVITY

In some countries, a private limited company has 'Ltd' after the name and public limited companies have 'plc'. What is used in your own country? Find out and make a list of 10 limited companies that operate in your town or region.

be an individual, with only a small sum of money invested in, say, companies like Singapore Airlines, Nestlé or Tata. Alternatively, the shareholder might be a huge pension fund, investing the savings of millions of pensioners in these companies. These shareholders would not buy shares in companies if they were held liable for business debts.

Shareholders → invest money in → limited companies.

Shareholders may be individuals or other companies. They are not responsible for the company's debts unless they have given guarantees (e.g. of a bank loan). However, they may lose the money they have invested in the company if it fails.

The protection of limited liability therefore makes it possible for companies across the globe to raise large sums of money. The Swiss multinational company Nestlé is famous for its products such as Nescafé and Quality Street sweets. The company has over 250 000 shareholders and no single shareholder owns more than 3 per cent of the shares in the company. Each of the 250 000 shareholders is willing to invest in the company because they think that it has good prospects to make profits, and they know that because of limited liability, the maximum amount of capital that they are risking is the value of their shareholding.

SUMMARY QUESTIONS

1. Which of the following would have limited liability?

   An incorporated business / a sole trader / an ordinary partnership / a company / a limited partnership

2. Singapore Airlines is owned jointly by the government of Singapore and by private shareholders. The Singapore government has the majority shareholding in the airline. The airline is an incorporated business. How much would an individual shareholder be liable for in the event that the airline had to meet debts?

3. In what ways might it be more risky to set up a sole trader business than a small incorporated company?

DID YOU KNOW?

Some forms of business organisation are specific to particular countries. Indian law recognises the joint Hindu family form of business ownership: members of a family own a business and the eldest member manages it. Every member of the family gets a share in the profit, regardless of how much they participate. Apart from the eldest member, the liability of the partners is limited.

KEY POINTS

1. Limited liability is a legal protection that reduces the risks involved in business.

2. A shareholder or other owner of a business with limited liability is only liable for the value of their investment in a business.

3. There are certain types of partnerships that have limited liability status. However, in ordinary partnerships there is unlimited liability of partners.

1.4.5 Business organisations in the public sector

TOPIC AIMS

Students should be able to:
- describe business organisations in the public sector, e.g. public corporations.

DID YOU KNOW?

Government-linked companies (**GLCs**) are companies in which the government owns some of the shares in the business.

What is a public corporation?

Public corporations are businesses owned by governments. Although the government owns the corporation, the controllers of the corporation are given considerable freedom to make their own decisions. Sometimes they are referred to as stated-owned enterprises (SOEs) or government-owned corporations (GOCs). In India the term public sector undertaking (PSU) is used.

A public corporation is created by passing a law to create the new form of business. The government then appoints a chairperson and a board of managers to lead it.

CASE STUDY | The Saudi Arabian Oil Company

The Saudi Arabian Oil Company is owned by the Saudi government because oil is such an important resource to the Saudi Arabian economy. The Saudi government controls the amount of oil produced, which in turn has an impact on the world oil price.

As in any business, governments usually set yearly targets for particular public corporations. The chairperson and the managers must then decide on the best way to meet these targets. With an oil corporation, the government may set a target for the number of barrels of oil to produce in a country. The managers of the oil company will then decide how much to produce from each oilfield and how to maintain supplies for future years. The managers will also supervise the marketing and selling of the oil. Agreements about how much oil to produce and the price to charge has to be agreed between members of OPEC (Organisation of the Petroleum Exporting Countries).

Questions

1 Why do you think the Saudi Arabian Oil Company is run as a public corporation rather than as a private sector business?

2 What types of decision are made by the Saudi Arabian Oil Company? How are these decisions important to the economy of Saudi Arabia?

STUDY TIP

The process of privatisation has taken place in many countries. You will need to be able to answer a possible question on the advantages and disadvantages of privatisation.

Purposes of public corporations

Public corporations are often created to make sure that important activities that affect the whole nation are carried out well. Indian Railways is a PSU: every day millions of people travel on Indian railways and goods are transported all over India. In most countries there is also a state broadcasting company, such as the British Broadcasting Company (BBC). The purpose of the BBC is to try to present news in a fair way that is not influenced by political or commercial interests.

Sometimes public corporations are set up to preserve jobs. The government is able to support public corporations through money it raises from taxpayers. This enables the government to provide services to locations where it is not economical to provide them, such as water supplies to areas of water shortage. In Libya water supplies are transported over 4000 kilometres, down a huge water pipe from under the Sahara Desert to major areas of population.

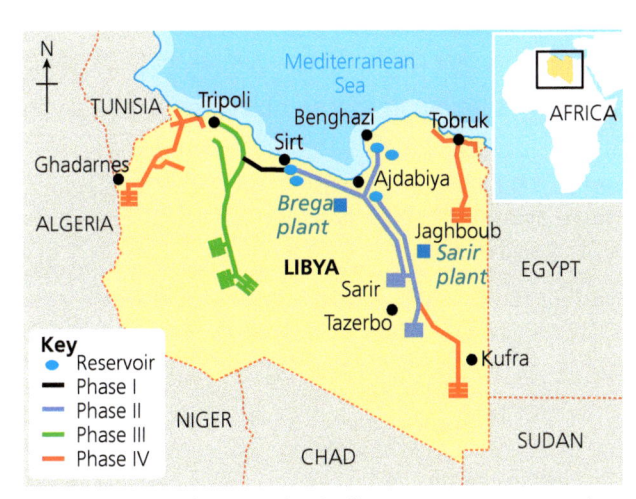

The great man-made river project in Libya was a government project bringing water from under the Sahara Desert along 4000 kilometres of water pipes to centres of population.

Government involvement in a particular industry can also reduce wasteful competition. For example, the government might provide the only electricity or water supply using one set of cables and pipelines. This saves having wasteful duplication of pipelines.

When a business or industry is taken over by the government this is described as **nationalisation**. Selling a public corporation to shareholders is termed **privatisation**.

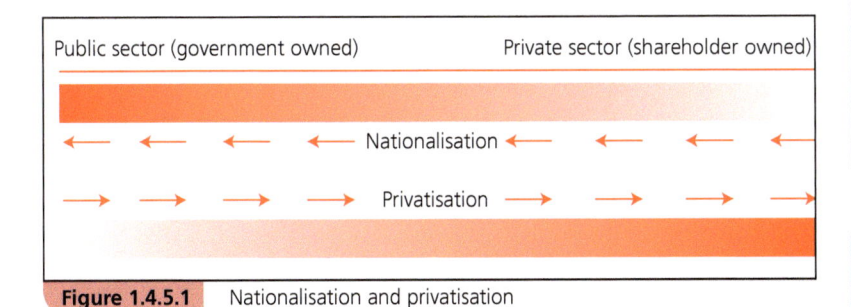

Figure 1.4.5.1 Nationalisation and privatisation

Disadvantages of public corporations

Public corporations can become too large and difficult to manage. The lack of competition can lead to higher prices and wasteful use of resources (although, as you read earlier, they can cut wasteful duplication). Subsidising a public corporation through taxes may prevent the revenues from being used more efficiently for other purposes.

ACTIVITY

Saudi Airlines was recently privatised. Carry out some internet research to find out why this happened. What do you expect the benefits of the privatisation to be? Who owned the airline prior to the privatisation? Who owns it now? Produce a report of your findings.

KEY POINTS

1 A public sector business is owned by the government.

2 These businesses have other objectives than just to make a profit.

3 Public sector businesses do not always use resources as efficiently as if they faced greater competition.

SUMMARY QUESTIONS

1 Give examples of three public corporations in different countries.

2 Suggest three reasons why governments set up public corporations.

3 Why are public corporations sometimes privatised?

1.5 Business objectives and stakeholder objectives

1.5.1 Business objectives

TOPIC AIMS

Students should be able to:
- demonstrate an understanding that businesses can have several objectives, and that the importance of these can change
- understand the need for objectives in business
- identify the importance of businesses having objectives
- demonstrate understanding of different objectives, such as growth, profitability and market share.

DID YOU KNOW?

Objectives should be **SMART**: **S**pecific, **M**easurable, **A**greed, **R**ealistic (or **R**elevant) and **T**ime-related.

New York City Football Club has a number of SMART objectives designed to secure their success in US soccer.

Aims and objectives

Businesses set themselves broad aims, sometimes referred to as goals, to provide a sense of direction. They also need to establish more precise objectives that give clarity about how the aims can be achieved.

A courier firm might set out its specific objectives in a statement like the following:

> 'To ensure that 99 per cent of all packages received at our offices by 18.00 are delivered to their final destination before 10.00 the following day within Asia.'

You can see that this provides a SMART set of objectives that make the business goal more precise:

- It sets out specific details about the delivery times.
- Success in meeting the objectives is measurable – 99 per cent.
- The figure of 99 per cent would be agreed by those responsible for delivering this high figure.
- The managers of the organisation will know from previous performance whether a figure of 99 per cent is realistic.
- The objectives are related to a given time period.

Business objectives:
- provide clear end purposes towards which to work
- enable everyone involved in a business to focus on these purposes
- make it possible to check on progress and to make improvements.

Businesses work towards a number of major objectives – for example, growth, profitability and market share. Some objectives will focus on profitable growth, while others may also set out the social responsibilities of the business, such as benefits to the local community.

Growth

A business can set out SMART objectives relating to growth. For example, it could seek to grow sales, or to grow the size of the company or the number of employees.

This could be set out in the following ways:
- to increase sales by 20 per cent by 2020
- to increase the number of employees by 10 per cent by next year.

Profitability

Profitability is an important business objective. Businesses require profits to stay competitive and to make improvements. A profit-related objective might be to increase operating profits by 5 per cent per year for the next 5 years.

Market share

The market share of a business is its percentage of sales in the market. The UK company Innocent sells 'smoothies', fruit drinks with no artificial additives. For example, Google's share of all mobile advertising revenues increased from 38 per cent in 2011 to 53 per cent in 2013. The company might set itself the objective of winning 60 per cent of the market share by 2017.

Objectives of social enterprises

A social enterprise is an enterprise that is set up to achieve objectives which relate to meeting the needs of society or the environment. They are sometimes referred to as 'not-for-profit' organisations. As a social enterprise an organisation seeks to make a 'surplus' rather than a profit. This is illustrated in the example of Guyana-based Help and Shelter, a social enterprise focusing on the protection of women, children, the disabled, the elderly and others, against domestic violence. Help and Shelter currently has about 8 000 clients (85 per cent of whom are female). The enterprise has a board of directors and a combination of paid staff and volunteers.

Help and Shelter's objectives can be summarised as:

- To work to build respect for the right of women, children, youth and men to live free of violence and the threat of violence, by actively fostering a high level of awareness about the prevalence, causes and costs of violence
- To assist those suffering from violence to develop alternative ways of handling power and resolving conflict through counselling for victims and perpetrators of violence
- To widen options for victims by providing temporary shelter for abused women, and to provide training and skills to enable greater self-sufficiency.

DID YOU KNOW?

In 2013 Manchester City Football Club partnered with New York Yankees to create New York City FC. The aim was to produce the best team possible in the US Major League Soccer (MLS). The initial objectives were to recruit a good squad of players to compete in the MLS by 2015, to develop a fan base and the infrastructure of a new club – SMART objectives.

STUDY TIP

One of the key functions of management is to direct and control a business. Without objectives, the managers of a business will not know exactly what they want the business to achieve.

KEY POINTS

1. Businesses work to broad goals, which may be broken down into objectives.
2. Objectives should be specific, measurable, agreed, realistic and time-related (SMART).
3. Broad objectives usually relate to profit, growth and market share.

SUMMARY QUESTIONS

1. Why do businesses need both goals and objectives?
2. An international soft-drinks manufacturer already controls 80 per cent of the market in Europe and the United States, but has less than 5 per cent of the market in Asia and Africa. Which of the following objectives do you regard as the SMARTest?
   - To maintain market share in Europe and the US and to grow market share in Asia and Africa.
   - To double market share in Africa and Asia over the next five years while retaining market leadership in the US and Europe.
   - To increase market share in Europe and the US by 1 per cent over the next five years, and to increase sales in Africa and Asia by 10 per cent within the next 10 years.
3. Choose a well-known global business, such as Tata, Toyota, Procter & Gamble, Nestlé, Shell or Nike. Explain how having clear business objectives will help its business managers to achieve targets.

1.5.2 Stakeholders and their different objectives

TOPIC AIMS

Students should be able to:

- state and explain the role of the different groups involved in business activity and their objectives: consumers, employees, managers, owners, financiers and shareholders
- identify, describe and explain the objectives of different stakeholder groups
- use examples to illustrate such objectives.

STUDY TIP

Make sure that you know the difference between stakeholders and shareholders. It is a common error to think that they are the same.

ACTIVITY

Choose a local company – for example, a farm, a retail outlet, a manufacturing or transport company. Identify the key stakeholder groups. Set this out in the form of a diagram. Are there any clashes between the interests of the stakeholders in this business?

What are stakeholders?

A **stakeholder** is someone who has an interest in the decisions taken by the business. Some stakeholders are internal: they are part-owners of the business or they work within the business. Examples are shareholders, managers and employees. Other stakeholders are external – for example, the customers and suppliers.

CASE STUDY | Shell Nigeria

Nigeria is a leading oil-exporting country. The oil company Shell extracts oil in Nigeria and pumps it in pipelines to refineries on the coast. The company provides jobs for many Nigerians and offers scholarships for students. It is also involved in a number of community projects. Tax revenues from the company make a major contribution to the Nigerian government. However, there are criticisms that oil production pollutes large areas of the countryside, and that the removal of oil directly from the pipeline can lead to injury or death.

Questions

1. Who are the stakeholders in Shell's activities in Nigeria?
2. Identify two groups of stakeholders in Shell Nigeria whose interests might clash. Explain how and why a clash might occur.

Oil spills and broken pipelines in Nigeria can have a devastating effect on the local environment.

Key stakeholders

The following table summarises the different stakeholders in a business.

Internal stakeholders	External stakeholders
1 **Owners:** may be single owner in sole-trader business or partners in a partnership. In a company, shareholders are the owners. Without owners the business would not exist; they are the risk takers. They like to see their share of profit increasing, and the value of their business rising.	1 **Customers** want a company to produce high-quality, value-for-money products.
	2 **Suppliers** want steady orders and prompt payment; they also want to feel valued by the company that they supply.
	3 **Local and national communities**: actions of businesses can have major effects on communities: Shell's pipelines in Nigeria run through people's lands, can be dangerous and cause pollution. (Shell might argue that the dangers come from local people tampering with the pipelines to take fuel out of the pipeline for their own consumption or to sell on.) Community leaders are an important stakeholder group.
2 **Employees:** their stake is that the company provides them with a living. They want security of employment, promotion opportunities and good rewards. Ideally, they want to work for a company that they are proud of.	4 **Governments** want businesses to be successful – to create jobs and pay taxes. They want to see prosperous businesses that take full responsibility for looking after the welfare of society.
	5 **Pressure groups:** organised with particular interests and points of view. Examples are the environmental campaigning groups Greenpeace and Friends of the Earth, who see themselves as defending the environment. They will have an environmental stake in the business.
	6 **Trade unions:** represent interests of groups of employees; seek to secure high wages and better working conditions for their members.
	7 **Employers' associations:** employers' equivalent of trade unions; they represent the interests of groups of employers.

SUMMARY QUESTIONS

1 In each of the following cases, explain what the conflict of interest might be between the two stakeholder groups indicated.

Decision	Stakeholder group	Stakeholder group
To give employees a wage rise	Shareholders	Employees
To open a new factory next to a populated area	Shareholders	Local community
To close down a factory	Shareholders	Employees

2 What arguments would you put forward to support the view that shareholders are the most important stakeholder grouping in an organisation? What arguments would you present against this view?

3 Identify a business that is just moving to your local area, or a new business that has set up there. Make a list of all of the stakeholder groups and their stake in the business.

KEY POINTS

1 A stakeholder is an individual or group that has an interest in decisions taken by a business.

2 Sometimes stakeholders have the same interests, but their interests may also differ and conflict.

3 Owners are very important stakeholders. They play a key part in setting up and ensuring the continual success of a business.

4 Main stakeholders are owners, employees, customers, communities, government, pressure groups, trade unions and employers' associations.

1.5.3 Aims of the private and public sectors

TOPIC AIMS

Students should be able to:
- demonstrate an awareness of the differences in the aims and objectives of private sector and public sector enterprises.

In 1.5 we saw that all organisations decide on broad aims (goals) to work towards and then break these down into more precise objectives.

The aims and objectives of businesses will be different depending on whether they are operating in the **private** or the **public sector**. Remember that private sector businesses are owned by individual risk takers, whereas in the public sector the government owns businesses on behalf of the nation.

Aims and objectives in the private sector

A major aim of businesses in the private sector is to survive. Businesses need to make a profit to survive and grow.

CASE STUDY | Railways in Japan

In Japan, railways are the major form of passenger transport. Since 1987 the railways have been privatised. Japan consists of a number of larger and smaller islands. There are six major rail companies that are part of the Japan Railways Group operating about 70 per cent of all passenger transport as well as freight transport. Most of the companies in the Japan Railways Group are fully privatised and owned by shareholders. In addition there are many other smaller private railway companies some of which run services on just one line while others run services on a number of lines. Japanese trains are famous for punctuality, and between major cities there are bullet trains (shinkanzen) running at 300 km per hour. Companies compete with each other with the objective of providing an efficient, safe and comfortable service.

Questions

1 Who will take the profits from the private rail operations in Japan?

2 How will the objective of maximising revenue enable Japanese railway companies to take more profits?

STUDY TIP

Make sure that you understand that a public limited company is not in the public sector of an economy.

The Japan Railways example indicates the way in which private sector businesses tend to focus on seeking to make high revenues and profits. By doing so, they are able to keep shareholders happy.

Other objectives of private sector businesses include:
- building a strong brand reputation
- winning customer loyalty
- coming up with exciting new ideas and innovations.

What other objectives can you think of for private sector businesses?

You can see that whatever these objectives are, they are usually related to enabling the company to make a profit.

ACTIVITY

Are the railways in your country run by a state-owned organisation or by the private sector? If your country has a rail service, how efficient is it? Does it give value for money? You could also look at the postal service, and national radio or television broadcasting organisations.

Aims and objectives in the public sector

Public sector organisations have wider responsibilities than just making a profit. They are expected to meet wider responsibilities to the community, such as providing a cheap and efficient train service for all members of society.

Public sector organisations therefore have broader aims than private sector organisations. They are expected to provide more of a public service. Today, they are increasingly required to combine public service with making a profit wherever possible. How possible do you think this is?

> **STUDY TIP**
>
> Make sure you can identify and explain the different objectives that private sector and public sector businesses set themselves.

CASE STUDY | Indian Railways

Indian Railways is the largest employer in India (over 1.6 million people) and operates the second-largest railway system in the world. The objectives of Indian Railways are to provide a modern, reliable, safe, customer-led and customer-focused service to the Indian nation. For a number of years, particularly between 2000 and 2005, the organisation made huge losses.

Railways in India were seen by the government as playing an important part in the life of the nation. The railway system provided a means of transport to remote parts of the country and an affordable means of transport to almost everyone. Trains enabled millions of people to get to work every day. The rail service was particularly important in times of national emergency, taking food to famine or flood victims. An important objective of Indian Railways is therefore to provide a public service.

Problems for Indian Railways have included safety, timekeeping and huge losses that had to be paid for by the government raising money from taxpayers. More recently, the government has set profit goals for Indian Railways. Some of these have been achieved by putting more carriages on trains and providing special routes for carrying freight. The safety record has also improved.

Indian Railways is a state-owned railway company with a near-monopoly of the country's rail transport.

Questions

1 Who takes the profit or pays for the losses made by Indian Railways?

2 How are the objectives of Indian Railways different from those of Virgin Trains?

SUMMARY QUESTIONS

1 In some countries, the postal service is run by a government-owned organisation. In other countries, post is carried by private companies that compete with each other. Make a list of possible objectives that would be set for a government-owned postal service. Make another list of possible objectives for a privately run postal service. How do the two lists differ, and why?

2 In what way are the aims of public sector organisations broader than those of private sector ones?

3 Describe the main objectives of Indian Railways.

KEY POINTS

1 Aims and objectives give organisations a direction to work towards.

2 Private sector organisations seek to make a profit, usually the main focus for their aims and objectives.

3 Public sector organisations may seek to make a profit but will focus on public service.

Unit 1 — Practice questions

SECTION 1: Short-answer questions

1. Explain, using examples, the difference between a 'need' and a 'want'. [2]
2. Does the fast-food company KFC provide a product or a service? Explain your answer. [3]
3. Identify and explain THREE ways in which Levi Strauss & Co. adds value to the original blue denim material. [6]
4. A cup of coffee in a cafe of a well-known multinational company costs $4. The ingredient costs are: coffee – $0.10, milk – $0.02, takeaway cup – $0.07. Work out the added value in this example and analyse how the company adds this amount of value to each cup of coffee. [6]
5. Define and explain the business meaning of the term 'opportunity cost' and give your own example. [3]
6. If the government of your country spends $10 million on road improvements, what is the likely opportunity cost? Explain your answer. [4]
7. Identify and explain TWO reasons why a public enterprise must be careful how money is spent by the organisation. [4]
8. Give TWO examples of organisations in your country that are owned and run by the government. [2]
9. Give ONE example from your country of a charitable organisation and explain the business objectives it is trying to achieve. [4]
10. Identify and explain the link between scarce resources and the need for consumers and businesses to make choices. [4]
11. Identify ONE example of a business in your local area in each of the following sectors:
    - primary
    - secondary
    - tertiary. [3]
12. Identify and explain TWO examples of businesses which operate in two or more sectors. [4]
13. For each of your answers to Question 11, identify and explain one appropriate measure of business size. [4]
14. Identify and explain the best measure of business size for the following organisations:
    - a state-owned health service
    - a large multinational car production company. [4]
15. Identify and explain TWO ways that a company making and selling chocolate bars could benefit from specialisation. [4]
16. Identify and explain TWO advantages and ONE disadvantage to a sole trader of entering into a partnership. [6]
17. Why might the government of a country offer a grant to an entrepreneur who has designed an innovative product that saves energy? [4]
18. Identify and explain ONE method of *internal* growth and one method of *external* growth for a farming business. [4]

SECTION 2: Longer-answer questions

The young enterprise company

A team of students from a private college in Dubai have set up their own company, Contact2U, selling computer and mobile phone accessories. They buy the accessories from a friend of one of their parents, who has a company based in China, and then repackage them, using their own business name and logo. The students add 30 per cent mark-up to the cost of the accessories to calculate their selling prices. The company also offers an installation service, for which a small fee is charged. The company aims to sell as many products as possible, but also to raise awareness of environmental concerns. They have pledged 75 per cent of all their profits to local 'green' organisations, which are trying to protect the area's natural marine species from pollution caused by the Dubai building and development programme. A combination of their low prices and charitable aims has led to very high sales and the company is going from strength to strength.

1 Identify and explain TWO ways that Contact2U adds value to its products. *[4]*

2 Identify and explain TWO suitable methods of measuring the size of the Contact2U company. *[4]*

3 Analyse how Contact2U's charitable aims may have led to increased sales. *[4]*

4 Identify and explain THREE ways in which the young enterprise company adds value to its products. *[6]*

5 'This company cannot possibly have serious environmental aims, when products are produced in and imported by air from China.' Do you agree with this opinion? Justify your answer. *[6]*

The new malaria clinic

The new clinic in rural Uganda is being funded jointly by the government and charitable organisations. The aim is to become a centre for the programme of vaccination against malaria and also offer other support, such as supplying mosquito nets for beds. Money raised by the charity in the US and Europe is sent directly to the charity representative in the local area, and government officials oversee the building and work of the clinic. Nurses at the clinic are mainly local, but they are supported by charity volunteers, who also provide basic training in the use of unfamiliar equipment.

1 Identify and explain TWO not-for-profit organisations that are involved in the malaria clinic project. *[4]*

2 Identify and explain ONE private benefit (to an individual) and ONE social benefit (to the whole society) that will be provided by the malaria clinic. *[4]*

3 Identify and explain TWO examples of opportunity cost for the organisations providing funding for the clinic. *[4]*

4 To what extent do malaria clinics help to provide sustainable development in countries such as Uganda? Explain your answer. *[6]*

5 Evaluate the view that 'clinics like these provide for an essential need, rather than a want, and should therefore be fully funded by the government'. *[6]*

The seed money enterprise

Lydia and Abigail are two young women from rural Zambia, who have received seed-money grants from the Camfed charity to start an enterprise in their village. They are very excited by this opportunity and have decided to lead a basket-making project, so that other women in the village can also benefit. The initial grant has been used to buy essential materials, such as dye, and they have found a way of selling the finished products in the nearest big town. The girls take the baskets to market each month and pay the women who make them 80 per cent of the selling price. The remaining 20 per cent is used to pay a small wage to each of the girls and cover extras such as transport.

1 Identify and explain TWO objectives of Lydia and Abigail's enterprise. *[4]*

2 Analyse ONE possible objective that the Camfed charity may be trying to achieve with 'seed money' grants. *[4]*

3 The materials for each basket cost $1 and the baskets sell for an average of $3. Explain how Lydia and Abigail's enterprise adds value in this example. *[4]*

4 Lydia and Abigail have used their grant to become entrepreneurs. Identify and explain THREE reasons why their new business may be successful. *[6]*

5 Evaluate the view that seed-money enterprises like Lydia and Abigail's will make a major contribution to sustainable development in sub-Saharan Africa. *[6]*

2 People in business

2.1 Motivating workers

2.1.1 Motivation

TOPIC AIMS

Students should be able to:
- explain the concept of motivation
- understand what is meant by motivation
- explain why motivation is important to a business
- understand how motivation can be influenced
- understand the factors that influence motivation, such as job satisfaction, job rotation and job enrichment.

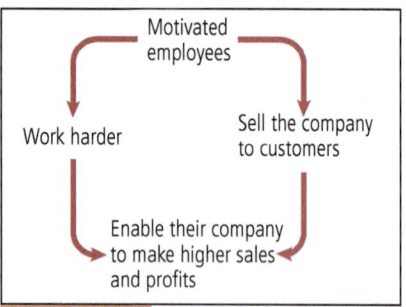

Figure 2.1.1.1 Motivated employees help a company to be profitable.

DID YOU KNOW?

The management theorist Frederick Herzberg argued that only intrinsic motivation should be counted as a true motivating force. When we do something because we want to do it, we are truly motivated. Do you agree? Why, or why not?

ACTIVITY

Create a job satisfaction survey for a job of your choice – perhaps one in your school, or one that your parents do. It should contain 10 questions designed to find out how satisfied employees are with their work.

Motivation is what causes people to act or do something in a positive way. By understanding why people behave in the way they do, managers can make work more fulfilling for people, and thus motivate them. A well-motivated workforce will work harder and contribute more to the success of a business.

Many people believe that real motivation comes from inside an individual. This is intrinsic motivation. It is associated with meeting higher-level needs. For example, an individual will take pride in completing a task or project if this makes them feel good about themselves and they have the opportunity to use their talents and skills.

The other form of motivation is extrinsic. This occurs when some form of reward or punishment is given. A bonus or commission can be positive extrinsic motivators. Fear of losing a job can be seen as a negative extrinsic motivator.

The importance of motivation to a business

Motivated employees work harder. They also feel proud to work for their employer. This is particularly important where they come into contact with customers. In these situations they are much more likely to be positive and present the company and its products in a positive way.

Motivation of employees is closely related to Maslow's hierarchy of needs. The higher the level of needs that can be fulfilled, the more likely employees are to be motivated.

Factors influencing motivation

There are a number of factors that can increase motivation, outlined in the following paragraphs.

Job satisfaction

The happier people are with their jobs, the more satisfied they will be. Jobs should be designed to increase this satisfaction. Employers will often measure job satisfaction by using rating scales for employees to report their reaction to their jobs. A rating scale could be set out from 1 to 5 (where 1 represents 'not at all satisfied' and 5 represents 'extremely satisfied').

A number of factors influence job satisfaction, including:
- the nature of the work, including how interesting it is
- variety of work tasks
- encouragement from others
- suitable rewards
- feelings of being treated fairly
- good relationships with colleagues and managers.

CASE STUDY | The 100 best companies to work for

Each year, the American business magazine *Fortune* carries out a survey of employees to find out America's best company to work for. The 2013 survey contains a series of questions given to a sample of 400 employees. Questions relate to views about management, job satisfaction and friendship among the workforce. In 2013, Google came out top because not only was it providing high pay and fringe benefits, but also the opportunity for employees to develop their careers and to put their own ideas into the company.

Google staff: Google employees report some of the highest levels of job satisfaction – with high pay and interesting jobs.

Questions

1. Write down five questions to include in a survey to find out about the best companies to work for. Why would you choose these questions?
2. In the survey outlined above, employees were asked about their opinions on their current level of job satisfaction and the effectiveness of management. How would studying the answers to these questions have aided managers to make changes that would enhance motivation?
3. Carry out an internet search to find the most recent report on America's 100 best companies to work for. What are the top three companies? Why do employees rate them so highly?

Job rotation

Job rotation widens employees' experience and increases motivation by moving them through a range of jobs. Variety and change provide greater interest, and the experience gives employees a better understanding of how the jobs fit together. They are also more likely to feel that they are being challenged and thus meeting higher-order needs.

Job enrichment

While job rotation involves increasing the variety of tasks, job enrichment involves increasing the challenge involved. Work activities become more complex and demand a greater range of skills. In job enrichment, it is important to clarify the objectives of the tasks to be carried out and to give the employees clear feedback on their performance. Job enrichment should not be confused with job enlargement. Job enlargement just means giving employees more of the same type of work to do without adding variety or increasing the challenge.

STUDY TIP

Think about whether it is better for the management of a business to use incentives or threats to make employees work more effectively.

SUMMARY QUESTIONS

1. Explain how job rotation and job enrichment are likely to motivate employees.
2. What are the differences between intrinsic and extrinsic motivation?
   Which of these is likely to lead to true motivation?
3. Think of a job that you know something about (e.g. a job done by a member of your family). How could the design of that job be improved to make job holders more motivated?

KEY POINTS

1. Motivation involves wanting to do something rather than having to do it.
2. Intrinsic motivation is a drive from within an individual. Extrinsic motivation comes from external rewards and punishments.
3. Businesses can encourage motivation by making work more interesting and thus satisfying.

2.1.2 Why people work

> **TOPIC AIMS**
>
> Students should be able to:
> - understand the concept of human needs, such as physiological and social needs
> - understand how work can help satisfy such needs.

> **ACTIVITY**
>
> Find out how many hours people work in different jobs in a typical week in your neighbourhood. Produce your findings in the form of a pie chart.

Time spent at work

To some people, work is a great pleasure that gives them a sense of personal fulfilment. For others, it is more of a necessity, a way to make a living.

Working hours

Many people spend a large part of their lives at work. Statistics from national household surveys in different countries show that the annual hours worked by employees vary considerably. For example, in the following Asian economies in 2007, people worked on average more than 42 hours a week:

- South Korea
- Bangladesh
- Sri Lanka
- Hong Kong
- Malaysia
- Thailand.

This contrasts with Western European countries – for example, Germany 41.2 hours per week, Belgium 38.6 hours per week. Workers in France are only required to work 35 hours per week, but in practice some work longer.

A major reason for these lower working hours is the existence of laws that prohibit employees from working more than a maximum number of hours in a week. For example, employees in France are supposed to work only 35 hours a week in contrast with Mexico (40 hours) and South Korea (45 hours).

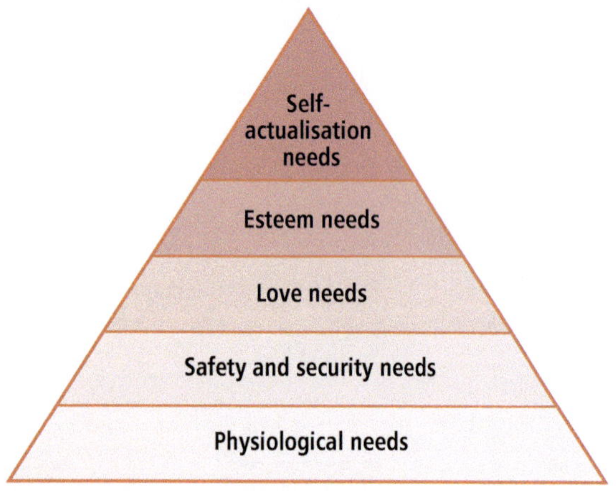

Figure 2.1.2.1 Maslow's hierarchy of needs. People are motivated to move up the pyramid (see 2.1.1).

Pyramid levels (bottom to top):
- Physiological needs
- Safety and security needs
- Love needs
- Esteem needs
- Self-actualisation needs

Work satisfies human needs

Through work, we are able to satisfy our needs. At a basic level, we need food, shelter and clothing to survive. These are physiological needs and are associated with biological well-being. Hopefully, a job of work will provide us with the income to meet these needs. However, because we spend 35 hours or more a week at work, it is desirable that work does more than meet just these basic biological needs.

Abraham **Maslow** set out what he referred to as a **hierarchy of needs** (see Figure 2.1.2.1).

> **STUDY TIP**
>
> The fact that people have a range of needs does not mean that money is unimportant!

The following table sets out the needs identified by Maslow.

Need	Description
Physiological needs	Life essentials, such as food, shelter and clothing; must be met in order to keep the body functioning. There are many people in the world who struggle to meet their physiological needs.
Safety and security needs	In order to be safe from danger, people need to be able to work in a clean and orderly space. Work needs to be secure, and employees should have the right to take part in pension and sick-pay schemes.
Love and social needs	Humans need to be able to give and receive love and friendship. This involves building up good relationships and a feeling of belonging. In the workplace, these needs can be satisfied by the companionship of fellow employees, the pleasure of working in a group or team and company social activities.
Esteem needs	Based on our desire for self-respect and the respect of others. Employees have a need to be recognised as individuals, to have a job title or some form of status or prestige, and to have their efforts noticed.
Self-actualisation needs	Humans need to develop skills and creativity and achieve full potential as individuals. Employees need the chance to progress and develop through training and use creative talents and abilities to the full.

Fewer people achieve the top levels in the hierarchy than the lower levels. Barack Obama, the President of the United States, not only earns a top income, but also does a job where he has a direct influence on the lives of people across the globe. This is likely to give him a lot of personal satisfaction. In a similar way, footballers like Cristiano Ronaldo and the tennis stars Venus and Serena Williams not only earn high salaries, but are also able to express themselves through their sport, which for them is their work.

Barack Obama: someone who is likely to self-actualise from his work as President of the United States

SUMMARY QUESTIONS

1 Which levels of satisfaction in the hierarchy of needs would the following jobs provide for you?
- Street seller of cheap toys
- International footballer
- Market research analyst
- Managing director of the international company of your choice
- Production line operative in a large company
- Owner of your own retailing business

2 What jobs can you identify that would enable you personally to fulfil all the elements of the hierarchy of needs?

3 In South Korea, employees work longer hours than in France. Does this mean that South Koreans are likely to have more of their needs met than employees working in France? Explain your answer.

STUDY TIP

Remember that work can make you happy and satisfied, but it can also be unpleasant and stressful. It is important for employers to create good working conditions at work, which in turn make for happy workers who are productive and efficient. Spending money can be cost-effective and help make bigger profits.

KEY POINTS

1 Human needs range from basic physiological needs to the need for personal fulfilment through work.

2 A job can fulfil human needs by providing money, a safe environment, a sense of belonging, self-esteem and the opportunity to develop skills.

2.1.3 Key motivational theories

TOPIC AIMS

Students should be able to:
- outline the key motivational theories of Taylor and Herzberg.

Motivation

Motivation is:
- the reason why people act or behave in a particular way
- a desire or willingness to do something.

What motivates people? Does the drive to work hard come from an inner need within the individual or some external motivator such as reward or punishment?

In 2.1.2 we saw that Maslow's work indicated that real motivation comes from within. Self-satisfaction and a belief in one's own worth are the greatest motivators. Maslow's ideas challenged prevailing views that had dominated mass-production industry management at the start of the 20th century.

Taylorism

Ideas of scientific management dominated thinking about how to manage mass production industries (such as the car industry) in the early 20th century. F.W. Taylor drew on his experience of working

---

CASE STUDY | **Fordism**

Fordism is a good example of scientific management theory put into practice. In the 1920s Henry Ford organised his car company as a giant system to mass produce motor vehicles – in particular the Model T Ford. His car factories turned out millions of vehicles that could be afforded by the masses. Cars were produced using standard repetitive operating processes. Workers were paid higher wages than those in similar industries and the high rates of pay were seen as being a key motivator. Workers tended the machines, using systems created by organisation planners and directed by production managers. The weakness of the system was that the aspirations and needs of individual employees were secondary to the industrial system. Labourers were often doing repetitive tasks on the production line and did not develop broad skills.

2 How might Fordist approaches have fallen short in creating real motivation?

Questions

1 What motivational techniques were used in Fordist car plants?

in engineering to develop a theory of efficiency. He used the term 'scientific management' to describe this approach. In 1911 he published the book *Principles of Scientific Management*, in which he focused on the design and analysis of individual tasks. Taylor believed that employees are inclined to seek maximum reward for minimum effort. To overcome this, managers should give detailed instructions for each task and manage employees closely to ensure that tasks are completed. Pay should be linked to performance in order to motivate employees.

Taylor's theory has three implications for working practices:

- managers collect knowledge about work processes systematically
- workers' discretion and control over what they do is removed
- managers lay down standard procedures and time for carrying out each job.

Herzberg's motivational theory

Herzberg's motivational theory provides a clear challenge to scientific management. Herzberg developed his theory by asking samples of engineers and accountants to identify occasions when they had felt motivated at work and occasions when they had felt unmotivated at work.

Herzberg showed that some factors – motivators – spur people to action, whereas other factors – hygiene factors – do not have the same type of impact and lead to dissatisfaction if they are not met.

- Motivators ('satisfiers') are factors relating to an employee's personal development, achievement, recognition, promotion and responsibility and the actual nature of the work itself. These satisfy and motivate people to work.
- Hygiene factors ('dissatisfiers') are factors that relate to the working environment, such as effective company policy and management practices, good working conditions and relationships, and salary. If these factors are not met then employees become dissatisfied.

Herzberg concluded that financial rewards are not long-term motivators. Of course, people are happy to receive a pay rise or financial incentive, but the impact of this extrinsic reward soon wears off. More recent research, however, indicates that money *can* act as a motivator, if the person receiving the pay increase associates this reward with recognition of his or her efforts and competence.

Herzberg's work suggests that managers need to consider both motivators and hygiene factors to improve performance and ensure that there is no dissatisfaction.

> **DID YOU KNOW?**
>
> Fordist–type management techniques are still used in some industries where employees have little control over their work, e.g. in call centres and fast-food outlets.

> **KEY POINTS**
>
> 1. Motivation is the drive to do something.
> 2. Taylorism and Fordism assume that work should be organised for workers who for their part seek high financial rewards.
> 3. Herzberg identified 'motivators' as the real drivers that motivate people at work including personal development, achievement, recognition, promotion, responsibility and the work itself.

> **SUMMARY QUESTIONS**
>
> 1. Identify job roles that include a lot of hygiene factors but do not necessarily lead to employee motivation. Explain why motivation may be missing in these jobs.
> 2. Outline some practical steps that you feel a manager could take to apply Herzberg's ideas.

2.1.4 Financial rewards

TOPIC AIMS

Students should be able to:
- explain the different payment systems, such as time rates, piece rates, bonus payments, performance rates and profit sharing
- evaluate the merits of different systems in given situations.

Payment systems

The payment for a normal working week is the basic wage or salary. Many employees receive extra benefits on top of their basic wage, either as money or in some other form. Payment systems may include some form of bonus, or incentive, to encourage employees. The bonus payment might be for high-quality work, or for completing a task ahead of schedule.

Not all employees receive a wage or salary. Salespeople may be paid on a commission basis – that is, a percentage of the revenue, or profit, that they make for the company by selling the firm's products.

The main ways of calculating pay are described below.

Flat rate

This is a set rate of pay, based on a set number of hours – for example, $200 for a 40-hour week. This is easy to calculate and administer, but it does not give the employee any incentive to work harder.

Time rate

Under this scheme, the worker receives a set rate per hour. Any hours worked above a set number are paid at an overtime rate. The overtime rate may be time and a half (i.e. 150 per cent of the normal rate) or double time (i.e. 200 per cent of the normal rate).

Piece rate

This system is sometimes used in the textile and electronics industries, for example. Payment is made for each item produced that meets a given quality standard. The advantage of such a scheme is that it encourages effort. However, it is not suitable for jobs that require time and care. Also, the output of many jobs in service industries is impossible to measure accurately. For example, how could you measure the output of a teacher, bus driver or doctor?

Bonus

A bonus is paid as an additional encouragement to employees. It can be paid out of additional profits earned by the company as a result of employees' efforts and hard work. Bonuses may also be used as an incentive to workers just before the firm closes down for a holiday period. The bonus incentive encourages employees to keep up a high work rate.

Commission

This is a payment made as a percentage of the sales a salesperson has made. For example, in a retail store, an employee might receive 10 per cent of each sale made, or may be paid an hourly rate plus 5 per cent commission on every sale made. The commission thus acts as an incentive to sell more.

In some parts of the world, diamonds are found close to the earth's surface and are literally washed out of riverbeds or from the earth with high-pressure hoses. What would be a suitable payment system for people working in these conditions?

ACTIVITY

Working in groups of two or three, identify the payment system that is used to reward employees in a given workplace. This may be a workplace where friends or relatives work. Compare the advantages and disadvantages of the different payment systems.

Performance rates

Performance rates are a good way of encouraging high performance. An employee will be set targets to achieve, based on some form of work measurement. For example, a standard time may be set to do a particular task. An employee who meets the standard will receive a set rate of pay. For exceeding the target, the employee will receive additional payments. The higher the target reached, the higher the level of pay.

Profit sharing

Under profit sharing, pay varies with the level of profit a company makes. The organisation sets a target for profit. If profit reaches this target, or exceeds it, the organisation will pay either a set sum for each employee, or will calculate the pay as a percentage of each employee's salary. Schemes such as this recognise the importance of hard-working employees in helping companies to make higher profits. The profit-sharing reward will usually be in addition to other payment schemes. The table summarises the benefits of different payment schemes.

Payment scheme	Key benefit
Flat rate	Easy to calculate, cheap to run.
Time rate	A good way of encouraging employees to work longer hours.
Piece rate	Acts as an incentive to employees to produce higher levels of output.
Bonus	Rewards high levels of performance and can be targeted at high performers.
Commission	Directly relates pay to sales made or other measures of output.
Performance rate	Directly links pay to meeting or exceeding targets.
Profit sharing	Enables employees to see the direct link between their efforts and company profits.

> **STUDY TIP**
>
> Make sure that you understand the difference between a bonus and time rates. Bonuses are usually paid for performance in excess of an agreed target. Time rates are always linked to hours worked.

> **KEY POINTS**
>
> 1. Payment systems reward effort and should act as incentives.
> 2. Time rates are based on the numbers of hours worked; piece rates vary with the number of units produced.
> 3. Bonuses, commission, performance rates and profit-sharing systems create incentives for meeting or exceeding targets.

SUMMARY QUESTIONS

1. What types of financial reward systems would be suitable in the following situations? Briefly justify your choice.
   - Firefighters (i.e. employees with responsibility for putting out fires and attending other emergencies).
   - Professional footballers playing in a knockout cup, where it is hoped that they will reach the final.
   - Homeworkers who are producing textile garments for a supplier who provides them with equipment and materials to produce high-quality textiles.
   - Shopworkers whose job it is to put new goods onto the shelves.
2. A company specialises in making handmade furniture using skilled craft workers. Each item of furniture is unique. The company is keen to make high profits and believes that the craft workers play an important part in the success of the business. Suggest a payment system, or combination of payment systems, that would enable the company to be successful and its employees to receive appropriate rewards for their efforts. Explain the reason for your choice.
3. A call centre sells insurance over the phone. The employees have been making several mistakes and there is a high turnover of staff. The current payment system is flat rate. Suggest alternative payment systems that might encourage higher levels of employee performance. Explain the reasons for your suggestions.

2.1.5 Non-financial rewards

TOPIC AIMS

Students should be able to:
- show understanding of non-financial methods such as fringe benefits
- understand when benefits such as discounts on products, free accommodation, use of a company car might be used.

Fringe benefits

Fringe benefits are non-financial incentives given to employees. They can act as a real incentive to attract employees into a particular job and then to retain them in the company.

In designing fringe benefits, it is important to consider factors that are likely to be attractive. Subsidised or free housing is a strong incentive in city areas where accommodation is expensive and there are long waiting lists for houses. Some jobs may have accommodation provided – for example, a dormitory or hostel for workers at a mine or factory. Some hotel workers are provided with accommodation at their place of work.

Fringe benefits are a useful way of meeting employee needs. The table shows how fringe benefits relate to Maslow's hierarchy.

Level in the hierarchy of needs	Example of fringe benefit
Physiological needs	Housing provides shelter. Subsidised canteen meals provide cheap food.
Safety and security needs	Insurance and health care benefits (e.g. the company pays the health insurance of its employees).
Love needs	Sports clubs or social activities where employees can meet and enjoy recreation together.
Esteem needs	Company cars, laptop computers and other status items.
Self-actualisation needs	The company pays for employees to go on training and development courses, which enable them to develop their skills and master their line of work. These might include courses in higher education.

One fringe benefit that is an important incentive is payment of school fees. In most countries in the developing world, education is highly regarded because it enables children to go on to get better jobs. However, school fees can be high for low-income families. An offer to pay all or part of children's school fees can be a powerful incentive. For example, the oil company Shell provides 2 600 scholarships a year to help with school fees for post-secondary school pupils in the areas of Nigeria where Shell is operating (Shell Secondary School Scholarship Scheme). Fringe benefits related to education and health insurance are powerful tools for winning employee loyalty.

It makes sense for a company to identify the sorts of fringe benefits that will provide the greatest incentive.

Companies need to design fringe benefits to give the greatest possible benefit to their employees. For example, in a rural area it may be sensible to offer senior employees the use of company cars. In a congested urban area, the employees may be more interested in subsidised use of public transport.

Fringe benefits are a cost to the company. Some may be relatively low cost and may be related to the company activity. Purchases of company products may be subsidised. Many transport companies allow employees and their families to travel for free or at very low prices.

A company may build a school or a clinic as a fringe benefit to encourage loyalty.

Some fringe benefits are intended to make employees feel good about working for their company: tickets may be provided to sports events and concerts, and company away-days or short holidays to attractive locations may be offered. Fringe benefits may relate directly to unsocial hours that some employees are expected to work – for example, a free evening meal and taxi home for those working after a certain time. Some employees, such as sales representatives, may benefit from a petrol or car allowance.

> **ACTIVITY**
>
> Working as a small group, choose an occupation. Design three fringe benefits that would be likely to attract and retain the motivation of employees in your occupation.

SUMMARY QUESTIONS

1. From the following list of fringe benefits, identify the ones that would be most attractive to employees in the situations listed below. In each case, justify your choices.

   Subsidised school fees / subsidised public transport / subsidised canteen services / car petrol allowance / low-cost company goods / free accommodation
   - Employees live a long way from their place of work.
   - There is a shortage of housing and what is available is very expensive.
   - Employees do not have access to cooking facilities and have to travel a long way to work.
   - Education is expensive and there is a strong emphasis placed on educational qualifications.

2. A large international confectionery company (producing sweets and chocolate) is seeking to develop rewards systems that encourage high performance. What sorts of fringe benefits could it create that would act as an incentive for high-performing employees?

3. In what circumstances are fringe benefits likely to act as stronger incentives to motivate employees than alternative financial rewards?

> **DID YOU KNOW?**
>
> In some countries, employees have to declare fringe benefits when they fill in their income tax forms, even if the benefits do not involve money (i.e. are non-financial).

> **STUDY TIP**
>
> Examination questions are often set on methods of motivating workers. Make sure you can explain the difference between a financial and a non-financial benefit, and that you can give examples of both.

KEY POINTS

1. A fringe benefit is a property or service provided in addition to financial reward.
2. Fringe benefits act as incentives for an employee to join a company, stay with the company and work hard for the company.
3. Fringe benefits should be designed to best meet employee needs.
4. Health, education and housing benefits are good non-financial incentives.
5. Subsidised products and petrol and car allowances also help to subsidise an employee's income.

2.2 Organisation and management

2.2.1 Roles and responsibilities

TOPIC AIMS

Students should be able to:

- draw, interpret and explain simple organisational charts
- understand the roles and responsibilities and interrelationships of people within organisations
- understand the concepts of span of control, hierarchy, chain of command and delegation
- comment on the central features of organisational structure
- show analytical awareness of the features of a given chart
- appreciate that organisation charts change as a business expands.

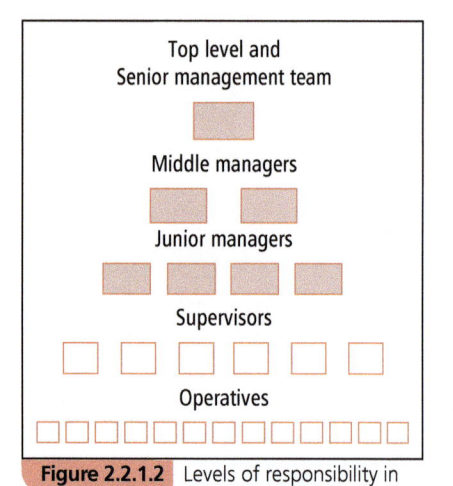

Organisation charts

An **organisation chart** shows the roles of people in an organisation and the relationship between them. For example, Figure 2.2.1.1 shows that a senior accountant in an organisation's accounts department has three junior accountants working for her.

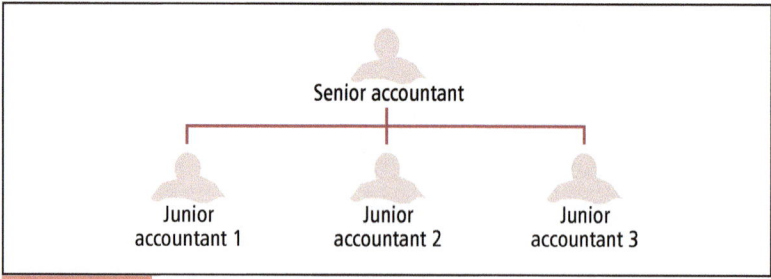

Figure 2.2.1.1 A simple organisation chart

Every organisation can be set out in this way, to show the departments, how they link together and the main lines of authority. It shows lines of decision making and levels of responsibility.

Role refers to what an individual does in an organisation. For example, a sales manager in Nigeria will be in charge of the company's sales team in that country. Their task will be to make sure that there is a clear sales plan and that the sales team receives the right level of training and support. The sales manager will be responsible for people and resources and for making sure that targets are achieved.

Levels within an organisation

An organisation chart usually indicates positions that have roughly equal amounts of responsibility on the same level. Figure 2.2.1.2 shows the **hierarchy** of an organisation – that is, how employees are arranged by rank or seniority. The managing director and the senior management team are at the top level. At the next level are the middle managers. Then there are junior managers, supervisors and, finally, operatives at the bottom level.

The diagram also illustrates a chain of command. Operatives are responsible to supervisors. Supervisors report to junior managers, and so on. The person that an individual reports to is often called their line manager.

Figure 2.2.1.2 Levels of responsibility in an organisation

DID YOU KNOW?

Empowerment describes the way in which employees lower down an organisation have been trusted to take on responsibility, e.g. when sales staff in a department store advise customers on good buys.

Span of control

The span of control of an individual is the number of people he or she manages or supervises directly. Figure 2.2.1.3 shows an organisation with a narrow span of control.

Choosing the best span of control means finding a balance between having control over people below you (subordinates) and being able to trust them. There is a limit to the number of people who can be supervised well by one person. The diagram shows an organisation in which no one is directly responsible for more than two subordinates.

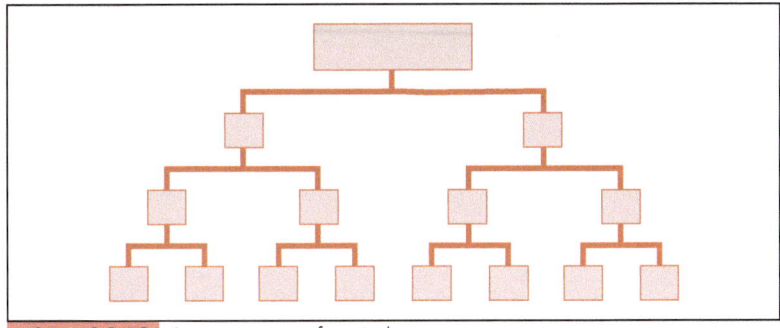

Figure 2.2.1.3 A narrow span of control

Tall and flat organisations

A narrow span of control makes it possible to control people and to communicate with them closely. However, the disadvantage is that this may lead to too many levels of management. This kind of tall organisation can be difficult to run.

In a flat organisation, managers delegate responsibility to subordinate staff. In this arrangement, managers need to have far more trust in their subordinates than in a tall organisation. Fewer managers are needed, and the hierarchy has fewer levels. Advertising agencies often give a lot of responsibility to their designers to come up with creative ideas. The designer will meet with the client and work on ideas themselves. This works well when the designer is comfortable with taking on responsibility and has good creative skills.

Some managers believe that the more senior an individual is, the fewer people he or she should have in their direct span of control. However, there are many examples of organisations that work well when senior managers have an extensive span of control. The best span in an organisation will depend on the skills of its managers.

When a business expands it may have to reorganise its structure. It may need to create a new hierarchy by adding extra layers of management.

Figure 2.2.1.4 A flat and a tall organisation

SUMMARY QUESTIONS

1. Define the following terms.
   Span of control / hierarchy / chain of command / delegation
2. What are the benefits and disadvantages of having a large span of control within an organisation?
3. Some organisations are said to be 'too hierarchical'. What is meant by this and why is it a problem to be 'too hierarchical'?

STUDY TIP

Make sure that you understand what sort of tasks are delegated. A secretary in an office might be given the task of arranging business meetings with clients, but would not be allowed to decide how much money should be spent on promoting products.

Delegation means giving authority for carrying out a task to someone at a lower level. Delegation means that people at the top of an organisation do not have to make all the decisions themselves.

ACTIVITY

Draw a chart for an organisation that you are familiar with. This could be your school, a club that you are a member of or even your place of work. Comment on the structure of the organisation, using terms such as span of control and hierarchy.

KEY POINTS

1. Organisation charts show the roles of members of an organisation and show the links of an organisation between its members.
2. There is a limit to an effective span of control.
3. Tall organisations are hierarchical and may be difficult to run.

2.2.2 The role of management

TOPIC AIMS

Students should be able to:
- explain the functions of management
- outline the importance of delegation.

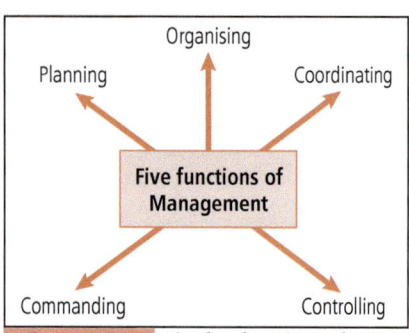

Figure 2.2.2.1 The five functions of management. Managers have to steer an organisation to achieve its objectives.

STUDY TIP

Make sure that you are able to state what managers actually do. The function of management is to acquire and allocate resources in a manner that best allows a business to achieve its objectives.

Planning

Managers need to create clear plans for others to follow. These plans are converted into general aims, more specific objectives, and tasks to be completed.

Plans should define:

- the end goal
- what needs to be done (tasks) and by whom
- the timescale for achieving tasks and objectives
- how achievement of the objectives will be recorded.

Different types of plans are established at different levels within an organisation. For example, a strategic plan is a top-level plan that covers the whole, or a significant part, of the organisation. It sets out how the organisation will achieve its objectives. A tactical plan typically involves middle management and is shorter term than a strategic plan. It set out the means through which particular objectives will be met, for example at departmental level. An operation plan is concerned with how specific operations and processes are carried out.

Organising

Managers are expected to organise themselves, their work and their workers by setting up systems, procedures and structures in a logical and efficient way. To do this, managers need to make the most of the resources available. An organised manager gives priority to the most important tasks and ensures that these are completed on time. Organisation involves:

- prioritising and selecting tasks
- deciding who will undertake the tasks
- assigning the tasks
- delegating authority and responsibility
- coordinating different activities and individuals
- making sure that things are done on time in an ordered way.

Coordination

Coordination is closely related to organisation and involves making sure that the interrelated activities that need to be completed are carried out in a structured way. The coordinator (manager) brings together the activities of different people, projects and plans in an integrated way.

Commanding (leadership)

Commanders (or leaders) give direction and through their leadership ensure that directions are followed. They will have responsibility for making sure that all employees perform their jobs well in the interests of the organisation (see 2.2.3).

Controlling

Managers need to create an effective control system to make sure that plans are kept on track (for example targets and deadlines are met) and that resources are used in an appropriate way. A control system includes targets and performance indicators, so that performance can be measured and managers can track performance against the targets set. When the organisation is falling short of its targets, appropriate control actions can be taken (for example allocating more resources to tasks).

Importance of delegation

To delegate means to hand over responsibility for carrying out a task to someone else in the organisation. Good managers need to know:

- what to delegate
- when to delegate
- who to delegate tasks to.

Tasks can be delegated if they can be completed accurately and safely by someone else in the organisation and on time to the required standards. They should only be delegated to someone that is competent, qualified and authorised to do the delegated task.

Some managers are reluctant to delegate because they want to keep control of activities themselves and do not trust others. The problem here is that a manager may take on too many tasks themselves and not be able to complete all of them well. However, this needs to be balanced against trusting others (typically subordinates) to carry out work that they are not able to do.

Good delegation enables more work to be completed with better results. Delegation also has a motivating element in terms of trusting and empowering others to take on more responsibility.

> **DID YOU KNOW?**
>
> A control system consists of methods such as targets and performance indicators, used to identify whether a business is on track to achieve its objectives, and where it is not, taking actions to put it back on track.

> **ACTIVITY**
>
> Select a story from the national press identifying a situation where a manager in an organisation has failed to carry out his or her responsibilities as expected. Which aspect of management, e.g. planning, controlling etc., has been poorly executed? Was the manager competent to carry out the tasks delegated to him or her?

> **SUMMARY QUESTIONS**
>
> 1. What is the relationship between planning, organising and control?
> 2. Identify tasks that have been delegated to you by others (e.g. in home/study/work situations). Which of these tasks was it appropriate/inappropriate to delegate to you?

> **KEY POINTS**
>
> 1. Management is the process of planning, organising, leading and controlling the efforts of organisation members.
> 2. Delegation is the process of handing over responsibility to others.
> 3. Work should only be delegated to others who are capable, authorised and can be trusted to carry out the delegated tasks.

2.2.3 Leadership styles

TOPIC AIMS

Students should be able to:
- understand the importance of the role of management in motivating employees
- understand leadership styles, such as autocratic, democratic and laissez-faire
- recommend and justify an appropriate leadership style in a given situation.

Managers as motivators

People are the essential resource in an organisation that helps it to achieve its objectives. Managers help to steer the organisation towards meeting these objectives. As people work best when they are motivated, an important task for management is to motivate employees. This is often referred to as human resource management or people management.

Good human resource managers listen to their employees and use approaches such as job rotation and job enrichment to create job satisfaction. They realise that employees are all human beings, with their own hopes and fears.

Many companies use an annual appraisal interview as a way of motivating employees. The employee meets with his or her manager to set targets to identify performance strengths and weaknesses over the past year. A training and development plan can then be created for the employee which sets out ways for improving work performance and enjoyment of work. Suitable training may also be identified.

Leadership styles

Leadership style refers to a manager's pattern of behaviour. There are three main styles: autocratic, democratic and laissez-faire.

- **Autocratic** means taking decisions by oneself. Autocratic managers make decisions on their own and then tell staff what they will do and how to do it. This tightly controlled approach may be called 'tell and do'. The autocratic manager may provide clear instructions, but staff may be demotivated because there is little opportunity for their own ideas.
- **Democratic** means decision making by people, after considering everyone's ideas. Persuasive democratic management usually means that the leader makes the decisions, and persuades the followers that these are the right decisions. In consultative democratic management, the group will have a lot of input into the discussion – that is, they are 'consulted' – even if the leader still makes the final decision.
- **Laissez-faire** is a French phrase that means 'let [them] do [it]' and it is used to describe a loose management style. Managers create guidelines and objectives, but then leave staff to carry out the tasks for themselves. This can be successful if the employees are motivated and good decision makers. However, it can lead to chaos if staff need strong direction from the manager and are unable, for various reasons, to make decisions themselves. The table summarises the three styles.

DID YOU KNOW?

Managers need to be able to delegate, that is give responsibility to another person for carrying out a task.

Appraisal involves managers sitting down with employees to discuss and agree targets and training plans.

Leadership style	Advantages	Disadvantages
Autocratic	Rapid decision making. Good for armed forces, fire and other emergency services.	Can lead to dissatisfaction. Motivation can drop.
Democratic	Makes use of many ideas. Involves consultation about decision making.	Can be slow in making decisions. May lead to disagreement and arguments.
Laissez-faire	Employees have freedom to manage their own work within given guidelines.	Lack of clarity can lead to low motivation and disagreement.

Good leaders match their style to the needs of different situations. They may be autocratic when urgent quick action is required and democratic when it will be advantageous to involve others in the decision-making process.

Some organisations are more suited to particular styles. In an advertising agency, it is helpful to share ideas between lots of people, so democratic or laissez-faire styles are helpful. Where decisions have to be made quickly and to a set pattern, a more autocratic style may be useful.

> **STUDY TIP**
>
> It is a common error to think that a democratic leadership style means that workers vote on issues and that the majority view is carried out.

KEY POINTS

1. Human resource management involves treating people as an organisation's most important resource.
2. Good managers make employees feel valued and identify their needs at work.
3. Autocratic managers direct others by making most, or all, decisions.
4. Democratic managers listen to others and share responsibility for decision making.
5. Laissez-faire managers create guidelines but leave their staff to carry out the tasks.

ACTIVITY

Working in a small group, decide on the most suitable leadership style to use in the following scenarios. Explain how the style you recommend would be suitable.

1. A business has received a large order for goods from a new customer. These goods need to be produced within a very short time frame.
2. A fault has occurred on the production line in a car-producing plant. It is not clear what is causing the fault, so the views of everyone working on that line are to be taken into consideration.

SUMMARY QUESTIONS

1. Copy and complete the paragraph below using the following words.

   Laissez-faire / autocratic / democratic / leadership style / human resource management

   It is important to match _____ with the situation and the type of organisation. For example, _____ management may be most suitable when it is important to consider the views of a range of people with specialist knowledge in an organisation. In contrast, when decisions need to be made quickly and with clarity, an _____ style may be more appropriate. A third approach, referred to as _____, gives greater freedom to individuals within the organisation to make their own decisions. People are the most important resource in the organisation. Looking after their individual interests is referred to as _____.

2. With which type of leadership styles would you associate the following potential problems?
   - Employees are demotivated because they feel that there is little room for them to think for themselves.
   - Employees are demotivated because they feel that they are not being led or directed properly.
   - Employees are demotivated because it is taking too long to arrive at decisions.

3. Suggest ways in which a manager can make his or her staff feel more valued in the workplace.

2.2.4 Trade unions

TOPIC AIMS

Students should be able to:

- describe the work of trade unions
- understand the concept of a trade union
- show awareness of the benefits that union membership can provide for employees
- show an awareness of how trade unions can influence business behaviour
- use examples to show how business behaviour might be modified in terms of levels of pay and treatment of employees.

Trade unions

A **trade union** is an association of the employees formed to protect and promote the interests of its members, and to achieve other jointly agreed aims. Trade unions are formed, financed and run by their members, who pay an annual subscription. The unions try to influence some of the decisions made by the owners and managers of a business, although they do not always succeed. They are able to exert more influence on an organisation if all or a high proportion of employees are union members.

In the UK, the National Union of Teachers (NUT) seeks to improve pay and conditions for teachers. In some countries, such as Germany, there are very large trade unions that represent all the workers in the same industry. In India, there are 11 major trade union groups representing workers in a range of industries, and many smaller unions representing sometimes only a few hundred people in a particular area.

Figure 2.2.4.1 shows some of the aims of trade unions. You can see that the main aim is to secure the best possible conditions of work

French workers taking strike action and protesting to protect their jobs and their right to only work a maximum of 35 hours per week.

Figure 2.2.4.1 Aims of trade unions. Not all countries allow trade unions to exist.

for members. Unions know that the decisions a firm makes will affect the livelihoods of workers and their families.

Negotiation

One of the purposes of a trade union is to negotiate – that is, discuss – with employers. Talks take place between representatives of the employees (union officials) and representatives of the employer. Both sides try to reach agreement on issues such as conditions of employment (e.g. hours worked, safety of the workplace) or wage levels. This negotiation can take place at a local level (e.g. within a factory) or at national level, where the union represents all the members of the trade union in the country.

The benefits of trade union membership to individuals

Typical benefits of belonging to a trade union include:

- knowing that you are not alone in the workplace; you are part of a group that represents you and your fellow workers
- belonging to a body that is negotiating better terms and conditions (e.g. pay increase, improved conditions) for you
- direct benefits (e.g. sickness benefit) for employees
- support for members if there is a grievance or disciplinary procedure (a grievance occurs when a member of a trade union feels they have been treated badly at work; a disciplinary procedure occurs when a union member has been disciplined for, say, poor timekeeping)
- direct action to support members (e.g. if negotiations over pay break down with employees, union officials may call a strike; this means that union members stop work).

The ability to strike gives unions a lot of power: if airline or railway workers go on strike, their companies lose money, profit and their reputation for reliability. Other actions that unions can take include working more slowly (a go-slow) and working to rule – only doing things which fit with the rules set out in a contract of employment.

The impact of trade unions

Strong trade unions can impact on business behaviour. In France, the trade unions are very strong. They were influential in setting a 35-hour working week in the European Union. Unions in France have often succeeded in creating national strikes: workers from many trade unions stop work for a day, or longer, to put pressure on employers and the government.

Over time, union action, or the threat of it, can influence businesses to:

- increase pay
- provide better conditions, such as cleaner washrooms, healthier working environments, longer holidays, safer workplaces.

ACTIVITY

Find out about some of the trade unions in your own or a neighbouring country. Use the search terms List of Trade Unions to search on the internet. Compare your findings with those of a partner. What is the purpose of these unions? Can you find a news story which illustrates the activities of a union? (In some countries, the government does not allow trade unions.)

STUDY TIP

Remember that trade unions do not pass laws. They can put pressure on employers, but not force them, to pay higher wages or improve working conditions.

SUMMARY QUESTIONS

1. What is a trade union? Who are its members?
2. Provide examples of two issues that trade unions become involved in, and explain why.
3. What benefits would an individual worker gain from being a member of a trade union?

KEY POINTS

1. A trade union is an association of employees, set up to protect their interests.
2. The nature of trade unions varies between countries; essentially, all unions are created to negotiate wages and conditions of employment.

2.3 The workforce

2.3.1 The recruitment and selection process

TOPIC AIMS

Students should be able to:

- explain the methods of recruiting and selecting employees
- understand the difference between internal and external recruitment
- understand the main stages in recruitment and selection of employees.

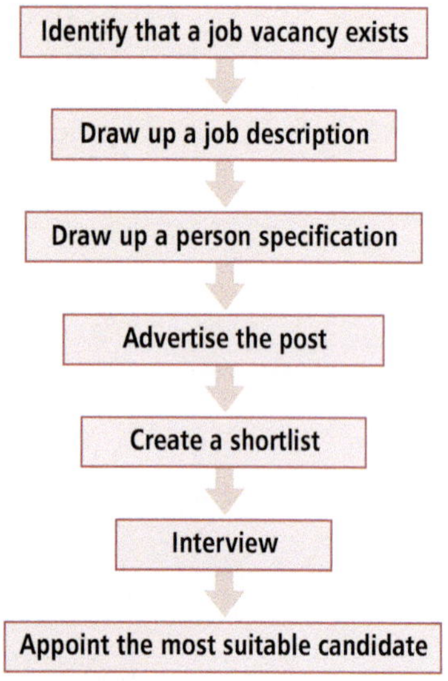

Recruitment

Recruitment involves attracting the right standard of applicants to apply for vacancies. Figure 2.3.1.1 summarises the typical stages in the recruitment process.

Recruiting may be *internal* or *external*. Internal recruiting means employing someone already working for the organisation: this may mean promotion. External recruitment involves appointing someone from outside the organisation.

The table shows the advantages of the two types of recruitment.

Advantages of internal recruitment	Advantages of external recruitment
There is less risk because the employer already knows the person and their capabilities.	New ideas are brought into the organisation from outside.
The cost of advertising is saved, so the recruitment process is cheaper. (In some countries and organisations, however, equal opportunities legislation means that all positions have to be advertised.)	Advertising externally may reach more widely into the business community (e.g. a teacher might be attracted to an educational publishing company and bring useful experience and knowledge to the job).
The opportunity for promotion within the organisation encourages people to work hard.	Internal jealousies are avoided from promotion.
Induction costs are saved.	

Advertising the job

Once a business is clear about the job it is offering, it can draw up an advertisement for the post. How this is set out depends on:

- who the business is trying to attract
- where the advert is going to be placed – that is, what media will be used (newspaper, radio, TV, website, etc.).

A good job advertisement will include the following features:

Feature	Description
Job description	The major requirements of the job, setting out the key responsibilities and tasks involved
What the business does	A brief description of the business and its activities
Location	Where the job will be based
Salary expectation	Figures are not always necessary, but an indication of salary level should be given
Address and contact	How to contact the recruiter (e.g. e-mail address)
Closing date	This gives candidates the time limit for applications
Qualifications	Certain jobs require a minimum entrance qualification
Experience	Experience that candidates should have
Fringe benefits	Mention additional benefits (e.g. company car)
Organisational identity	A logo or badge associated with the company

Identify that a job vacancy exists
↓
Draw up a job description
↓
Draw up a person specification
↓
Advertise the post
↓
Create a shortlist
↓
Interview
↓
Appoint the most suitable candidate

Figure 2.3.1.1 The recruitment process

Selection

Selection involves choosing the most suitable applicant for a vacancy. Screening applicants is a very important part of this process. Figure 2.3.1.2 illustrates the various stages in screening applicants.

The recruiters put together a shortlist of candidates who most closely meet the person specification for the job. These candidates will be invited for interview. This may involve a panel of interviewers, who will ask questions and score candidates on the extent to which they meet the specification.

The interview process may take one or two days. As well as being interviewed, the candidates may be asked to take tests and perform tasks: these are considered good indicators of a person's ability to carry out the job, and of whether a person will fit into an organisation. An aptitude test might be set; this is a practical test to assess suitability for a post. For example, a prospective airline pilot might be tested for reaction time to moving objects. Another test might be a psychometric test, used widely for management posts and some jobs with international companies. This is a personality test in which students are asked for their views on a particular subject, or to indicate how they would act in a given situation. The test may be carried out with pencil and paper or online.

The recruiting process for jobs at a lower grade may simply involve a short interview of students.

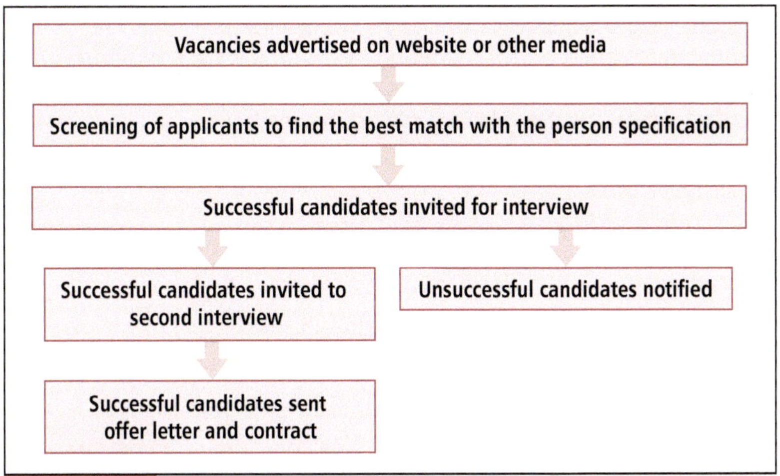

Figure 2.3.1.2 The screening process

SUMMARY QUESTIONS

1. What are the most important steps in recruiting and selecting a new employee to join an organisation?
2. Why does an organisation shortlist students?
3. Outline the difference between external and internal recruitment. For a food-exporting company, what would be the benefits of recruiting a new sales manager:
   - internally?
   - externally?

STUDY TIP

Job descriptions outline the tasks, duties and responsibilities of the job holder. Person specifications identify the qualities, experience and qualifications that the job holder needs to have.

DID YOU KNOW?

In most countries, equal opportunities laws govern recruitment and selection. All candidates should be asked the same questions and not be favoured on the grounds of, for example, sex, race, ethnic group, disability or being an existing employee of the company.

ACTIVITY

Identify the main stages that were involved in the recruitment of a friend or relative who has recently started a job. How closely do these stages mirror the stages outlined in this chapter?

KEY POINTS

1. Recruitment is the process of identifying the need for a new employee, defining the job, and finding and selecting the right person to do that job.
2. Recruitment may be internal or external.
3. Creating a well-structured job advertisement is important for attracting good students.
4. Companies also create a person specification and job description for recruitment purposes.

2.3.2 Recruiting and selecting in practice

TOPIC AIMS

Students should be able to:
- draw up a job description
- draw up a job specification
- choose suitable ways of advertising a vacancy.

The job description

When a business starts to grow, it may need to employ new staff. From time to time, it will need to replace existing staff who leave or retire. Whenever a business recruits, it is essential to set out a clear description of what the job entails. The table sets out the information that should be included in a **job description**.

Title of the job	Indication of what the job involves and the level of responsibility (e.g. sales manager, South East Asia)
Department and location of the job	Organisational department and its location (e.g. marketing and sales department, Beijing, China)
General terms of what is involved in carrying out the job	Indication of what is involved in the post (Many job vacancies describe the job in fairly general terms, particularly if these might change over time.)
Responsible to whom	Who the employee will report to, their line manager
Responsible for whom	Other employees for whom the employee will be responsible and manage
Other responsibilities	Resources for which the employee will be responsible
Scope of the post	Sets out the level of the post (e.g. managerial)
Education and qualifications	The level of education required to carry out the post
Name of compiler and approver and date of issue	The person who designed the job description and the date on which the description was written

Business effectiveness is most likely to be achieved where clear criteria are established for recruiting new employees, e.g. appropriate skills, experience and qualifications. Here is an example of a simple job description for the role of a market researcher.

STUDY TIP

Good recruitment is about selecting the most suitable person for the job, not the most highly qualified. Do you understand the difference?

ACTIVITY

Create a job description and job specification for one of the following jobs.
- A job carried out by a friend or member of your family. Find out what the job entails, and what qualifications and skills are required to carry out the job.
- A job that you have seen advertised in a newspaper, and is one with which you are familiar, which gives some general guidance about the nature of the job.

ABC Markets, plc
Job description

Job title	Senior Market Researcher
Department	Marketing, Accra, Ghana
Responsible to	Kojo Agyeman
Responsible for	Junior and part-time market researchers
Scope of the post	The market researcher's main role is to conduct interviews in line with guidance provided by the Head of Market Research
Responsibilities	The post holder is expected to: arrange interviews ask questions of interviewees record interviews on forms, on computer or on video carry out interviewing over the telephone keep accurate and detailed records.
Compiled by	Akwesi Sarpong (Market Research Manager)
Date	12 June 2014

ABC Markets Accra plc, Ghana
Person specification

Post title: Senior Market Researcher

Criteria	Essential	Desirable
Qualifications/ knowledge	A business studies university-level qualification (The successful candidate will have successfully completed at least 3 years of study at university.) Information technology qualification – including information processing and presentation	
Work-related experience	1 year's experience of working in a market research role	Experience of having managed a small market research team
Skills/abilities and special attributes	Good planning and organisation skills Ability to prioritise tasks Excellent communication skills Team-working skills	Team-leadership skills Advanced mathematics skills

Job or person specification

A **job specification** (sometimes referred to as a person specification) sets out the skills, characteristics and attributes needed for a particular job. Job descriptions and person specifications then provide the basis for job advertisements. They help job applicants and post holders know what is expected of them and should:

- contain enough information to attract suitable people
- act as a checking device for the business to make sure that applicants with the right skills are chosen for interview.

The job specification gives a list of requirements related to the person doing the job. It will include an introduction, giving details of the job title, post reference number and management responsibilities. It will then set out the attributes that the organisation wants that person to have – for example, their type of personality or educational level. It describes essential requirements and the other the desirable requirements. The interview panel will choose someone who has all the essential requirements. If they have to choose between candidates who fit all the essential requirements, they will use the desirable requirements.

Different media for advertising jobs

Jobs can be advertised in various media:

- Websites can target local, national and international job seekers.
- National newspapers often advertise certain types of jobs on particular days. Magazines are often targeted at special interest groups e.g. accountants or marketers who may be looking for jobs.
- Local radio can attract local recruits, particularly in urban areas.
- Vacancy boards/noticeboards in locations such as supermarkets.
- Other suitable media include adverts on the sides of trains, buses and in bus and train stations.

The cost of advertsing is also a consideration. For example, a top executive job with a high salary is likely to be advertised nationally via a costly media, such as a national newspaper. However, a local sales job might be advertised in a shop window, job centre or local newspaper.

KEY POINTS

1. A job description should set out clearly what a job entails.
2. A job specification sets out the skills, characteristics and attributes needed for a specific job.
3. The job description and job specification can be used as a basis for framing interview questions and suitable tests.

SUMMARY QUESTIONS

1. Explain the differences between a job description and a job specification.
2. Draw up a job description and a person specification for a business studies teacher.
3. What would be the most suitable media for advertising a senior marketing post in an international company?

2.3.3 Training

TOPIC AIMS

Students should be able to:
- identify and explain different training methods (internal and external)
- analyse and evaluate on-the-job and off-the-job training
- analyse and evaluate the relevance of training (including induction training) to both management and employees.

The main types of training

Training is the process through which the employees learn the knowledge and skills needed to do their job well. Because modern jobs are continually changing, employees usually need to receive training throughout their working lives. For example, they may need new training to keep up to date with technological developments, or with new laws that affect the business. Figure 2.3.3.1 shows the two main types of training.

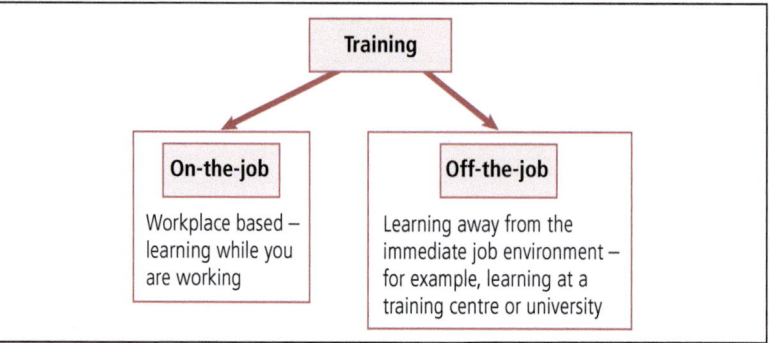

```
                Training
               /        \
         On-the-job    Off-the-job
     Workplace based –   Learning away from the
     learning while you  immediate job environment –
     are working         for example, learning at a
                         training centre or university
```

Figure 2.3.3.1 On-the-job training allows employees to learn specific skills for their job, is usually at their place of work and is cheaper. Off-the-job training is more expensive and may be less relevant to the specific needs of individual companies and employees.

The main purposes of training

Training is important for both employees and managers. Through training, individuals are better prepared to carry out their work tasks. However, if staff move on quickly to work for competitors once a business has invested in training, this can be a disadvantage. The main purposes of training are explored below.

- **Induction**: this introduces an employee to a new job and to the company and/or the workplace. It will usually include an overview of the company, but there will be information specific to certain industries, such as health and safety training for employees involved in the manual handling of goods or driving forklift trucks. Another important part of induction is that it allows people to know other employees and to get started on their work quickly because they get company procedures.
- **Understanding the job requirements**: initial training should focus on making sure that an employee is able to fulfil the basic requirements of the job.
- **Development of job skills**: specialist skills will need to be developed to enable an employee to do a job well. These might be interacting with customers or using important IT applications.
- **Broadening knowledge of the business**: the more trainees know about the wider activities of the business and the nature of its work, the more they will be able to help the organisation meet its objectives.
- **Changing attitudes and skills**: organisations frequently have to make changes. Training needs to be designed to help individuals adapt to new attitudes which move the organisation forward.

STUDY TIP

Training requires time and money, but should produce a return in the long run: it is an investment in people. All investments incur risks. What risks are there to a business of investing in training?

DID YOU KNOW?

An annual performance appraisal is a meeting between an employee and their manager, and is a good time to consider what is going well, or less well, and to identify training needs. The employee discusses with the manager how the work is going, and together they set targets for the coming year. Employees may need additional training to meet these targets, to become more skilled and increase their job knowledge.

CASE STUDY: Group training in Australia

In Australia, there is a network of around 150 group training organisations. These employ over 40 000 apprentices. (An apprenticeship is a structured process for training in a set of skills that is recognised by a particular industry.) There are group training organisations for most industries in Australia, including automotive, construction, electrical, plumbing, engineering, horticulture, community service, retail and hospitality. The group training organisations carry out preliminary training at the apprentices' premises. The Master Plumbers Group Training Organisation runs workshops for apprentice plumbers. When the apprentices are sufficiently skilled, they are taken on by plumbing businesses. The apprentices will then work for the employer for a set period of time. This may be for just a week or for several years. Trainees can work towards particular qualifications. The employer pays a part of their wage, with the government topping this up. The group training organisation handles all the paperwork and payment of the apprentices. They only provide apprentices to companies that they feel are competent to carry out work-based training.

Apprenticeships enable young people to learn a skill, working for a company for a short or long period of time.

Questions

1 In what ways do the group training schemes involve on-the-job training?

2 How do they additionally involve off-the-job training?

3 How do employers and apprentices in Australia benefit from the group training schemes?

Training is important for employees at every level in the organisation and at every stage of their career. New employees will learn how to fit into the organisation and how to develop the skills they need. Experienced employees can upgrade their knowledge and skills.

Management training is also important. Managers need to learn how to manage and motivate others. They also need to learn complex job skills and keep up to date with the latest developments in their field. A new manager will often work for a few months in a number of departments in a company to gain an understanding of how the various parts of the organisation fit together.

SUMMARY QUESTIONS

1 Martha completed a university degree in business studies and then went to work as an accountant for 2 years. She now wants to become a business studies teacher. What types of on-the-job and off-the-job training would be helpful to Martha in preparing her to become a skilled business studies teacher?

2 Prakesh is about to start a job at a supermarket involving a range of general duties that include shelf stacking and managing a cash till. What sort of induction activities should Prakesh be given in his first week at work? Explain why you have suggested these activities.

3 What sort of training would you expect to receive for a job that you are currently interested in doing once you leave school? Where is this training likely to take place?

KEY POINTS

1 Training improves employee knowledge and skills and helps an organisation to have effective workers with the right skills.

2 On-the-job training takes place internally within an organisation. Off-the-job training takes place externally.

3 Induction training enables new employees to settle in quickly and learn their responsibilities.

4 Ongoing training keeps employees up to date with new developments and enables them to learn new skills.

5 Management training enables motivation and effective management of employees.

2.3.4 Dismissal and redundancy

TOPIC AIMS

Students should be able to:

- explain the difference between dismissal and redundancy
- use examples to illustrate the difference
- appreciate why the workforce of a business may need to be reduced
- understand the circumstances when downsizing a workforce occurs (e.g. automation, closure of a factory)
- recommend and justify which workers to recruit or to make redundant in given circumstances
- understand the benefits and limitations of part-time and full-time workers.

Employers cannot guarantee everyone a job for life. There are times when a company has to close down all or part of its operations because it is not profitable; in these situations, jobs will have to be cut.

At other times, an employer may have to dismiss an employee – for example, because he or she is not competent in their job, or because they have behaved in an unacceptable way. In all countries, there are laws with which employers must comply when they dismiss employees. A distinction is made between fair and unfair dismissal.

Dismissal

Dismissal occurs when an employer terminates a worker's employment contract. There are many reasons for dismissal, which may be fair or unfair. Employees can be fairly dismissed for, say, poor timekeeping, stealing company property, gross misconduct, bullying and harassing other workers or criminal damage to the workplace. The exact legal requirements vary from country to country. There are instances, however, when law courts decide that unfair dismissal has occurred. A worker might prove, for example, that the true cause for dismissal was some form of prejudice, which would be unfair.

Redundancy

Redundancy occurs when a job role is no longer required. The person in that role therefore loses their job. Decisions are usually made by assessing which job or skill is no longer needed. Sometimes, when reducing numbers of staff for a particular job activity, who leaves is determined by who was the most recent to join.

Redundancy involves either the closure of a business as a whole, closure of a particular workplace where the employee was employed, or a reduction in the workforce. As a result of redundancy, employees are no longer required to perform particular job roles.

It is important that managers handle redundancy very carefully. Poor handling can lead to bad feelings among those made redundant, as well as among remaining workers and in the community as a whole. At the least, managers must make sure that they comply with employment law, particularly in relation to fairness. Typically, the law will set out requirements for a redundancy payment; this is related to how long the employee has worked for a company.

Why do redundancies occur?

Redundancy may occur when a business downsizes and reduces its labour force. This happened in most countries across the world in 2008 and 2009. A world economic crisis resulted from poor decisions in the banking industry (see 6.1.2) and millions of people worldwide lost their jobs. Some businesses shut down, others closed down some of the plant, while many others made some of their workforce redundant. In manufacturing, many factories, particularly in the automotive industries, were closed. At the same time, many services jobs were cut – for example, there were many bank closures. In some cases, this involved the closure of branches of a bank; in others, the whole bank was closed. The American bank Lehman Brothers was a famous example.

The global economic crisis in 2008–9 led to many companies creating redundancies by closing down plants and cutting their workforces.

Retrenchment means cutting down expenditure to become more financially stable. In many companies, the wage bill accounts for 70 per cent of costs, so this is often the easiest area to reduce. Other causes of redundancies are:

- Focus: sometimes, directors of a company believe that it has grown too large, is trying to do too many things and, as a result, is not performing well. The directors will then seek to focus the business on what it does best and announce redundancies in 'non-core activities' or 'non-core markets'. So a company that has retail outlets in India, China, the United States and Norway might decide that the Norwegian market is too small and decide to focus on the other three areas.
- Automation: machinery may take over work previously carried out by people. Computer systems often reduce numbers of staff. Most banks, for example, offer phone services so that a customer can call the bank and hear a message giving details of their accounts. Phone messages are automatically generated by computer rather than a human operator.

Benefits and limitations of part-time and full-time workers

A key change in many economies has been the reduction in full-time work and the increase in part-time work. From the employers' point of view part-time workers are typically cheaper in terms of wage costs, and are sometimes easier to dismiss using employment laws because part-time work often provides a less secure contract. Whole industries rely on large numbers of part-time workers, e.g. retailing (supermarkets), and call centres serving utility companies. Disadvantages of part-time workers are that they may be less committed to the organisation and may have less skill and experience than full-timers. The advantage of part-time work for the employees is that they can combine work with other commitments (e.g. to their family or to study). Part-time work provides a source of income for those who might otherwise be unemployed. Disadvantages are lack of job security and lower rates of pay and benefits.

SUMMARY QUESTIONS

1. Write down definitions of the following terms: redundancy, dismissal, retrenchment, downsizing.
2. Provide two examples of situations in which an employee might be made redundant. Then provide an example of a situation where an employee might be dismissed for reasons other than redundancy.
3. In your view, would the following examples illustrate fair or unfair dismissal? Justify your answers.
   - A business sustains losses for several years and is forced to close one of its factories. In consultation with the trade union, it agrees which of these factories to close. In line with legal requirements, it provides redundancy pay, depending on how long employees have worked for the company.
   - A company needs to make cutbacks because it has lost a major order. It informs the employees that those who have been working the longest will be made redundant because their wages are too high.

STUDY TIP

Understand the difference between redundancy and dismissal: a worker is made redundant because their job has disappeared. Workers made redundant may get financial help, while those who are dismissed do not.

ACTIVITY

Find out about the law covering dismissal from work in your country. For what reasons can an employee be fairly dismissed? In what situations would the law courts decide that the dismissal was unfair? What does an employer need to do before they can 'fairly' dismiss an employee? Does an employee need to be warned before they can be dismissed?

KEY POINTS

1. A business cannot guarantee a job for life. At times, it may need to reduce the number of employees.
2. Dismissal takes place when an employee's contract of employment is terminated (ended). There are legal requirements relating to dismissal.
3. Redundancy results when a business shuts down, closes part of its operations or cuts down the workforce. There are legal requirements relating to redundancies.

2.3.5 Employment legislation

TOPIC AIMS

Students should be able to:

- describe the main features of an employment contract
- understand why employees need protection against discrimination and unfair dismissal
- understand legal controls over employment contracts, health and safety, unfair dismissal, discrimination and minimum wage
- use examples to demonstrate such protection in terms of racial and gender discrimination.

An important aspect of employment legislation is making sure that all groups in the labour force are paid the same wage for doing work of equal value.

STUDY TIP

Remember that dismissal is different from redundancy. If employees are dismissed, they are removed from the job usually because of some misconduct. If they are made redundant, the job no longer exists, so the employee is no longer needed.

Employment legislation

Employment legislation is intended to protect employees in the workplace. Laws cover areas such as health and safety as well as areas such as employment contracts and protection from unfair dismissal, and racial, sexual or age discrimination. Many governments have established a legal minimum wage for their workers so that no worker can be paid any less than this for a job. Countries that have a minimum wage include Barbados, Brazil and the Democratic Republic of the Congo.

Employment contracts

A contract is an agreement between people or organisations to deliver goods or services, or to do something on jointly agreed terms.

A **contract of employment** sets out the relationship between the employer and the employee who has been contracted to work for them.

A contract of employment is usually set out in writing and typically includes the following details:

- the names of the employer and the employee
- the job title
- the date when the employment began
- the scale or rate of pay and method of calculating pay and bonuses
- when payment will be made
- the hours to be worked
- holiday entitlement and holiday pay
- sick pay and injury arrangements
- entitlement to a pension scheme
- the conditions of termination (length of notice that the employer must give).

Protection of employees against discrimination and unfair dismissal

In most countries, there are rules about the dismissal of employees. At the heart of this issue is the difference between what is described as **fair** and **unfair** dismissal.

When employees are dismissed unfairly, they may have grounds for taking the case to court to receive compensation or to be reinstated in their job.

Grounds for fair dismissal might include the employee:

- deliberately destroying company property
- harassing another worker, either verbally or physically
- continually being late
- being unable or unwilling to do the job
- committing an act of gross misconduct
- continually taking time off.

However, in some instances, employees may claim that dismissal has been unfair, on the grounds that they have been discriminated against because:

- of their race or religion
- they have joined a trade union
- they are a woman, or too old.

Protection against discrimination

National legislation is required to make sure that individual workers are not discriminated against at work. **Discrimination** is treating one person or group less favourably than others. This may be because of, for example, race, religion, gender, age or disability.

> **CASE STUDY** | The Employment Equity Act, South Africa
>
> South Africa has passed an Employment Equity Act which applies to all employers and workers and protects workers and job seekers from unfair discrimination. It also provides a framework for implementing affirmative action. This involves making sure that everyone who is suitably qualified for a particular job has equal opportunities.
>
> In the past, certain groups have found it difficult to get jobs. The new legislation aims to ensure that the different groups of people in the country are treated equally and with respect and dignity. All levels of jobs should be open to everyone who is qualified to do them. This may mean that companies have had to make changes to their employment procedures.
>
> **Questions**
>
> 1 What examples of recruitment, selection and training practices can you think of that might discriminate against designated groups? What practical steps could an employer take to remove these obstacles?
>
> 2 How could an employer make sure that designated groups are equally represented in all job categories and levels in the workplace?

> **SUMMARY QUESTIONS**
>
> 1 Describe the main features of an employment contract.
>
> 2 In what ways can employees be discriminated against in the workplace? Give two examples of groups that may be discriminated against in the workplace in your country. How can employees be protected against discrimination?
>
> 3 Briefly explain how the following types of legislation can protect workers.
> - Fair pay legislation
> - Legislation against unfair dismissal
> - Race equality legislation

> **ACTIVITY**
>
> Carry out some research to find out about protection that employees in your own country have against discrimination at work. You could carry out an internet search using the keywords [Name of your country], Employment Legislation, Discrimination. Alternatively, your teacher may provide you with sources to research this information. Present your findings in the form of a report headed 'Employment discrimination in [Name of your country]'.

> **DID YOU KNOW?**
>
> Health and Safety laws and requirements are intended to make sure that businesses behave responsibly. Enforcement varies among countries – in some there may be incentives to encourage businesses to act responsibly. There may be penalties if regulations are not followed. Example of requirements include protection from dangerous machinery, provision of safety equipment and clothing, hygienic conditions and laws of work.

> **KEY POINTS**
>
> 1 Employees need protection against unfair treatment.
>
> 2 Certain groups need additional protection against discrimination.
>
> 3 There may be specific encouragement for businesses to support these groups.
>
> 4 Legislation may exist, but not be enforced.

2.4 Internal and external communication

2.4.1 Communication

TOPIC AIMS

Students should be able to:

- explain the different methods of communication
- understand the concept of communication
- appreciate the importance of communication within a business
- understand how communication takes place
- describe the barriers to effective communication
- understand why such barriers exist
- explain how the barriers can be overcome
- understand the difference between internal and external communication.

Communication

Communication – that is, passing on or exchanging information, ideas or feelings – is vital to a business. Instructions, orders, lists and specifications all need to be transmitted to others within the organisation. The organisation also needs to communicate externally – that is, to people outside it – to place orders, find things out and, very importantly, to promote and sell a brand and its related products.

Communication involves sending a message or messages to a receiver. The sender must select the best method of communication such as oral, written or electronic. The sender must then select the best medium to send the message, such as email or telephone.

Communication takes place both within a business and between the business and other organisations.

Effective communication depends upon:

- clearly defining the objective of the message
- taking account of the needs, attitude and knowledge of the receiver
- being aware of how distractions (noise) can distort the message
- selecting the best medium for communication

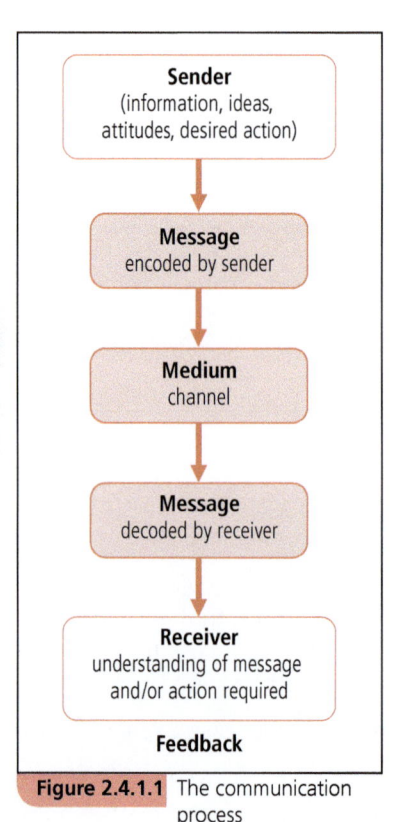

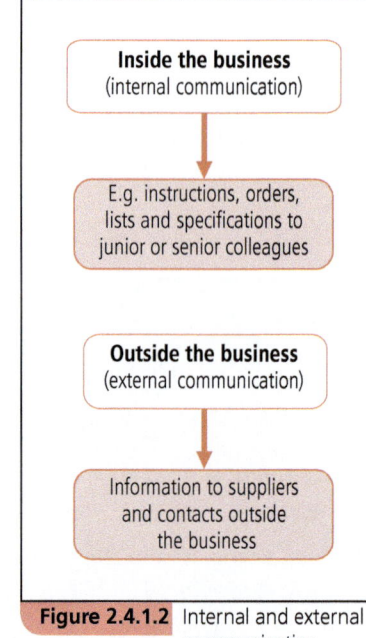

STUDY TIP

Good communication is essential if a business is to be successful. Communications take place within a business (internally) and outside a business (externally), for example, with suppliers and customers. The methods used should reflect the nature and purpose of the message.

Figure 2.4.1.1 The communication process

- **Sender** (information, ideas, attitudes, desired action)
- **Message** encoded by sender
- **Medium** channel
- **Message** decoded by receiver
- **Receiver** understanding of message and/or action required
- **Feedback**

Figure 2.4.1.2 Internal and external communication

- **Inside the business** (internal communication)
  - E.g. instructions, orders, lists and specifications to junior or senior colleagues
- **Outside the business** (external communication)
  - Information to suppliers and contacts outside the business

- checking that the message has been understood through feedback
- listening to feedback and responding.

Common communication problems

There are a number of barriers to communication.

1. **Language**. The sender may not be a good user of language, or may use jargon, unfamiliar technical language or abbreviations. Problems may arise in international communication where a receiver's first language may be different from that of the sender. It is essential when creating a message to think about the needs of the receiver and be clear and direct.
2. **Emotional state**. The sender or receiver may be upset or angry and set out a message poorly or fail to listen carefully to a message. The receiver may read or hear what they want to hear rather than the message sent.
3. **Communication method**. The method chosen may be inappropriate for the receiver. For example, mobile phone communications may 'break up' or emails may not get through. In some countries or remote areas internet services may not be available. Some topics may be better handled in person than by phone.
4. **Cultural differences**. The receiver's interpretation of the message may be different due to differing cultural experience and language. Organisations need to have a good understanding of the culture of countries that they communicate with.

Solutions to communication failure

All employees in an organisation need to be aware of the importance of effective communication. This involves making them aware of the problems of poor communication, and familiarising them with the best communication methods through training. For example, when making an order over the phone, numbers of items requested may easily be misheard. It is better to use written communication such as email or to fill in an order form.

Organisations need to have the right resources to enable effective communication. This involves investing in good communication technologies and making sure that employees know how and when to use different types of communication.

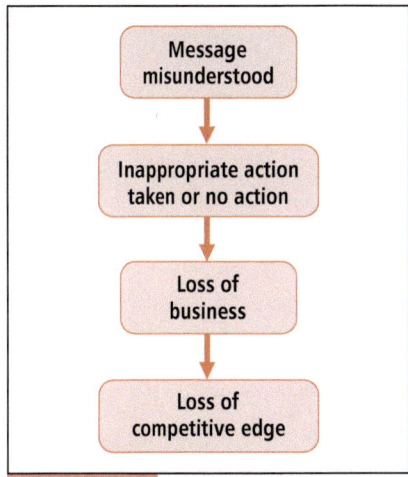

Figure 2.4.1.3 Consequences of communication failure

DID YOU KNOW?

New technology frees people from the office and from the need for a fixed location. Emails can be dictated into a mobile phone or workers can use a laptop on a train to connect to their company's intranet. Sales staff and others can keep in close contact with their office even when they are at a distant location. However, email 'overload' can be a negative consequence of too much electronic communication.

ACTIVITY

Identify some of the messages that you have received recently about your schoolwork. How were these messages communicated to you? Give examples of situations where 'noise' affected some of these messages. What could have been done to reduce this?

KEY POINTS

1. Communication involves exchanging ideas and messages with others.
2. Communication takes place within an organisation (internal) and with those outside the organisation (external).
3. Careful attention must be given to framing clear messages, and using an appropriate medium in a way that recipients find easy to understand.

SUMMARY QUESTIONS

1. Who are the main parties involved in the business communication process?
2. What is the difference between internal and external communication?
3. What are the main barriers to effective communication? Explain one method of dealing with one of these barriers.

2.4.2 Internal communication

TOPIC AIMS

Students should be able to:
- understand different methods of communication
- comment on the appropriateness of different methods of internal communication
- understand when to use a given method of communication.

Video conferencing facilities enable face-to-face communication without travel costs.

STUDY TIP

Make sure that you can evaluate the effectiveness of different communication methods in different situations. Effective communication is much more than just telling someone what to do. It involves the interchange of information, which is all about developing understanding of issues so that everyone appreciates what has to be done and what part they have to play.

Internal communication

Internal communications take place within an organisation. Figure 2.4.2.1 shows several purposes of internal communication.

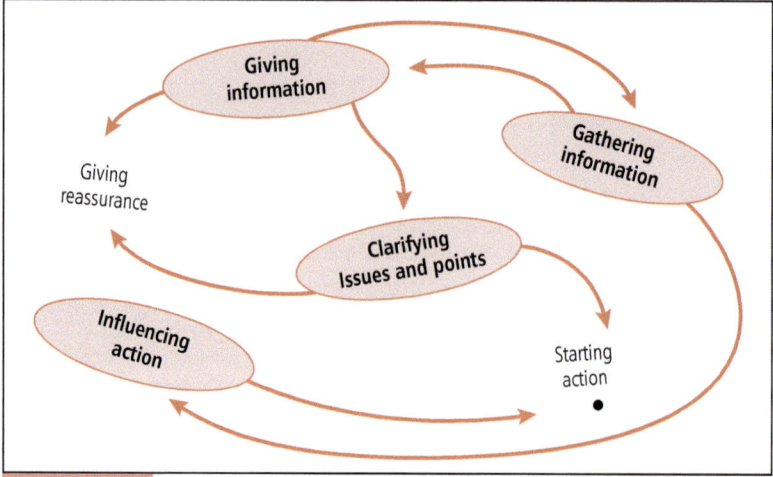

Figure 2.4.2.1 Purposes of internal communication. All methods of communication have limitations, such as they can be slow to implement and expensive, messages can be misunderstood and sometimes people are left out of communications.

Types of communication

Formal communication takes place through the official channels in an organisation (e.g. in a formal meeting). In contrast, informal communication does not follow set guidelines (e.g. an informal online chat between two employees). Electronic communication takes place through email, telephone (including mobile phone), video conferencing and using a company website for employees, an **intranet**.

Formal written

Memo is a shortening of 'memorandum', a thing to be remembered. Memos are used to pass on information, instructions and enquiries. Today, this form of written communication has largely been replaced by email messages.

A report is a written communication from someone who has collected some facts or issues. A report is written for a particular purpose and is set out in a particular format:

1 Title page
2 List of contents
3 Terms of reference (why the report is being written)
4 Procedure (how the report has been put together)
5 Findings (what has been discovered that is of interest)
6 Conclusion (a summary of the findings)

Fax is short for 'facsimile'. A fax machine is connected to a telephone line. Documents such as drawings and notes can be fed into one machine, and are received and printed by another.

Businesses also communicate internally through posters (e.g. to convey messages about safe working) and through in-house magazines. The advantage of written communication is that it can be carefully analyzed and checked for meaning.

Formal verbal

Verbal communication takes place all the time within an organisation. This includes telling someone what to do (giving instructions) and giving feedback about their performance. The advantage of verbal communication is that it provides an opportunity to check understanding and ask questions.

Meetings are held regularly in most businesses. Some of these are formal meetings, with a chairperson to conduct the meeting, an agenda (list of items to be discussed) and a minute taker (someone who keeps a written record of what has been said). Training sessions are organised to help employees to develop the skills and knowledge required to do their job well. **Appraisal** interviews are another form of two-way communication at which an employee is given targets to work towards (see page 2.3.3).

Informal

Much of the communication within a company takes place informally, using what is referred to as a grapevine. This helps to develop working relationships. An example of this might be senior business people having a round of golf together. Networking describes building informal contacts with others.

Electronic

Electronic links have transformed communication within businesses. Most companies have an intranet. This is a network of linked computers and databases of information. The intranet serves as an internal company website, providing lots of information about the company and its departments to people inside the organisation.

Telephone links are also important in maintaining external and internal relationships. Mobile phone links are particularly useful when employees are working away from the workplace. A company website created on the internet enables everyone involved with a business to find out more about its activities. **Video conferencing** enables visual link-ups between members of the same company at different locations. However, in remote areas and developing countries internet services and mobile phone reception are not always available.

> **ACTIVITY**
>
> Identify different types of internal communication in your school. What types of information and instructions are given using these different types of communication? Identify one advantage and one drawback of each method when compared with an alternative method of internal communication.

> **DID YOU KNOW?**
>
> A **team** briefing is a formal method of verbal communication. The team leader will usually brief (inform) the team about the latest developments within a company and what is expected of the team in contributing to those developments.

> **KEY POINTS**
>
> 1 Internal communications take place within an organisation.
>
> 2 Communication methods need to be appropriate to the type of audience to be reached and the messages to be sent.
>
> 3 Electronic communications, such as emails, fax, intranet, internet and video conferencing, have replaced many traditional methods.
>
> 4 Electronic communications enable immediate, relatively low-cost links in which a lot of information can be exchanged.

> **SUMMARY QUESTIONS**
>
> 1 Which of the following forms of communication are most likely to involve an electronic element? Explain your answers in each case.
>
> Fax / email / reports / meetings / memo / video conference / appraisal interview
>
> 2 VG Fashions is a manufacturer of cotton textiles in Pakistan in the process of introducing new advanced machinery for spinning cotton in some of its mills. This will require upgrading the skills of some of its existing employees. What methods of internal communication could it use to inform employees of the changes and to prepare them to upgrade their skills? Explain the benefits of each method selected.

2.4.3 External communication

TOPIC AIMS

Students should be able to:
- understand the difference between internal and external communication
- understand different methods of external communication
- understand the concept of effective communication.

Internal and external communication

We have seen in 2.4.2 how the prime focus of internal communication is the people who work within an organisation – employees, managers and, in some cases, shareholders. Internal communication to these groups takes the form of organised information through a company intranet, employee magazines and newsletters, and shareholder reports, notices and letters.

External communication indicates how a business communicates with individuals and other businesses outside itself. It must be effective because it gives the outside world a view of the company, its brands and products. The table sets out the purposes of external communication.

Purpose	Example
1 Providing information and making sales	Most large companies have a website giving product details and inviting customers to make purchases. Bus, train and airline companies provide sites through which passengers can check timetables and purchase tickets. Sites also include terms and conditions of sale, costs of purchase, etc.
2 Giving instructions	Telling suppliers where to deliver goods or telling customers how to use products.
3 Confirming arrangements	May include confirming meetings or conferences or details of transactions.
4 Improving customer service	Helplines to deal with customer issues and complaints. Can help to reduce errors, provide customers with plenty of feedback and deal with enquiries. Customers view the communications they receive from a company as part of the service. For example, they expect to be communicated with on time and in a polite and helpful way.
5 Public relations (PR)	Brochures and advertising material. Effective PR projects a positive image, that a company is professional in its dealings with its stakeholders.

Kenya Airways is Kenya's best-known airline. Its website enables it to sell to international consumers as well as across Kenya.

Methods of external communication

There are a number of different methods of external communication.

1 **Personal relationships** are the contacts and relationships that people in an organisation build up with others. They are vital to the success of the business.

2 **Business letters** are very important forms of formal written communication. A letter will usually contain the following features:
- addresses of the recipient and sender
- date
- greeting (e.g. Dear Sir/Madam)
- subject heading – the title of the topic the letter refers to (e.g. Price list request)
- body of the letter
- close (e.g. Yours faithfully)

A business letter gives a good idea of how professional the business organisation is. It should look attractive and it should not contain any spelling or punctuation errors.

3 **Email** has become the most widely used form of communication and now has the same 'weight' as a traditional letter. Many companies today set out structures for emails that give them the official appearance of a traditional letter, with the company logo

and a particular layout and style. Writers need to take care with the contents of business emails.

4 **Company websites**. Most companies have a website for many forms of external communication. An effective site will have a distinctive name (e.g. lastminute.com, iwantoneofthose.com). The site should be welcoming, with interesting material to encourage the user to revisit. It should be easy to access and to navigate (i.e. to move around). It needs to be broken down into clear subsections, so that users can quickly access the part of the site that interests them. There should also be clear links to other parts of the site.

A successful site must be easy to use for purchasing: this includes order forms and credit card security measures. Many users are concerned about security – hackers may be able to access a company database and the credit card details of all their customers. Website designers need to find a way of making purchasing safe, but not so cumbersome as to put off purchasers altogether.

5 **Customer newsletters**. The company can send mail directly to customers giving details of new developments (e.g. a store opening, forthcoming sale, products that are on offer in a particularly period).

6 **Advertisements**. Found in various media (e.g. television, newspapers and magazines).

7 **Telephone**. These links are important to businesses such as banking, insurance and utilities. These types of companies run call centres, which operate helplines to deal with customer queries, sell products over the phone or handle billing and other payment systems.

8 **File transfers**. Large quantities of data (e.g. in the form of pictures and statistics) can be sent electronically. File transfer involves sending 'bunches' of data from a sending to a receiving computer.

9 **Electronic data interchange (EDI)**. Many international food manufacturers and retailers set up large-scale systems of purchasing goods electronically. EDI is a network link that allows retailers to pay suppliers electronically, without using invoices and cheques. This reduces time, paperwork and costs.

10 **Video conferencing**. Workers at different locations can see and talk to each other on screen using electronic links. This avoids the expense and inconvenience of travel.

SUMMARY QUESTIONS

1 What is the difference between internal and external communication?
2 What arguments might a business put forward to justify setting up a company website?
3 What are the advantages of communicating with customers by business letter rather than through electronic communication?

DID YOU KNOW?

Payment systems today are usually encrypted. Purchasers' bank card details are put into code, making them very difficult to copy. Companies also protect their databases by making sure that only specified users with passwords are able to access them.

ACTIVITY

Compare three well-known commercial (selling) websites. Choose one that sells clothes, such as ASOS; another that sells books, such as Amazon; and a sportswear retailer, such as Nike or Reebok. Compare the sites in terms of the following criteria:

- quick to access
- easy to navigate
- easy to find information
- presents a good image of the company
- goods easy to order
- easy to make transactions
- other factors you consider important.

KEY POINTS

1 Internal communication takes place within a business; external communication is with individuals and businesses outside a given business.
2 Electronic communications such as emails are replacing traditional methods.
3 Company websites enable an organisation to present itself in a positive way to consumers all over the world.

Unit 2 — Practice questions

SECTION 1: Short-answer questions

1. Identify and explain the most appropriate method(s) and type(s) of communication in the following situations.
   - There is a fire in the building and everyone must leave.
   - The managing director wants to tell staff about the company objectives for this year.
   - The marketing manager wants to tell customers about a new product. [6]

2. Identify and explain TWO reasons why people work. [4]

3. Explain what is meant by 'maximum weekly working hours'. [3]

4. With reference to Maslow's hierarchy, analyse why working in teams may act as a motivator for workers. [4]

5. Explain the difference between overtime pay and bonus pay. [4]

6. Identify and explain TWO reasons why big companies frequently offer profit-sharing schemes to their employees. [4]

7. State and explain ONE example of a fringe benefit that may be suitable in the following occupations:
   - shop or supermarket worker
   - car factory worker
   - airline stewardess. [6]

8. Identify and explain TWO factors that could increase job satisfaction for workers in a telephone call centre. [4]

9. Analyse how a well-conducted yearly appraisal interview may motivate an employee. [4]

10. Good managers use different management styles according to the situation. Using the example of a large restaurant business, identify and explain which management style you would recommend in each of these scenarios.
    - There is a fire and the manager needs his staff to take all the customers out of the building.
    - The restaurant manager wants to get ideas from staff about new menu items.
    - The restaurant manager wants all staff to comply with health and safety rules, such as hand-washing and tying back long hair. [6]

11. Analyse ONE reason why employees may be demotivated by a laissez-faire leader. [4]

SECTION 2: Longer-answer questions

The Sea Breeze Hotel

Jon is the newly appointed manager of the Sea Breeze Hotel and restaurant, which has been acquired by a new owner. The hotel has become run down in recent years, partly due to a poor manager, who was absent much of the time and failed to give staff direction and leadership. When he was present he was overpowering, shouting orders at the staff and keeping for himself any extra gratuities left by guests. Jon has a major job on his hands and knows he must start by winning the respect of the hotel workers. His first move on taking over was to call a staff meeting and explain that he would be consulting his staff over proposed changes and emphasising a new focus on 'excellent' customer service.

1. Describe the management style of the previous manager of the Sea Breeze Hotel. [4]
2. Identify and explain TWO reasons for the current low staff morale. [4]
3. Analyse TWO ways in which Jon can win the respect of the hotel staff. [6]
4. Do you agree that Jon's consultative management style will lead to an improvement in the guests' experience at the Sea Breeze? Explain your answer. [6]
5. Jon is proposing to offer workers an hourly rate of pay, plus a performance-related bonus, based on comments from guests and his own observations of customer service standards. To what extent will this help to raise standards? [6]

The Vegetarian Treats Company

Ashok is a successful entrepreneur who has built his company up from a very small start. He now owns six shops in different areas of Mumbai and wants to expand into other Indian towns and cities. His sweet and savoury products are made in a central kitchen, to old family recipes, based on secret spice mixes that give the products their unique flavour. Ashok employs managers and teams of staff for each of his shops, and also a senior product manager and chefs for the kitchen. Other members of Ashok's family are keen to get involved in his success and are trying to persuade him to form a partnership with his brothers.

1 Draw an organisation chart for Ashok's business and describe the structure. [4]

2 Identify and describe TWO communication methods that Ashok may use when trying to communicate weekly sales targets to all his shops. [4]

3 Analyse TWO barriers to communication which Ashok may face if he opens new shops in other cities. [6]

4 Explain THREE objectives that Ashok may have in trying to expand his business. [6]

5 Do you agree with Ashok's family that he should form a partnership with his brothers? Explain your answer. [6]

The new low-cost airline

Skyways is a new privately owned airline, based in Malaysia. The company has a growing fleet of Airbus planes and is expanding its network of routes on a weekly basis. Fares are low, which is encouraging new air travellers. Skyways is finding it difficult to recruit suitable cabin crew staff as there is a shortage of trained personnel available, so the airline is now looking abroad for pilots and senior crew. Skyways has also introduced its own staff training programme for more junior customer service agents and ground staff.

1 Identify and explain TWO reasons why Skyways needs to recruit trained staff. [4]

2 Identify TWO items that may appear in the job description and TWO items from a likely person specification for a Skyways cabin crew vacancy. [4]

3 Analyse TWO possible business problems that may occur as a result of Skyways recruiting air crew from other countries. [6]

4 Identify and explain THREE tests, other than a face-to-face interview, that Skyways might use to screen job applicants. [6]

5 Skyways' general manager has expressed the view: 'If we spend a lot of money on staff training it will be wasted, as staff will leave for jobs with other airlines'. Do you agree with him? Justify your answer. [6]

The ICT skills training company

The TeachIT company is a privately owned enterprise in Kenya. It provides businesses with staff ICT training at its own training centre in Nairobi. The company also receives money from the local Ministry of Education to advise on ICT education in schools. The company is successful, but as children are leaving school and starting work with good ICT skills there is less need for TeachIT's services. The company is now trying to diversify into training in leadership skills, as its market research indicates that this is a growing area of need in business.

1 Identify and explain TWO possible reasons why businesses may outsource their ICT training to companies such as TeachIT. [4]

2 Identify and explain TWO reasons why ICT training in schools may be a priority for many governments around the world. [4]

3 Analyse ONE advantage and ONE disadvantage for a business providing this type of off-the-job training in ICT skills. [4]

4 Evaluate the view that 'all managers will benefit from training in leadership and team-building skills'. [6]

5 TeachIT's managing director tells his customers that 'good staff training is one sure way to business success'. To what extent do you agree with him? [6]

3 Marketing

3.1 Marketing, competition and the customer

3.1.1 The role of marketing in a business

TOPIC AIMS

Students should be able to:
- understand marketing aims to identify and satisfy customer needs
- appreciate the importance of maintaining customer loyalty and building customer relationships.

STUDY TIP

Remember that marketing is much more than simply **selling**. Students often think that they are the same thing.

ACTIVITY

Write down five questions that could be used to find out what benefits people look for in a skin cream or shampoo.

A product sold in several countries needs to adapt to different uses.

The role of marketing

Businesses would not exist without customers. It is essential, therefore, to find out what customers want and need. A business then needs to satisfy these needs by providing what can be memorised as the four Ps:

- **product**: the right goods and services
- **price**: at the right price
- **place**: where or how customers want to be able to buy
- **promotion**: by providing the right sort of encouragement.

The four Ps summarise the role of **marketing** and the marketing department in a company: anticipating and identifying consumer wants and needs and then planning the means to meet these requirements. You will learn more about the four Ps in 3.3.1.

When customers buy products they are looking for particular benefits – that is, what a product will actually do for them. A benefit of a particular model of mobile telephone may be that as well as making and receiving calls and messages, it has a camera and GPS system and allows internet access. Customers may be interested in 'features' – physical qualities of the product, such as what it looks like – but it is the benefits that will persuade them to keep purchasing.

CASE STUDY | Bonux, Romania and Nigeria

Marketing seeks to find out what customers want and then to provide it. In October 1995, Procter and Gamble (P&G), one of the world's largest producers of washing powder, took over a well-known Romanian company that produced washing powder and soap. One of its brands, Perlan, was particularly popular. Customers liked it because it provided a clean wash at an economical price. P&G invested a lot of money in improving the production plant in Romania. The washing powder was rebranded as Bonux. It came in two varieties: one for hand-washing and the other for washing machines. P&G spent a lot of time interviewing customers to find out ways to improve the product. They introduced a number of improvements, so that Bonux can now offer consumers a threefold benefit: cleaning, a pleasant scent and savings.

P&G market researchers have found through questionnaires and field tests that this formula is what consumers are looking for in other countries as well. In 2006, they opened a detergent factory producing Bonux in Nigeria. The product is produced

Market research carried out by P&G for Bonux washing powder revealed that global consumers want: cleaning, pleasant smell and saving.

using a special formula which improves cleaning in dusty conditions. The product is exported from Nigeria to other parts of West Africa, South Africa and East Africa. More customer interviews showed that they liked to purchase the powder in larger packets. Customer questionnaire answers indicated that although this is initially more expensive, it works out cheaper over time. More larger packs are now supplied to the market.

In 2013, P&G employed 1 800 people in Nigeria.

Questions

1 What particular benefits does Bonux offer customers?

2 How was P&G able to find out the sorts of benefits that Bonux customers were looking for?

3 Why do you think that P&G has set up a factory in Nigeria? How would knowledge of the market have enabled P&G to decide to set up there?

ACTIVITY

Choose three of the products from the list below. Using your own knowledge, state what sorts of benefits customers would look for from each product.

- BIC razors
- BIC biros
- Mercedes-Benz motor cars
- A bar of soap that you use in your home
- A bottle or can of drink that is popular in your country

KEY POINTS

1 Consumers look for particular benefits when purchasing goods and services.

2 Marketing involves finding out what customers want and expect in order to provide them with appropriate goods and services.

3 Businesses are most likely to make a profit when they meet customer requirements.

Businesses are most likely to make a profit when they provide the benefits and products that customers want. Finding out what customers require involves careful research and analysis of the findings. Think of a product that is successful and you can be certain that the company that produces it has a very good marketing department.

You will find more information on market research in 3.2. Other aspects of marketing covered below include advertising, promotion and pricing.

SUMMARY QUESTIONS

1 Chad has come up with a brilliant idea for a new energy-saving device that can be used in the home. He has tried it out in his own house and it works well. He now wants to borrow some money from the bank so that he can produce and sell these devices on a larger scale. However, a friend has suggested that he should first investigate the market. Do you agree with the friend? What would be the advantage of finding out information about the market? What sorts of information should he find out?

2 In the Bonux case study, you read how P&G decided to invest in the Romanian factory and change the name of the product. They also altered the formula of the washing powder and started selling it in different containers. How do you think market research would have helped them to decide to make all these changes?

3 Identify a product that your family or friends use that in your view might benefit from some changes. What sorts of questions would marketers need to ask in order to find out what changes they should make to this product?

3.1.2 Market changes

TOPIC AIMS

Students should be able to:

- show understanding of market changes and how these might be responded to by business
- show understanding of why consumer spending patterns may change
- show understanding of why markets have become more competitive
- evaluate impact of increased competition on consumers and businesses.

Consumer spending patterns

Consumer spending patterns are the typical goods and services bought by individuals and groups of consumers. Spending patterns are heavily dependent on income. The more income an individual has, the greater the proportion they are likely to save, and spend on luxuries.

As incomes rise, patterns of spending change. Increasing numbers of consumers are earning more. This is particularly so in huge countries like Brazil, Russia, India and China (the BRIC group of countries), and in other newly industrialised countries (NICs), which include a number of South East Asian countries, such as Indonesia, Malaysia and Vietnam, as well as rich oil states such as Kuwait and Dubai. Consumers here are spending more on internationally branded products – for example, Nike trainers rather than a cheaper pair made locally.

Spending patterns are also affected by **lifestyles** of groups of consumers. A lifestyle is a way of living and a pattern of buying associated with individuals. It is possible to have a unique personal lifestyle, but most people can be grouped with others.

'American lifestyles' or 'Western lifestyles' are associated with high levels of consumption and energy use. However, within these there are a number of separate groups. In the US there are 'lifestyle groups' – for example, 'affluent consumers', 'middle-income consumers', 'young families'. Each of these has its own distinct spending patterns.

More consumers are moving into the affluent lifestyle groups: they are more likely to consume a wider range of products, use more energy and create more waste.

China is the world's largest producer of iron ore and steel, but it still has to buy additional steel on competitive world markets to meet all its needs.

DID YOU KNOW?

While the number of affluent consumers continues to rise, the vast majority of the world's population is still not able to afford modern lifestyles. United Nations statistics show that numbers of people living in extreme poverty (less than $1.25 per day) in the developing world halved (from 40 per cent to 20 per cent) between 1990 and 2010. There will still be 1 billion people living in extreme poverty by 2015.

ACTIVITY

Identify a product or market in which there has been a change in consumer spending among your friends or family in recent years. Examples might be fashion clothing or takeaway food. What have been the main changes in consumer spending? Why have these changes occurred?

Competitive markets

World markets have become more competitive for several reasons.

1. **The shrinking globe**. It is easier to transfer products and services across the world than ever before. Goods can be transported from Sydney, Australia to Nairobi, Kenya in hours rather than days. Services such as banking and insurance contracts can be supplied online almost instantly to large areas of the globe. The telecommunications and transport revolution has made this high level of competition possible.
2. **Access to overseas markets**. Over the last 30 years, international governments have made agreements to reduce taxes and other barriers that previously prevented imports from entering the home market; examples are in the trading of grain, steel and cars.

3 **Low cost of setting up new businesses**. Many small and medium-sized enterprises can be set up at relatively low cost. This is particularly the case with businesses that are prepared to inject the initial capital to create a simple website, selling goods and services, tickets, banking, insurance and other services.

4 **Privatisation of industries**. From the 1950s to the 1980s, many industries and businesses were government-owned. However, from the 1980s, a number of governments across the world have sold off some of these enterprises to private businesses. Instead of having a single government-owned business, there are now a number of competing companies in a range of industries. These include water supply, electricity, gas and transport networks such as private bus companies.

> **STUDY TIP**
>
> Globalisation has brought benefits and costs. It has allowed the growth of multinational companies, but many businesses worldwide have collapsed because of globalisation. Change is not always for the better.

CASE STUDY | The global steel market

The global market for steel is very competitive. Steel is required as a material for building and manufacturing a range of products. In 2012, the main companies producing steel were as follows:

Company	Steel production (in million tonnes)	Country
Arcelor Mittal	93.6	Luxembourg
Nippon Steel	47.9	Japan
Hebei Steel	42.8	China
Baosteel	42.7	China
POSCO	40.0	South Korea

Each of these steel producers manufactures over 40 million tonnes of steel a year, but they each control a limited share of the total market (the total market being 1 548 million tonnes). Purchasers of steel, such as construction companies, try to purchase from suppliers who can offer them the best deals. For purchasers, it is good to have so many suppliers because competition will help to cut prices. However, for suppliers, competition will restrict their profits, because they have to offer the best deals.

Questions

1 Who do you think benefits most from the competitive global steel market – producers or purchasers? Justify your answer.

2 Why do you think that the market for steel is so competitive?

In competitive markets, businesses mainly seek to win custom by:

- producing high-quality products (e.g. Rolls-Royce aircraft engines, Parker pens, Apple Macintosh portable computers).
- selling cheap products at lower prices than rivals (e.g. the German supermarket chain Lidl offers very cheap products in stores with basic layouts and the minimum of customer service).

KEY POINTS

1 Consumer spending patterns change in response to changes in income and lifestyle choices.

2 In competitive markets, businesses must aim to offer higher quality or lower prices than their rivals.

SUMMARY QUESTIONS

1 How is consumer spending likely to change as a result of:
  - rising incomes across the globe?
  - the development of 'lifestyles' common to groups of people worldwide?

2 Choose two of the following products and give two reasons that have led to their global market becoming more competitive.
  - Oil • Computers • Confectionery • Books

3 Today consumers across the world can purchase CDs, books and films over the internet. How has this increased competition affected:
  - buyers? • sellers of these items?

3.1.3 Market segmentation

TOPIC AIMS

Students should be able to:

- show how markets can be segmented according to age, socioeconomic groupings, location or gender
- demonstrate an understanding of why such segmentation can be of use to a business
- recommend and justify a method of segmentation appropriate to given circumstances.

Segmentation

Groups of customers with similar characteristics can be divided into separate groups known as segments. It is useful for marketers to identify groups with similar buying patterns. They can then target their products, promotions and advertising. The different ways of segmenting markets are summarised in the following diagram.

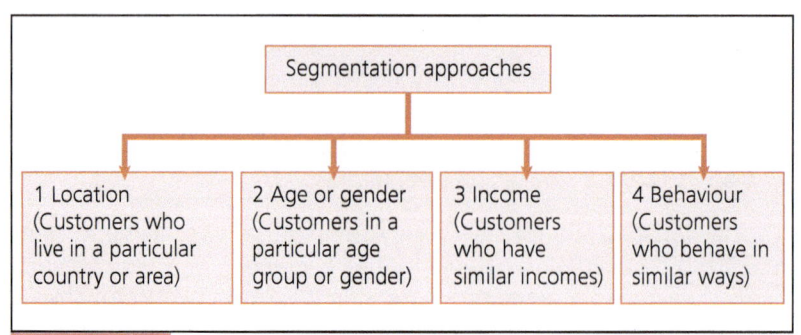

```
                    Segmentation approaches
                              |
   ┌──────────────┬───────────┴──────────┬──────────────┐
1 Location        2 Age or gender        3 Income        4 Behaviour
(Customers who    (Customers in a        (Customers      (Customers
live in a         particular age         who have        who behave in
particular        group or gender)       similar         similar ways)
country or area)                         incomes)
```

Figure 3.1.3.1 Approaches to market segmentation

Customers in the same location may have similar purchasing patterns, but other differences, such as age, may put them into different segments of the market.

Location

People in certain countries and regions have common characteristics which influence buying attitudes. In marketing to different countries, it is important to look at aspects such as income per person and the culture and tastes of people. For example, in Egypt, green beans are very popular in many food dishes; in the north of France, butter is widely used in cooking. Electrical products sometimes require different technical specifications for sale in different countries (e.g. they may be required to be fitted with a different plug). Different languages are spoken in different parts of the world, requiring the use of different labelling and product instructions to meet local consumer requirements.

Age and gender segmentation

Customers may be divided into discrete segments either by age (e.g. for clothes retailing) or by gender (e.g. for the sale of cosmetics and magazines). It is very important to understand how population patterns can create groups of similar customers. Consumers in similar age groups often have broadly similar interests. For example, in Saudi Arabia, more than 41 per cent of the population is under 14 years old, and a further 18 per cent between 15 and 24 years old. Many of these young people have broadly similar tastes, although there is a significant difference between the products that young males and young females want to purchase. Marketers therefore target this group by finding out what sorts of toys and books appeal to the under-14s, and the types of clothes and music favoured by young people aged 15–24.

ACTIVITY

Visit a local shop and identify products that are targeted at specific groups. Try to identify products targeted at the following age and gender groups.

- Older people (over 65)
- Younger people (under 14)
- Young males
- Young females

Income and social class segmentation

Income is a major factor influencing purchasing decisions. Rising incomes across the world over the last 10 years, particularly among younger people, has led to a boom in demand for branded products, including many high-status clothing items (e.g. expensive trainers and designer-label shirts and sweaters). Products such as cars, jewellery and perfume are targeted at particular income groups. For example, some perfume is sold at very low prices, while other perfume is much more expensive and is designed to appeal to more sophisticated tastes and richer consumers. Many societies are also divided by occupations (e.g. manual workers, who work with their hands, and professional workers, who work in offices or in a profession like a doctor, lawyer, etc.). The type of occupation a person does influences their income and thus their likely buying patterns. Richer people will be able to afford to buy cars, washing machines and televisions, whereas poorer people may only be able to afford a bicycle and radio.

Behavioural segmentation

It is also possible to classify customers by **behavioural segmentation** – for example, how often they buy a product and how loyal they are. Some people may buy a newspaper every day, others only when they want to read about an interesting event. Some people will always buy the same brand of washing powder, while others will compare prices and other aspects before making a choice. Items that people are loyal to include a particular newspaper (because of the quality of the way it presents the news, e.g. *The Times of India*, or *The Daily Gleaner*, Jamaica) or a type of soap.

> **DID YOU KNOW?**
> Many countries in Western Europe have an ageing population, referred to as 'the grey consumer'. This segment is targeted by marketers of health care products such as vitamin pills and anti-ageing creams.

> **STUDY TIP**
> You should be able to explain how and why a business needs to segment a market if it is to market its products successfully.

> **ACTIVITY**
> To what extent are there different geographical markets for clothing in your country? For example, is there a difference between the fashions of young people living in cities and those living in rural areas? How have producers and marketers adjusted their product and advertising to appeal to different segments?

> **SUMMARY QUESTIONS**
> 1 Procter and Gamble is a global company that produces soap powders and other detergents. They have developed washing powders specifically for the Nigerian market because of the higher levels of dust in rural areas. What type of segmentation is this? How does this segmentation help Procter and Gamble?
> 2 What is the difference between segmentation by age and segmentation by income? What products can you think of where it would be helpful to use these types of segmentation? Explain your answer.
> 3 In many countries in Africa, the Middle East, South East Asia and South America, a very high percentage of the population is under 21. Identify products that will typically be bought by this age group in these countries. How can producers make sure that these products are targeted at this age group?

> **KEY POINTS**
> 1 Market segmentation is the process of dividing up a market into different groups of customers by identifying common characteristics of these groups.
> 2 Segmentation involves identifying customers in the same location, the same age group, of the same gender or with the same behaviour patterns.
> 3 Knowledge of these segments enables a business to target its products and marketing activities accurately and cost-effectively at distinct segments.

3.1.4 Mass markets and niche markets

TOPIC AIMS

Students should be able to:

- appreciate the difference between mass marketing and niche marketing
- understand the difference between and significance of mass and niche markets in terms of size and customer needs
- understand the benefits and limitations of each approach to marketing.

DID YOU KNOW?

Niche markets are smaller than mass markets. They cater for groups of similar customers, such as tourists who specifically visit countries like Jordan to see religious sites in line with their faith. The type of site they want to visit or the hotels they want to stay in are likely to be quite different from other tourists who visit Jordan for an outdoor adventure holiday.

ACTIVITY

Working in a small group, identify products and services that you enjoy that are targeted at:

- the mass market
- a niche market.

In each case, try to work out how the marketing mix is organised to meet the requirements of the mass or niche market that you have identified.

Mass marketing

Most markets can be divided into a number of separate segments. For example, the tea market is divided into a cheap, low-cost segment, a speciality tea segment, a high-quality premium segment, and other segments such as fruit and herbal teas. A **mass marketing** strategy ignores this segmentation and seeks to appeal to all of the customers within different segments. Marketing is to the widest audience. Advertising and promotional messages are designed to appeal to a broad audience. Hopefully this will lead to a large number of sales. Products are designed to appeal to the whole market. Another product that is mass marketed is a standard type of family toothpaste such as Colgate. Colgate was the first type of toothpaste to appear in a tube, over a hundred years ago. Today, it is still one of the best-selling brand names across the globe. It may be advertised on television, with the hope of attracting buyers of all ages, genders, ethnic backgrounds and income groups.

Niche marketing

Niche marketing is the opposite of mass marketing. A niche market is a relatively small segment of a larger market. Marketers will focus their marketing activity on the characteristics of consumers that make up a particular niche. The nature of the niche determines the type of product. For example, toothpaste may be designed to appeal to children. Children's toothpaste tends to come in a smaller tube, and to have some attractive packaging, such as an illustration of a children's cartoon character on the tube. The advantage of niche marketing is that it focuses on small, specific groups of individuals, and marketing is therefore more targeted. Niche marketing focuses on the specific needs of individuals who make up a sub-set of the total market, e.g. disabled athletes will have specific needs for product modifications which are different from the wider group of athletes in a specific sport.

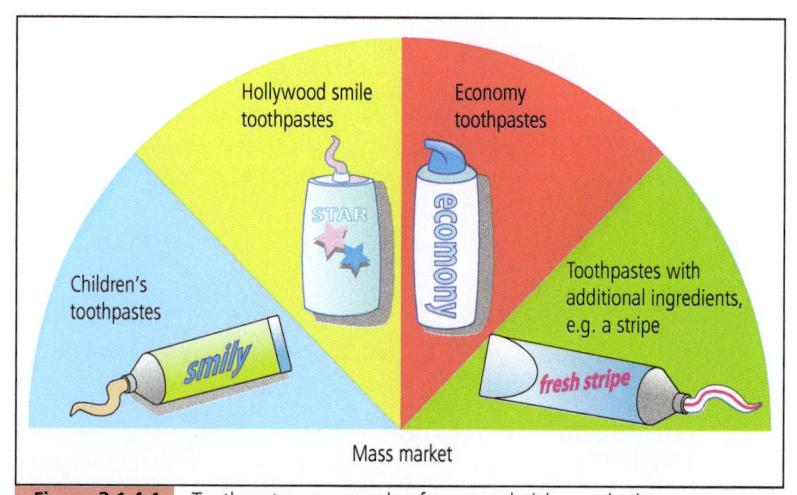

Figure 3.1.4.1 Toothpaste: an example of mass and niche marketing

CASE STUDY: Niche marketing of tourism in Jordan

Tourism is the largest productive sector of the economy in Jordan. Jordan has four main tourist sites – Petra Nabatean City, which is set in rocks; the Dead Sea; the River Jordan; and the Wadi Rum desert. Tourists visit Jordan for a number of reasons, including:

- health and wellness tourism – for their health
- cultural and religious tourism – to visit historical and religious sites
- ecotourism – to see deserts
- sports tourism.

Rather than targeting marketing activity at the mass market of all tourists, the Jordanian tourist board is focusing on market niches. This involves identifying groups of tourists who are very similar in what they are looking for. For example, in the health and wellness niche, tourists want to relax and get well. They want to visit spas where there are waters with healing properties and stay in quality hotels. In the ecotourism sector, tourists are looking for wilderness and desert adventures, and to meet local people.

The tourist board in Jordan is therefore targeting its marketing mix (including advertising) and its products (e.g. types of hotel facility) at specific customers who fit into these niches. At the same time, it is developing its main tourist sites to appeal to these customers.

Questions

1. What is the mass market and what are the niche markets described in the case study?
2. How can identifying the niche markets help the Jordanian tourist board to attract visitors to Jordan? Why is this likely to be more effective than mass marketing?

The Nabatean City of Petra – one of the main tourist sites in Jordan. The Nabateans were an ancient Arab people who built this magnificent city in the rocks. Religious and cultural tourism to sites like Petra provides one segment in the overall Jordanian tourist market.

KEY POINTS

1. In a mass marketing strategy, a business ignores differences between customers and aims to cover the whole market.
2. Niche marketing involves creating marketing activities designed for a small specific segment of a larger market.

SUMMARY QUESTIONS

1. What is the difference between a niche and a mass market? Illustrate your answer by reference to specific products (e.g. motor cars, cosmetics).
2. Who are the customers that make up a mass market that you are familiar with? How do they differ from customers in specific niches of the overall market that you identified?
3. In what ways does a business have to modify the marketing mix for niche markets? Give examples to illustrate your answer.

3.2 Market research

3.2.1 Primary and secondary market research

TOPIC AIMS

Students should be able to:

- appreciate the need for market research
- understand the concept of a market-oriented business
- show awareness of the use of market research information to a business
- understand how a business carries out market research; limitations of market research
- know of the difference between primary and secondary research, advantages and disadvantages of each
- know and understanding of how market research can be carried out
- understand the factors that influence the accuracy of market research
- appreciate the reasons why market research data might be inaccurate or of limited use.

Kenya provides 30 per cent of all flowers imported in Europe. Kenyan flower growers have carried out market research to identify which types of flowers are most popular in which European countries, and at what times of the year.

Market orientation

Without customers, a business would not exist. Businesses need to ask themselves: 'What would I, as my own customer, expect from my firm?' This focus on customer needs is market orientation. To orientate means to find your direction. A marketing-orientated company takes its direction from what customers want. For example, Kenyan flower growers provide 30 per cent of all fresh-cut flower imports in Europe. The Kenya Flower Council carries out marketing on behalf of all flower growers to find out what the market wants (which varieties of flowers, in what condition), when flowers are required and how to price the flowers competitively.

Market-oriented firms succeed because they listen to customers and give them what they want. For example, some sportswear manufacturers talk to top athletes to find out what sort of clothing they would like to enable them to perform better. In contrast, product-oriented firms concentrate on providing a good product, but without finding out first whether customers want to buy it. Product-oriented companies might include hi-tech businesses experimenting with very new technologies of which customers are not yet aware.

Market research

Market research means carefully gathering, making a record of and then analysing data about the market for goods and services.

Some typical market research questions are set out below. Answers to these questions provide market information.

- Who are our customers?
- What do they want?
- When do they buy/use?
- How much will they pay?
- Can we improve it for them?

Market research methods involve the collection of primary and secondary data. Primary data is new data collected by the company (or by researchers acting on its behalf). Secondary data has already been gathered and been published by someone else. Primary research can be focused on the types of questions that are specific to the business carrying out the research. However, it can be costly.

Primary data is obtained by interviewing a sample of the targeted market (expected customers). A sample is a group that is representative of the overall market. Primary data may be collected through a questionnaire, consisting of a sequence of questions. The questions should be clear and simple, and wherever possible tested on a few people in a pilot survey. It is often easier to analyse results if you ask **closed**, not **open questions**. Closed questions ask for an answer to be chosen from alternatives, for example:

How often do you shop here?

a Every day **b** Once a week **c** Once a fortnight **d** Hardly ever

Questions can be asked in person (often best because it involves face-to-face interaction and the interviewee is likely to elaborate on their answer), through the post (can be slow and produce a poor response), by telephone (quick and easy, but not always very reliable – some people do not like being called for this purpose) or via a website. Another approach is to use e-mail marketing, but this may give a low response rate. To increase rates, it can be helpful to offer a reward for completing a questionnaire (e.g. a $10 gift voucher for an 'on-the-spot' street interview, or a discount on online purchases).

Observation involves looking at how customers behave when shopping. For example, supermarket planners may observe the route that customers take round a store.

A group of customers may be brought together to talk about a product and the choices they make. This consumer panel might also be asked to discuss a list of topics, or test products and give their reactions. Researchers watch and listen to the customers for ideas about what products will and will not be successful. A customer panel is sometimes called a focus group.

Secondary research

Secondary research, as noted earlier, is carried out by someone else. It can be in the form of published research on set topics by market research organisations. It may appear in government statistics, or in books and magazines. It may indicate, for example, what households spend their money on, or numbers of women in part-time work.

Published reports can be expensive, but secondary research is often cheaper to conduct – the research is already published. However, it may be out of date and may not be closely related to a particular organisation and its targeted customers.

Both primary and secondary data may be inaccurate because:

- only a small percentage of the target market is researched
- a consumer panel may not be representative of typical consumers
- a survey may not be given to (or answered by) enough people, or may be given to the wrong people
- the data may go out of date quickly
- questions may be badly worded and misunderstood.

> **DID YOU KNOW?**
> Observation has revealed that shoppers in supermarkets and other stores usually like to start in the fresh produce department.

> **STUDY TIP**
> Market research results are not always accurate: there may be weaknesses in the way the data was collected. Researchers need to make sure, for example, that there is no bias in the samples used.

> **KEY POINTS**
> 1. Market research is a systematic process designed to find out about customer needs.
> 2. A market-oriented company uses market research to find out about customer wants and expectations.
> 3. Primary research involves finding out data first-hand; secondary research is the use of data generated by others for research purposes.

SUMMARY QUESTIONS

1. Which of the following are primary and which are secondary market research sources?
   - Conducting a survey of every fifth person in the street.
   - Asking each of your classmates 20 questions.
   - Copying out information from a magazine article.
   - Interviewing people through a phone survey.
   - Sending a questionnaire through the post.

2. A national radio station has carried out research to find out what types of programmes its listeners are interested in. It interviewed 1 000 people in the south of the country and held a consumer panel of 10 listeners in the north. Why might the results be inaccurate?

3. You want to find out whether there is demand for a new type of ice-cold drink. What types of primary research and secondary research could you carry out? What would be the benefits of using primary rather than secondary research?

3.2.2 Presentation and use of results

TOPIC AIMS

Students should be able to:
- analyse and interpret market research data shown in the form of graphs, charts and diagrams
- draw simple conclusions from data.

ACTIVITY

Carry out some primary market research to find out customers' views on two competing household products (e.g. brands of matches or canned drink). Questions you could ask might include:

- How often do you purchase the product?
- Which brands do you prefer?
- What quantities do you buy?
- How much do you pay?
- Does the product offer good value for money?

Set out your findings in a market research report. For each of the questions you ask, set out the data using an appropriate chart or graph.

Graphs and charts

Presenting information in a visual way makes it easy to understand and helps to break up text. Graphs and charts are a useful way of presenting key points of market research information. The following table shows the sales of different types of women's clothing from clothes shops in the United States in 2013. The charts that follow the table show ways of presenting this information in a more visual way.

Type of clothes item	Sales of these items as a % of all sales in clothes shops
Tops (e.g. T-shirts, shirts, blouses, sweaters)	30
Trousers, jeans, shorts and skirts	23
Dresses	20
Coats and jackets	15
Sportswear	7
Other clothes	5

A pictogram

A pictogram is a type of bar chart that uses pictures of the items it is connected with. Figure 3.2.2.1 presents the data in the table as a pictogram and it shows that 'tops' are the best-selling items.

Figure 3.2.2.1

The advantage of pictograms is that they are easy to understand because the picture represents the actual items. However, they take time to draw to scale.

Pie charts

Pie charts show a total figure split into various categories. Figure 3.2.2.2 presents the clothes sales data in the form of a pie chart.

Advantages of pie charts are that they immediately show the relative size of items (by the size of the slices of the pie). However, they are not very clear when showing the size of items which only take up a small part of the pie.

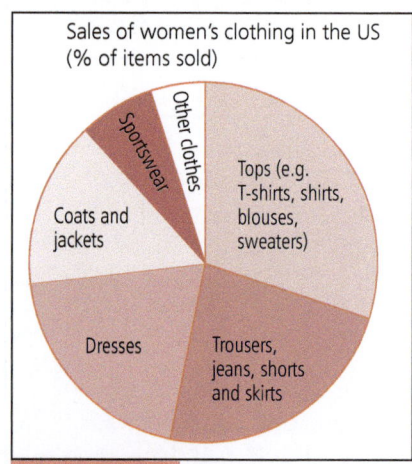

Figure 3.2.2.2

Bar charts

In a bar chart, a series of horizontal or vertical bars represent the values of particular items. The reader can quickly make comparisons.

Figure 3.2.2.3

Figure 3.2.2.3 sets out the sales of different types of women's clothes in the form of a bar chart.

The height of the bar makes it easy to compare one item with another – for example, figures for different years. They are less useful, however, if figures vary considerably from year to year.

Line graphs

A line graph can be used to illustrate how particular figures change over time. They show the size and speed of an increase, so that comparisons can be made. Figure 3.2.2.4 shows the number of women's clothes stores in the United States compared with the number of enterprises selling women's clothes. (A particular business enterprise may own just one store, two stores or a chain of stores.) The vertical axis of the chart shows the number of stores and enterprises. The horizontal axis shows the dates from 1995 to 2010.

Figure 3.2.2.4

The figure shows that the number of stores is rising at a faster rate than the number of enterprises. For example, in 2010 there were twice as many stores as enterprises. On average, each enterprise owned two stores. If we go back to 1995, we can see that there were 40 000 stores and 21 500 enterprises – roughly 1.8 stores per enterprise.

STUDY TIP

When drawing a line graph, remember to label each axis, use sensible scales, label lines where there are two or more or use a key. Always give the graph a suitable title.

KEY POINTS

1 Market research information can be displayed in graphs, charts and diagrams.

2 Line graphs may be used to show changes over time to specific variables.

3 Pie charts show how a total figure is split into various categories.

4 Bar charts are used to compare relative sizes of items and changes over time.

SUMMARY QUESTIONS

1 What types of graphs and charts would you use to illustrate the following?
   - The percentage market share a company has at a particular moment in time.
   - The rise in the market share of the company over time.
   - How total company sales are split between the various products that it sells.

2 What is a pictogram? Give an example of the sort of market data that a pictogram would be helpful in illustrating.

3 Why is it important to carefully select the scale of the axis used in a graph?

85

3.3 The marketing mix

3.3.1 The four Ps

TOPIC AIMS

Students should be able to:
- show knowledge and awareness of the four main elements of the marketing mix (product, price, place and promotion).

STUDY TIP

The correct marketing mix is all about getting the right balance between the factors that influence sales. Think about the consequences of getting this balance 'wrong'.

Product, price, place and promotion

As we saw in 3.1, the ingredients of the **marketing mix** are often referred to as the four Ps: product, price, place and promotion.

A mix is made up of ingredients that are blended together for a purpose. Think of the ingredients used to make a cake: no ingredient will work on its own. They have to be blended together to make a successful cake. In the same way that there are many cakes to suit all tastes, a marketing mix can be designed to suit the precise requirements of the market.

To create the right marketing mix, businesses have to meet the following conditions.

- The product has to have the right features (e.g. it must look good and work well).
- The price must be right. Consumers will need to buy in sufficient numbers to cover costs.
- The goods must be in the right place at the right time. Making sure that the goods arrive when and where they are wanted is an important operation. The method of selling must be suitable for the customers (e.g. through a small corner shop or a large supermarket or online).
- The target group needs to be made aware of the existence and availability of the product through promotion. Successful promotion helps a firm to spread costs over a larger output.

Figure 3.3.1.1 The marketing mix

ACTIVITY

Think of a product that you spend money on regularly – perhaps a type of sweet or a visit to the cinema. How effective is the marketing mix for this product? Before you start, make sure you know, with your teacher's advice, who the product is supposed to sell to (the target market). Is the product aimed at young people? Male or female? Choose a sample of 30 people to interview from the appropriate group (e.g. females in the age range 14–18). Ask your sample to compare the marketing mix of your selected product with three other rival products. Compare their views of the marketing mix of these products.

DID YOU KNOW?

An up-market product is one with a high price and of high quality: it tends to be sold from exclusive locations with expensive advertising and promotion. A down-market product is a cheap product with little or no advertising, sold from down-market locations. Can you identify some up-market and down-market products in the same product category?

CASE STUDY | The Tata Nano

The Tata Nano provides an excellent case study of the marketing mix in action. The car is designed to meet the mass market in India and other similar markets. It is the smallest and cheapest new car in the world. The captions in the diagram show how the *product* has been designed for simplicity. The car can be ordered direct from dealers in India, although it is hoped to launch a more expensive version in the European and American markets (*place*). The car has been *promoted* through a worldwide press launch and a lottery in India (which is the main market): the first million customers drawn in the lottery were to be first in line for the new car. The car was launched at a *price* of 100 000 rupees (about US$2 000). This made it the world's most affordable new car.

Labels on diagram:
- No air conditioning on standard model
- Windows wind down by hand
- Manual steering, no air bag
- height: 1.6 m (5 ft)
- 1.5 m (5 ft)
- length: 3.1 m (10 ft)
- Plastic and adhesive replaces welding
- Bodywork made of sheet metal and plastic
- 624 cc two-cylinder engine in boot giving max speed of 70 km/h (43 mph)

Questions

1 Do you think that the marketing mix for the Nano is likely to lead to high sales? Explain your answer.

2 How would you expect the marketing mix for the Nano to compare with the mix for an expensive car?

3 Is it going to be possible to sell this car in other markets (e.g. in the US and Europe)?

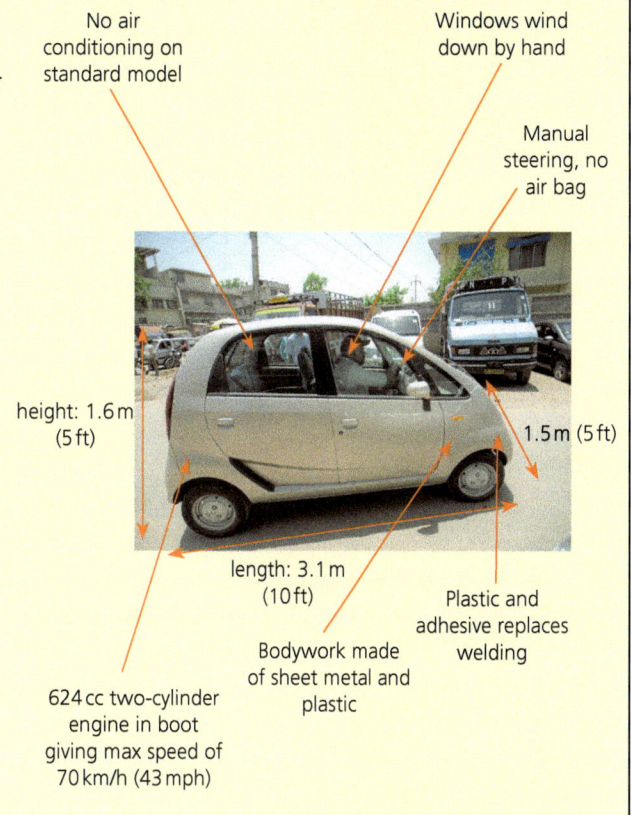

SUMMARY QUESTIONS

1 Match the following terms with the definitions below.

Product / promotion / place / price / marketing mix

- Advertising and other means of enticing customers to buy a product.
- Getting the product to where customers want to buy it.
- A combination of the four Ps.
- The good or service that is being sold.
- The amount charged for a good or service.

2 Choose a product that you have recently bought. What aspects of the marketing mix encouraged you to buy that product?

3 How is the marketing mix different for an exclusive type of tea such as Earl Grey tea when compared with a standard, cheap variety of tea?

KEY POINTS

1 A well-chosen marketing mix is required to attract the targeted customers to make purchases.

2 The marketing mix consists of getting the right product in the right place at the right price and supported by appropriate promotions.

3 The four Ps need to be blended together in the most appropriate way.

3.3.2 The product

TOPIC AIMS

Students should be able to:

- understand the importance of packaging
- show awareness of the concept of a brand name in influencing sales
- understand the importance of building and maintaining customer relations and loyalty
- draw and interpret a product life cycle diagram
- understand the four main stages of the product life cycle
- show awareness of extension strategies.

ACTIVITY

Look at the items shown in Figure 3.3.2.2. In your country, where is each of these in the product life cycle?

Identify products that your classmates purchase that are at different stages of the product life cycle.

Figure 3.3.2.2 Items in the product life cycle

Products

The most important part of the marketing mix is the product. It must meet an identified consumer need.

We like products because they provide us with **benefits**. A bicycle is not just something that sits outside our house; it provides the benefit of transporting us to school or to the sports club, or to meet friends.

Products have a number of features. For example, your bicycle has:

- shape   • design   • colour   • size   • packaging (when first bought).

In addition, there may be other benefits associated with your bicycle, after-sales service (repairs to the chain, replacement of the tyres by the seller) such as a guarantee (in some cases).

Starting with the packaging

The first time a customer sees many modern products is in the packaging. Figure 3.3.2.1 gives some of the many reasons that products are packaged.

Packaging adds value to products for all of the reasons shown in the diagram. However, there are some negative aspects: packaging can raise the cost and, as a result, the price of a product. It also creates pollution and waste.

Purposes of packaging:
- To enable the branding of the product
- To make the product look more attractive
- To enable the easy stacking, storing and transport of the packaging
- To comply with laws protecting customers
- To protect the product from contamination
- To provide details about how to use the product
- To keep the product fresh
- To protect the product from damage

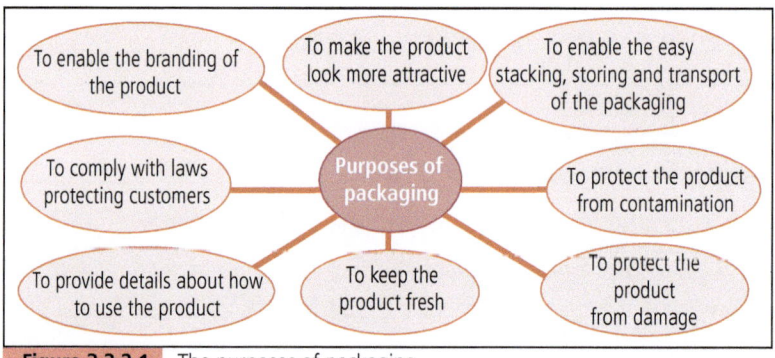

Figure 3.3.2.1 The purposes of packaging

Branding

A **brand** is a product or group of products with a unique, consistent and easily recognisable character. For example, we all recognise the Coca-Cola brand, not only by its logo, but by the shape of the bottle, the colour of the can, the taste of the product and other features.

The product life cycle

The life of a product is the period over which it appeals to customers. At the *introduction* stage, sales growth is slow. Only a small number of people know about a product or realise its benefits. Profits start to rise in the *growth* phase. More and more people find out about the product and want to purchase it. Competitors are coming into the market. In the *maturity* phase, most of the potential customers have been reached. However, there may be lots of repeat purchases. Competition from rival producers is strong. In the *decline* stage, the product becomes 'old' and sales start to fall. An updated or replacement product may have entered the market.

Giving new life

To prolong the life cycle, new life needs to be injected to the marketing mix. There are various ways of doing this.

1 Modify the product. In the 19th century, Lifebuoy soap was introduced to India with the promise of 'health and hygiene' to millions of rural customers. The product was sold as a basic red bar of soap. The brand went through a period of steady growth and eventual maturity in the 20th century. At the start of the 21st century, sales were falling by 15 per cent a year. The company then relaunched the soap in 2002, in a new shape, with a new, high-lather formula and attractive advertising. This has won back customer loyalty. Sales of Lifebuoy increased by 10 per cent per year in India. (Today, over 3 billion bars of Lifebuoy are sold per year in Asia and Africa.)

2 Altering distribution patterns to create more attractive retail outlets for consumers. For example, Hindustan Unilever, the makers of Lifebuoy, has created networks of women with business skills in rural villages to sell their products. There are over 25,000 of these women, selling in 100,000 villages and reaching 1 billion customers. Many other businesses have injected new life into their products by creating new channels, such as attractive websites, where customers can buy products online.

3 Changing prices. Prices can be lowered or raised to become more attractive to customers. Lower prices make goods more affordable, while higher ones make them appear more exclusive.

4 Promotional campaigns. Advertising, 'buy one get one free' offers and other promotions encourage new customers to try out a product and reward existing customers for their loyalty.

SUMMARY QUESTIONS

1 Draw a product life cycle for each of the following products.
   - A new product that has recently become popular in your country.
   - A product that has been available in your country for a long time, but has now become less popular.

   Explain your answer in each case.

2 List four products that are well-known brands. In each case, explain how packaging helps, or fails, to make the product more attractive.

3 How can a product's life cycle be extended?

STUDY TIP

In the long term, many products become outdated – the life cycle for the product category goes into decline (e.g. cassette tapes were replaced by CDs and, more recently, by MP3s).

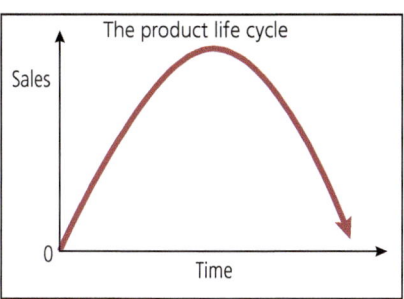

Figure 3.3.2.3

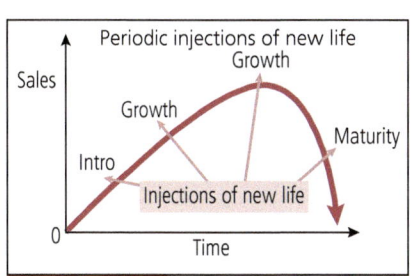

Figure 3.3.2.4

KEY POINTS

1 Products have life cycles that can extend from just a few weeks to hundreds of years.

2 Sales and profits increase during the growth and maturity phases of the cycle.

3 Businesses employ a range of extension strategies to inject new life into the product life cycle.

3.3.3 The price

TOPIC AIMS

Students should be able to:

- understand the main methods of pricing: cost plus, competitive, psychological, penetration, price skimming
- show awareness of the implications of the methods
- appreciate the difference between a price elastic demand and a price inelastic demand
- understand the importance of the concept in pricing decisions.

The price

The price a business charges will depend on the percentage of the market that they are trying to attract. The main decision is whether to charge:

- a *low price* in order to attract sales by undercutting the competition. This makes it possible to sell large quantities at a low cost per unit.
- an *average price*. If you charge an average price, you will need to compete with your rivals by other means (e.g. better packaging, advertising and promotion).
- a *higher price*. Firms can charge a *high* or *premium price* if they are seen as being better than their rivals in meeting the needs of customers.

Our glasses

		Glasses Direct	Spec-savers	D&A	Vision Express	Saving-Glasses Direct
Fully rimmed	○○	From £24	From £25	From £29	From £25	£1
Rimless	○○	From £24	From £99	-	From £99	£75
Semi-rimmed	○○	From £89	From £169	-	From £169	£80
Bendable	○○	From £39	From £125	-	From £125	£86
Titanium	○○	From £89	From £125	-	From £125	£36
Designer	○○	From £69	From £125	From £109	From £125	£56

Table comparing prices of spectacles. This advertisement is designed to attract customers to an online spectacle seller, Glasses Direct, by showing how prices are lower than those of rivals (competitive pricing).

ACTIVITY

Visit a local retail store and look at the prices displayed for different products. What examples can you find of penetration pricing, psychological pricing, skimming and competitive pricing?

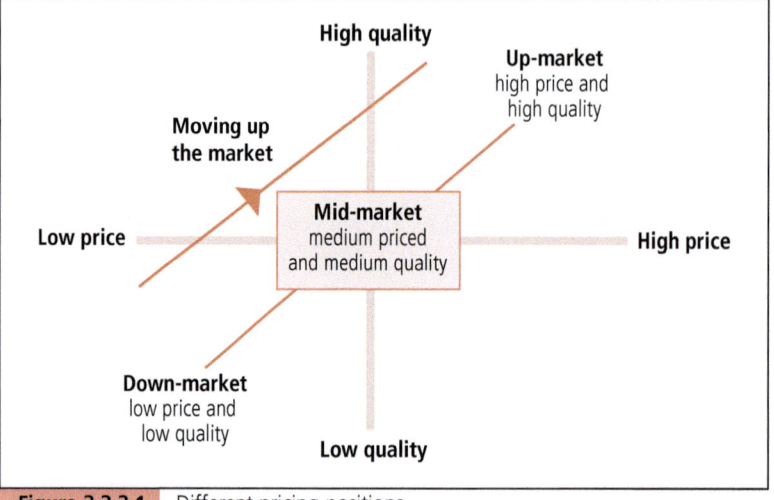

Figure 3.3.3.1 Different pricing positions

Price elasticity of demand – a measure of responsiveness of demand to a change in price

It is useful to find out how customers will react to a change in price. Price elasticity is used to measure this: this measures how much the quantity demanded changes following a change in price.

$$\text{Price elasticity of demand (PED)} = \frac{\text{\% change in quantity demanded}}{\text{\% change in price}}$$

Demand is *elastic* when the change in the number of goods demanded is high when compared with the change in price. For example, Ramesh sells fruit and vegetables from a cart. One week he lowered the price of his mangoes by 5 per cent (undercutting his competitors) and demand increased by 20 per cent. Demand for his mangoes in this case was elastic.

However, when the change in numbers of goods demanded is lower than the change in price, demand is said to be *inelastic*. For example, Ramesh sells oranges that are sweeter and contain fewer pips than those of his competitors. He decided to raise his price by 5 per cent. When he did so, sales of his oranges only dropped by 2 per cent. Demand for his oranges was inelastic. Knowledge of how elastic demand is helps sellers decide how much to charge for a product, and whether they will increase sales revenue from lowering or raising prices.

The main methods of pricing

Cost-plus pricing

A common way to make pricing decisions is to calculate how much it costs to do a particular job or activity, and then add on a given percentage as a profit for the job or activity. For example, a business may calculate that it will cost $100 to do a small repair job on a car, including parts, labour and equipment. The business also wants to make a profit, so may decide to add on another 20 per cent as profit, so charges $120.

Competitive pricing

A business may price its products lower than those of rivals. Businesses may make a loss in the short term by doing this, perhaps to force a competitor out of business.

Penetration pricing

When a firm brings out a new single-use product into a new or existing market (e.g. a new snack or drink), it may feel that it needs to make a lot of sales very quickly in order to establish itself and to make it possible to produce larger quantities. It may therefore start off by offering the product at quite a low price. A loss may be made until the new product has penetrated the market. When market penetration has been achieved, prices can be raised.

Skimming

When you bring out a new product, you may be able to start off by charging quite a high price. Some customers may want to be the first to buy your product because of the prestige of being seen with it. The word **skimming** comes from the idea of skimming off the top layer of cream. For example, you could sell an exclusive dress at an exclusive price to wealthier customers. The next season, you could lower the price, making it accessible to a less wealthy group of customers.

Promotional

This is a way of promoting the product by making the price more attractive, often when the product is first introduced. For example, a promotion might offers new chocolate bar half price to encourage new customers to try it.

> **KEY POINTS**
>
> 1 The simplest method of pricing is to add a percentage mark-up on costs.
> 2 Different pricing methods can be justified in different situations.

> **STUDY TIP**
>
> Charging a lower price might not increase the sales revenue of a business. This is because customers might not really be that influenced by the price. If they don't like the product it still won't sell, even if it is cheap.

> **SUMMARY QUESTIONS**
>
> 1 A local clothing business is considering lowering its prices (to increase sales and profits). An adviser carries out some research and reports back that there is elastic demand for the type of clothes being offered by the shop and that local consumers are highly influenced by psychological pricing. How might this affect the pricing decisions made by the business?
>
> 2 A sign-writing business that produces shop signs uses a cost-plus pricing method. It marks up prices by 20 per cent on the costs of painting shop signs. The owner has calculated that it will cost $50 to produce a sign for a restaurant. What price should the business charge for the job?
>
> 3 A new book has just been published by a best-selling author. Initially, the book is to be produced in hardback and will cost $100. Next year, it will be relaunched in paperback form and sell for $50. What pricing technique is being used, and why?

3.3.4 Place — distribution channels

TOPIC AIMS

Students should be able to:
- appreciate the importance of distribution channels and the factors that determine the selection of them
- show knowledge and understanding of a distribution channel
- recommend and justify an appropriate channel in a given situation.

Distribution

Supply, or *distribution* as it is commonly called, makes products available to customers where and when they want them. This is an aspect of place, a very important part of the marketing mix.

Something like 20 per cent of the total production cost of a product is taken up with freight charges. These are the costs of moving raw materials to the producer and then transporting finished products to the end-user.

Channels of distribution

A **distribution channel** is the means by which an organisation and its customers are brought together at a particular place and time to buy and sell goods. This may be in a shop, via a computer link or by television shopping.

The organisations that are involved in the distribution chain are:

- **Manufacturers** – firms that make the products.
- **Wholesalers** – firms that store goods in bulk which they purchase from manufacturers and then sell on to retailers.
- **Retailers** – the firms that sell goods to the final consumers.
- In Channel A, the manufacturer sells direct to the customer by mail order. The customer selects goods from a catalogue and purchases through the post.
- In Channel B, the manufacturer distributes direct to their own warehouses and company shops, which supply customers. Examples are products that are produced directly by large supermarket chains in their own factories. The manufacturer is responsible for distribution.
- In Channel C, sometimes referred to as the 'traditional channel', a manufacturer makes goods; a wholesaler buys lots of different

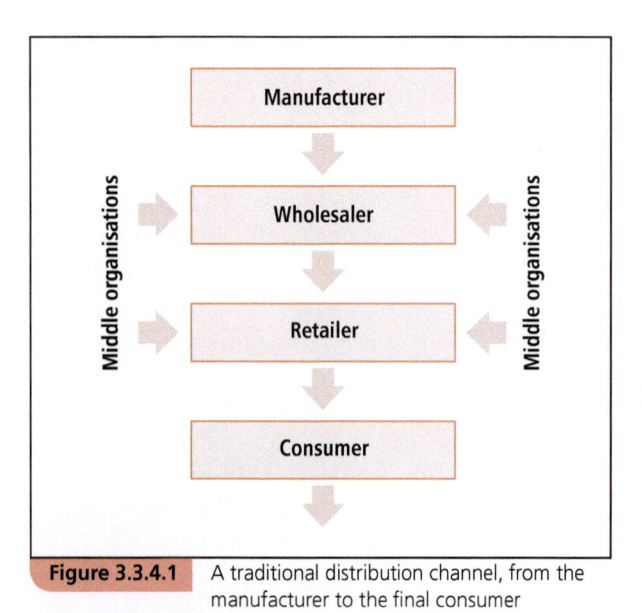

Coca-Cola has shortened its distribution channels to China by setting up joint ventures with the Chinese government and other Chinese partners to build bottling plants in China.

Figure 3.3.4.1 A traditional distribution channel, from the manufacturer to the final consumer

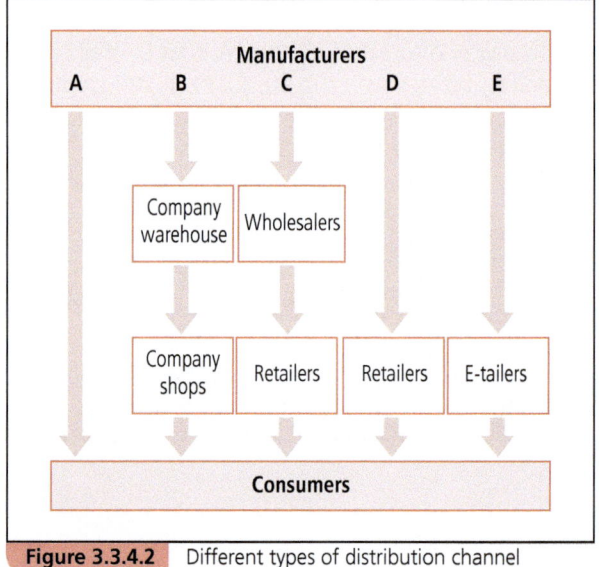

Figure 3.3.4.2 Different types of distribution channel

goods from several manufacturers. The wholesaler sells on to retailers. The manufacturer, wholesaler and retailer are all independent. (The term wholesaler refers to a business that stocks items in bulk until they are required by retailers.)

- In Channel D, retailers buy directly from manufacturers. This is easiest when the retailers have a very large storage area, or when goods can be bought in bulk.
- Channel E has become particularly important as more and more households become linked to the internet through computers and mobile phones. The e-tailer is the organisation that deals with customers through an interactive website, which enables customers to buy goods online.
- The more people involved the longer the distribution channel, and the move people taking a share of the profits. If the distribution channel is shorter there will be more profit for the manufacturer and the price to the customer can be lowered.

ACTIVITY

Interview the owner of a local shop to find out what channels of distribution they use for the various items they stock. (You will normally find that they use more than one channel of distribution.)

CASE STUDY: Coca-Cola in China

Distribution can become more expensive when it takes place internationally: the longer the supply chain, the greater the cost. The American company Coca-Cola's fourth biggest market is China. Eventually it could become the largest market.

In the 1970s, China had only one brand of soft drink, distributed nationally. It was difficult for foreign companies to enter the market. Coca-Cola started out by exporting Coca-Cola to China and selling it to retail outlets such as hotels. Over time, the company developed a relationship with the Chinese government. Bottling plants were set up that were owned by the Chinese government. The next stage was to set up a joint venture bottling plant (see opposite), owned jointly by Coca-Cola and the government. Eventually, Coca-Cola was allowed to set up its own bottling plants. In this way, the company was able to produce cheaply using local supplies of raw materials. By 2013, Coca-Cola had 42 bottling factories in the country. It now produces tea, coffee and bottled water, as well as Coca-Cola itself and many other soda drinks.

Questions

1. Why would Coca-Cola want to set up bottling plants in China rather than exporting bottles of Coca-Cola to China?
2. Illustrate how the supply chain was shortened when Coca-Cola set up its own bottling plants in China.

KEY POINTS

1. Distribution is the process through which goods are made available to consumers.
2. Channels of distribution are the series of stages involved in bringing goods to the end-consumer.
3. There are many different channels of distribution, depending on the type of product and the market. Increasingly, goods are distributed through shortened channels, often involving electronic selling.
4. The purpose of simplifying distribution channels is to reduce costs.

SUMMARY QUESTIONS

1. What is a distribution channel? How is a product that you are familiar with distributed? What are the various stages of distribution?
2. In what ways does e-tailing help to shorten the distribution channel?
3. Define the following terms.

   Distribution / manufacturer / wholesaler / retailer / e-tailer

93

3.3.5 Promotion

TOPIC AIMS

Students should be able to:

- understand the aims of promotion
- identify, explain and give examples of different forms of promotion
- understand how promotions influence sales
- justify an appropriate method of promotion in a given situation.

Promotion refers to ways of spreading information about a product, brand or company.

Promotion can be carried out in many different ways (e.g. advertising on television, radio, cinema, newspapers and, nowadays, using the internet and even mobile phones to get messages across).

Other forms of promotion include the sponsorship of events, sales promotion, merchandising (making products look attractive, e.g. in a shop window), trade shows and public relations. It is important to carry out promotions in the most cost-effective way possible, as the return on marketing is not easy to determine. The greatest possible return must be made.

The combination of different types of promotion is referred to as the promotional mix.

A distinction is made between promotions 'into the pipeline' and 'promotions out of the pipeline' (see Figure 3.3.5.1).

Advertising in Kenya includes simple billboards, advertisements on buses, radio, television and leading newspapers, as well as in the cinema.

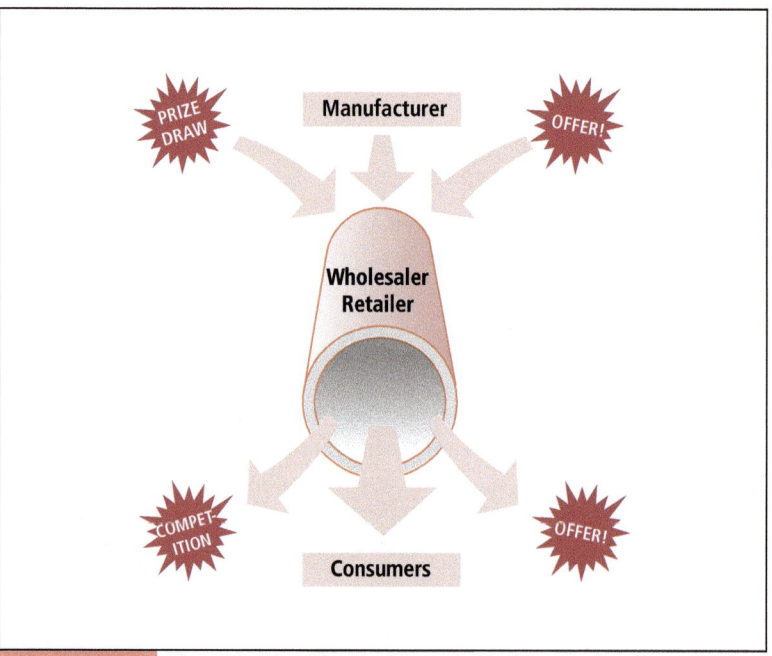

Figure 3.3.5.1 Promotion into the pipeline and out of the pipeline

ACTIVITY

Identify elements of the promotional mix for a product that you consume regularly. Explain why each of these elements is being used by the promoter.

Promotions into the pipeline are methods that are used to sell more products into the distribution system – that is, they are aimed at wholesalers and retailers rather than final consumers. Examples are 'dealer loaders', such as 20 for the price of 10, display units, dealer competitions, extended credit to dealers, sale-or-return, and so on.

Promotions out of the pipeline help in promoting and selling products to the final consumer. These include free samples, trial packs, coupon offers, price reductions, competitions, demonstrations and point-of-sale materials.

Different forms of promotion

Advertising

Advertising is a widely used form of above-the-line promotion. For example, in Kenya, advertising includes outdoor billboard advertising on street poles along major traffic routes, and advertising on the side of buses. In addition, there are around 90 radio stations and nearly all Kenyans listen to radio broadcasts regularly. Adverts can be placed in English and Swahili, as well as 17 other languages. There are eight television broadcast stations. Television covers the main centres of population. Television ownership tends to be among wealthier people, but there are televisions in most community and village centres. Leading newspapers are the *Daily Nation*, *East African Standard*, *The People* and *Kenya Times*. Stills and film clips are used extensively to advertise products in Kenya, including in mobile cinemas touring rural areas.

Advertising can increase sales by making consumers aware of new products, demonstrating how good products are and reminding consumers about products. Cinema and television advertising is highly visual and can build an image. However, due to the cost involved, in most countries TV advertising is normally only used by large companies that have big marketing budgets and are looking for mass market distribution.

Sales promotions

Sales promotions take place through media and non-media promotion for a limited time to increase consumer demand. Examples include:

- competitions
- special price offers for a limited period
- point-of-purchase displays
- free gifts.

Personal selling

Personal selling is oral communication with potential buyers of a product in the hope of making a sale. Initially, the seller will try to build a relationship with the buyer before going on to try to 'close' the sale.

Public relations

Public relations involves managing the flow of information from an organisation to its 'publics' in order to build the reputation of a company and its brands. Any form of activity which does this is termed *PR*. PR might involve publicising a charity, informing consumers about a brand or producing advertisements that show the company and its products in a positive light.

The purpose of each of the promotion methods described above is to increase the sales of the business.

Figure 3.3.5.2 The four main types of promotion

STUDY TIP

Price reduction is only seen as promotion if it is for a limited period of time. Permanently lower prices are part of the pricing strategy of the business.

DID YOU KNOW?

A good example of sales promotions are those offered by budget airlines such as India's Spice Jet. To attract new customers to the route, the airline will offer flights to new destinations at very low prices for a limited period of time. This has been very successful in winning new customers.

KEY POINTS

1. Promotion is the process of making consumers aware – that is, communicating information about a product or company.
2. There are four main types of promotion: advertising, sales promotion, direct selling and PR.
3. The ultimate purpose of promotion is to increase awareness, and therefore sales, of products and brands.

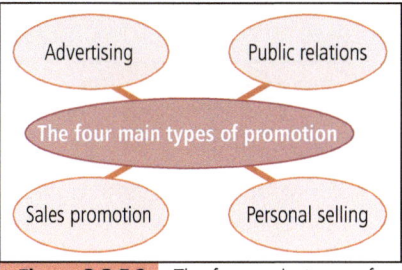

SUMMARY QUESTIONS

1. What type of promotion is involved in the following?
   - Giving out free samples of a new type of shampoo
   - Publicity surrounding a major charity event
   - Publicising a product on television or in a newspaper
2. What is the difference between promotions into the pipeline and promotions out of the pipeline?
3. What is the purpose of promotion? Illustrate your answer by reference to a promotion that you are familiar with.

3.3.6 Technology and the marketing mix

TOPIC AIMS

Students should be able to:
- define and explain the concept of e-commerce
- evaluate the opportunities and threats to both consumers and business of e-commerce
- understand use of the Internet and social networks for promotion.

The internet

E-commerce (buying and selling over the internet) has changed the way that a lot of buying and selling is done in recent years.

There are two main types of e-commerce:
- **B2B** (business-to-business) buying and selling
- **B2C** (business-to-consumer) selling.

B2B buying and selling

Most large businesses recognise the importance of the internet in trading with other businesses. The internet has helped to cut the costs of ordering new components, parts and stocks of goods. Buyers can use databases for information about items for sale all over the world. Major companies such as car producers have pooled together to create databases of supplies and suppliers of car components. This procedure is estimated to have reduced car production costs by as much as 20 per cent.

B2C buying and selling

Electronic commerce is having its greatest impact in B2C links. Businesses have realised that the internet provides them with a way of developing a relationship with customers.

DID YOU KNOW?

The **Internet** is an internationally linked set of computer networks with a common addressing scheme. The internet has been around since 1969, but was only widely used as a business tool in the mid 1990s, with the development of the first effective web browsers (the software required to navigate pages on the internet).

ACTIVITY

Carry out some research on an internet B2C site. Write a report that answers the following questions.
- How easy is the site to use?
- What are the benefits to consumers like you from using the site? What disadvantages are there?
- What are the advantages to the business of having only an internet presence?

STUDY TIP

Examiners often set questions about the suitability of a company using the internet to sell its products directly to customers. Think about what products can best be sold in this way. When would it be unsuitable? Why?

A traditional shop may attract customers by displaying goods in its shop window. In e-commerce, the shop window is the company's **website**. As it can reach anyone in the world with internet access, it is obviously a much more powerful sales and marketing tool than the traditional shop window. If the website is well constructed, buying over the internet can be a time-saving and less expensive way of making a purchase. A customer wanting to buy farm equipment, for example, can search for sites selling the item. They can browse through the details of different types of equipment available and purchase directly over the internet, or by using phone or mail links. It is important to develop a website that users will want to keep visiting.

The three main factors in a good website are content, community and commerce.

The following table sets out the benefits of a good website to providers and consumers.

Benefits to the provider	Benefits to the consumer
Low ongoing costs once the site has been established	Lower prices resulting from provider's low costs
The provider doesn't have to have a high street presence or other expensive location	Consumers can browse the website in the comfort of their own homes, or elsewhere
The provider can set out far more information about products or services on an easy-to-navigate site	Consumers can spend time navigating the website, finding out as much information as they need to before making a choice
The provider can access a wide market from a remote location	Consumers do not need to be near to the provider

There are some problems associated with e-commerce.

- The cost and time taken to create a website that is attractive and easy to use: businesses usually employ specialist website designers to create the site and manage it for them. Once the site has been built, there will be enormous cost savings for the business.
- Payment: making payment over the internet requires users to provide details of their bank accounts. The risk of fraudsters stealing users' bank details can make buyers reluctant to make purchases over the internet, and businesses lose custom.
- Importance of relationship: internet buyers and sellers do not have face-to-face contact, which can be important.
- Poor customer service has affected e-commerce development, for example, in India. Customers have found that deliveries are often late and they have been unable to contact customer services.
- There is limited or unreliable internet access in some countries, or deliveries may be unreliable.

Promotion

Promotion works best when satisfied customers spread the word about products and brands. The internet and social media sites are a great way of generating discussion about, and interest in, products. Companies build discussion forums such as wikis and blogs into their commercial websites. These encourage customers to talk about products. They spread the message to their friends through links to social media sites such as Facebook. Companies can encourage consumers to provide online feedback to them in discussion forums. At the same time, advertising is geared to provide 'talking points' about products to encourage customers to interact with each other.

Content
Content drives users to a website – content includes news, interviews and product information.

Community
Visitors to the site need to feel that they are part of a group and that they are valued.

Commerce
It generates income, through shopping, advertising, etc.

Figure 3.3.6.1 The three Cs of a good commercial website

DID YOU KNOW?

Social networking involves communities of internet users communicating with each other. They chat and pass on information (e.g. Facebook and My Space), share photos (e.g. Flickr), share videos (e.g. YouTube) and interact with each other. Companies can use social media to encourage positive conversations about their products and brands.

KEY POINTS

1. Businesses can use e-commerce to sell to a wider market.
2. There is an initial cost in setting up a website, but once established it opens up a potentially global market.
3. The website needs to be easy to operate, and easy for customers to make payments.

SUMMARY QUESTIONS

1. Define the following terms: Internet / website / e-commerce / B2B / B2C
2. What would be the benefit to a Pakistan-based clothes retailer of setting up a website to sell traditional regional clothes over the internet? What might be the drawbacks to the business of setting up this site?
3. What are the main ingredients of a good commercial website?

3.4 Marketing strategy

3.4.1 Elements of a marketing strategy

TOPIC AIMS

Students should be able to:

- understand how the marketing mix can be used to influence consumer purchasing
- understand how the marketing mix can change as the product goes through its life cycle
- select and justify marketing methods appropriate to a given situation
- understand the importance of different elements of the marketing mix
- recommend and justify a marketing strategy in a given situation.

What is a marketing strategy?

A marketing strategy is a plan of the marketing activities for a range of products, or for a single product. In effect, this means choosing the right combination of marketing mix elements to support the product/s.

The best possible mix will depend on the stage of the product life cycle.

The elements of a marketing strategy

The table shows the four key elements of the marketing strategy. The case study that follows gives an example of a marketing strategy used by Ford and Mahindra & Mahindra to enter a new market in India.

Product	Price	Place	Promotion
What product are we selling to our target customers? What does the product look like? What benefits does it provide?	What is an appropriate price for our product and the relevant target audience?	Where should we sell it? What are the most suitable channels of distribution?	How do we promote the product in a way that fits with the product image and the type of customers?

CASE STUDY: The Ford Figo in the Indian market

A joint venture between Ford and Indian company Mahindra & Mahindra is developing products designed for the Indian consumer. They have developed a new car designed specifically as a result of market research in India. The car is called the Ford Figo and it is designed specifically for a target customer – named 'Sandeep'.

Sandeep is defined by Ford India's markets as an individual with his head in the clouds but his feet on the ground. Sandeep is young, just married and lives at home with his parents. He is aspirational and reasonably well educated. He is looking to move from a motorbike to an affordable car. The Ford Figo is targeted at the small cars segment of the car market (which accounts for 70 per cent of all car sales in India).

The car was promoted through a lottery system that rapidly captured public imagination. Names drawn from the lottery dictated who would be eligible to purchase the first cars from Ford's network of dealers in India. There was a great deal of media and customer attention. In the first month that the car came on the market 10 000 were ordered, and sales have gone from strength to strength with 100 000 being produced within the first 15 months. The Ford Figo is now exported to a number of other countries.

Questions

1. What elements of price, place, promotion and product are mentioned in the study?
2. How do you think the marketing strategy outlined in the case study will enable the Ford Figo to gain a strong position in India's car market?
3. Why do you think 'Sandeep' was chosen to represent the target market for the new Ford Figo?

| CASE STUDY | Unilever washing powder in Brazil |

In the mid 1990s, Unilever had gained 81 per cent of the Brazilian washing powder market. The only sector it had not captured was that of the very lowest income households. The company therefore set out an 'Everyman' campaign to win even this sector of the market. Market research showed that washing in the poorer areas was typically carried out by hand, using washboards and bars of laundry soap. Washing was a major social event, with people coming together to talk at the river and taking pride in their work. Though many people owned television sets, many could not read or write, so it would be difficult to convince them to change washing habits with a 30-second TV commercial. Typically, this group of consumers shopped at local, family-owned stores, which manufacturers find difficult to reach through large wholesalers.

Questions

1 What marketing strategy would you suggest to reach the low-income sector of the Brazilian market for soap powders?

2 How would this involve blending each of the elements of marketing into a consistent mix?

The changing marketing mix

Over time, it may be necessary to change a marketing strategy. This involves changing the marketing mix. For example, we saw earlier (see page 89) how Lifebuoy soap was successfully relaunched in India with a new advertising campaign and strategy.

At the start of a product life cycle, the emphasis is on gaining a hold in the market. This may involve promotional activity and promotional pricing. Distribution may be through a small number of outlets. Over time, the business will adopt new promotional activities, alter its product and employ different distribution channels.

SUMMARY QUESTIONS

1 What is meant by the term 'marketing strategy'? Illustrate your answer by using the example of a product or brand that you are familiar with.

2 How is the marketing strategy different for a low-price, low-specification product, compared with one for a high-price, high-specification product? Use examples of products from the same market segment to illustrate your answer.

3 Why is the marketing strategy for a product likely to change over the course of its life cycle? Explain with reference to a specific product.

ACTIVITY

Identify a product and create a marketing strategy for it in your domestic market. Your marketing strategy should include a description of the product, its benefits and its target customers. Justify the pricing strategy, the locations for selling the product and the channels of distribution. You will also need to justify promotions to support each of the other elements.

ACTIVITY

Recommend a strategy for the relaunch of a product of your choice. Choose a product that is widely used in your country that has been losing popularity in recent times.

KEY POINTS

1 A marketing strategy is a plan setting out approaches that will be used to market a product or range of products.

2 The strategy covers each element of the marketing mix and how the elements fit together.

3 Marketing strategies need to be adjusted over the course of time.

3.4.2 Legal controls related to marketing

> **TOPIC AIMS**
>
> Students should be able to:
> - outline the nature and impact of legal controls related to marketing
> - show how legal restrictions on the marketing mix impact on marketing strategy.

> **DID YOU KNOW?**
>
> Most countries have laws preventing businesses from having a monopoly (i.e. being the only business in the market) and raising prices. Governments may break up monopolies to allow competition.

> **ACTIVITY**
>
> Produce a two-page leaflet that shows how regulations in your country impact on the marketing strategy for goods. The regulations should relate to the promotion of goods, where goods can be sold from (place), restrictions on pricing activity, and limitations on how goods can be produced and sold.

Controlling commercial and marketing activity

In creating a marketing strategy businesses need to understand what they can and cannot do. There are standards governing what constitutes appropriate marketing activity.

Some of these standards are laid down in law (legislation) so they are mandatory, some are voluntary codes or practices within an industry, while others are set by individual businesses. The legal system will set out a fair framework for trading, for marketing activities and to settle disputes that may arise.

Misleading promotion

This relates to advertising in particular. Most countries have advertising standards bodies that are set up by advertisers on a voluntary basis to prevent and discourage misleading advertising. Advertisers will be prevented from making false claims, e.g. relating to 'hair restorers', 'miracle weight loss cures', etc. Typically voluntary codes are backed up by consumer protection laws relating to how goods and services are sold and to the sale of dangerous products. Misleading offers such as 3 for the price of 2, and 30 per cent off which unfairly distort the offer being made are illegal and can lead to fines for dishonest companies and other punishments through the courts.

Faulty or dangerous products and services

The law of a country typically states that goods should be 'fit for the purpose' for which they are sold. For example, when you buy a bicycle you expect to be able to ride it. The buyer would have a justifiable complaint if, for example, some spokes were broken or a wheel was bent.

Goods should also match the description of them given in promotions and sales literature. This is particularly important for goods sold in packets. The pictures or descriptions on the packet should accurately match the products inside. Goods should also match the description of their quality. In addition, buyers should be given the correct weight or quantity of goods that they have paid for.

Consumers are usually protected by law against dangerous or harmful products. For example, children's toys should not have sharp edges. Electrical goods should be safe to use. Food products should contain edible and safe ingredients.

Similarly services should be carried out with reasonable care and skill. They should also be provided within a reasonable time. For example, if a consumer has asked a repair business to repair a radio, it would be unreasonable to wait for months for the repair to be completed. The service should also be provided at a reasonable cost.

Pricing controls

Legislation relating to pricing also impacts on marketing strategy. While producers and sellers have considerable leeway over what prices they can charge there are some aspects of pricing that are illegal. These include:

- colluding with other providers of goods and services to jointly set prices. This practice is regarded as uncompetitive and can be seen as 'ganging up' on consumers. Fines and even prison sentences for directors may be the penalty for collusion on pricing.
- charging prices that are different to those that have been agreed. When a supplier agrees to sell goods at a certain price this is typically seen as being contractually binding. Should the supplier seek to then increase the price after supplying the good he would be deemed to have acted in an illegal manner.
- hidden pricing. This often relates to purchasers who buy goods on credit terms. They believe they have entered into a credit transaction with a given set of terms only to find that there are additional (hidden) extras that they have to pay.

Controls on place of sale

There are also legal restrictions on where certain goods and services can be sold from, e.g. cigarettes, alcohol and pharmaceutical products may only be allowed to be sold from licensed premises.

Aligning strategy with expectations

The marketing and legal departments of companies must make sure that the marketing strategy being employed is legal, decent and honest, i.e. that:

- the way that the good is promoted is honest and fair
- pricing is clear and free from collusion with other suppliers
- goods are sold through appropriate licensed locations
- the product meets the required legal standards and specifications.

Reputable companies will do more than meet legal requirements. In addition they will meet voluntary industry standards and set their own standards for excellence.

> **DID YOU KNOW?**
> The Consumer Protection Law in Egypt requires manufacturers or importers to place a label on commodities stating that they meet Egyptian standards. The label must be written in Arabic, in a legible and clear form. Price, specifications and characteristics of products must be made clear.

> **KEY POINTS**
> 1. Commercial activity and marketing strategy is constrained by laws and by voluntary standards.
> 2. Laws govern what promotional messages are acceptable, the legality of a pricing strategy, where goods and services can be provided, and the nature of products that are allowed to be sold.
> 3. Reputable companies will ensure that their marketing strategies not only meet the legal requirements but also set standards for excellence.

> **SUMMARY QUESTIONS**
>
> 1. A cigarette manufacturer wants to sell its products through a chain of supermarkets and would like the supermarket to place the cigarettes near to the checkout counters where people pay for their goods. It wants to advertise these products on national television saying that they are good for people who want to live a healthy lifestyle. It has made an agreement with a rival cigarette company to charge the same price for a packet of 20 cigarettes as that charged by the rival. What laws is the cigarette manufacturer contravening with this marketing strategy?
> 2. What is likely to happen if a company ignores the laws and customs of a particular country when establishing a marketing strategy to market its products in that country?

3.4.3 Problems of entering new markets abroad

TOPIC AIMS

Students should be able to:
- demonstrate an understanding of problems of a business when entering a new market abroad
- demonstrate an awareness of methods of dealing with such problems
- understand growth potential, benefits and limitations of new markets.

Merchants have traded goods for thousands of years. Traders selling goods such as nutmeg, pepper and silks were using the route known as The Silk Road between China, India and the Arabian peninsula over 2000 years ago. They travelled vast distances in the hope of selling at a profit in new markets. In recent years, we have seen different markets around the world increase at very different rates, countries like China, Brazil and Russia are experiencing rapid growth, with income per head increasing. This creates opportunities for marketing.

However, it is not easy to enter a new market. There are a number of obstacles that create difficulty. A first major difficulty is that consumers in the market that you want to sell into may not be familiar with your brand or product.

This can be illustrated by the example of Heinz baked beans. The HJ Heinz company is a large American multinational producing many food products. One of its products is tinned beans. They are produced to different recipes in different countries, in different sized and shaped tins. Most commonly they are produced with a tomato sauce base. The variety of bean typically used is the haricot bean.

In the late 1990s the company started selling their beans in Eastern Europe, where beans are very popular. However, because customers were not sure what was inside the tin they were wary of buying the product. As a result the company changed its labelling to include pictures of the beans. This resulted in a large increase in sales. The company has also changed 'beans' to 'beanz' on the tin to support its advertising slogan of 'Beanz meanz Heinz'.

Other problems of entering new overseas markets include the following:

- **Lack of local knowledge**: businesses particularly want to find out about consumer tastes and preferences. They also need to know about rules and laws about what can be produced. For example, in Thailand a very popular drink for people working long hours was called 'Krating Daeng', which translates as 'Red Bull'. The drink helps to keep people awake because it contains substances called caffeine and taurine. It was sold in a brown bottle. Before it could be introduced to other markets, some of the ingredients needed to be changed because of health and safety laws in other countries. The drink has now been reformulated under the name 'Red Bull' and it sells across the globe.

- **Contacts**: it is very important to have contacts in overseas markets. These contacts may be with people who can help you to sell your product. They may be with government officials who can explain details of local laws.

- **Different cultures and tastes**: many products have to be altered for local conditions. This is particularly true in the food and drink market.

- **Language differences:** there can be challenges associated with setting up and operating in a foreign country. Without knowledge of local languages lots of mistakes can be made.

Illustrating the Beanz!

STUDY TIP

Students often think that the only problem a business faces when entering a foreign market is a tariff barrier (import tax). Make sure that you understand the non-financial obstacles that also have to be overcome.

Dealing with problems in overseas markets

One way of selling to overseas customers is to make sales visits to countries to sell your products. This could be supported by telephone links and the creation of a sales website (although unreliable web connections in some countries may make this unsuitable). This is a low-cost method, but has the disadvantage that the exporter only builds limited overseas contacts.

Another approach therefore could be to use an overseas sales agent or partner. The partner would share the profits from the sales.

On a larger scale, a business can open up an overseas production or sales operation. This is much more costly. Building an overseas operation helps a company to plan for the long-term. Customers will take the company much more seriously if it has a local base. For example, in South Africa, Volkswagen makes a range of cars for the African market from its base there. The company is sourcing an increasing number of components from local manufacturers. Another example is Oxford University Press, which has its own publication department in Africa – producing books for the East African market.

Another good way to enter an overseas market is to form a **joint venture** with a local partner. Here a joint business is set up between the two companies. Many Western companies have set up joint ventures in China and India. The local partner will have a lot of local contacts with government officials and business people in the home market. The local partner will also have a good knowledge of local tastes and preferences.

The table below gives examples of joint ventures in India.

Tata and Fiat	The joint venture manufactures cars from Tata and Fiat. Tata motors buys diesel engines for its cars from Fiat. Fiat distributes Tata cars in Europe.
Mahindra and Renault	The venture will manufacture Renault's Logan cars in India. Renault gains access to the Indian market. Mahindra gains technical knowledge about car production.
Bharthi–Wal-Mart	The Indian government restricted the growth of foreign retailers in India. The joint venture therefore gave Wal-Mart access to the Indian market.

KEY POINTS

1. When entering a new overseas market companies are faced by a number of problems. These include language differences, lack of local contacts, lack of knowledge of the local market, and different rules and regulations.
2. There are cultural differences between different markets. As a result, customers in different countries have different tastes and preferences.
3. There are a number of ways of entering new markets that reduce the risk. These include working with local partners such as sales agents or setting up a joint venture.
4. It is possible to set up a new operation in an overseas market.

DID YOU KNOW?

McDonald's, the fast food restaurant, has introduced more spicy and vegetarian dishes in India to suit local tastes.

ACTIVITY

Visit a local shop. Can you identify one product that is produced in your own country that would need to be adapted if it were going to be sold in other countries? How would the product need to be altered, and why?

SUMMARY QUESTIONS

1. A Japanese company sells cameras in Europe through agents who deal directly with camera retailers. However, with the development of new digital camera technologies sales have started to increase substantially in Europe. The company wants to increase business in Europe. What methods would you recommend for increasing its presence in the European market?
2. What would be the main advantages to a Western company from creating a joint venture when seeking to increase sales in China?
3. In 2009 Tata Motors of India launched the Tata Nano – the world's smallest mass-market car. The car is designed to solve car-parking problems in cities and to have very low petrol consumption. Tata hopes to sell variations of the car in Western markets. What problems might Tata have in selling to these markets? How might Tata deal with these problems?

Unit 3 — Practice questions

SECTION 1: Short-answer questions

1. Identify and explain TWO objectives of the marketing department within a business. [4]

2. Using a mobile phone or laptop computer as an example, explain the difference between 'features' and 'benefits' of a product. [3]

3. Identify and explain TWO reasons why a business might carry out market research. [4]

4. Explain the statement: 'The consumer is king in a market economy'. [4]

5. Explain why primary research may be known as 'field' research and secondary research may be known as 'desk' research. [4]

6. Analyse TWO reasons why primary market research results may be inaccurate. [6]

7. Explain, with examples, the difference between a consumer survey and a focus group. [4]

8. State and explain ONE example of data that would be best presented using a pie chart and ONE example of data that would be best presented as a line graph. [4]

9. Explain, using examples, the following approaches to market segmentation:
   - geographical
   - gender
   - socio-economic group. [6]

10. For each of your answers to Question 9, explain a market for which this method of segmentation would be appropriate. [6]

11. Identify and explain a niche market within the market for food in your country. [4]

12. Identify and explain TWO benefits to a small business of aiming its product at a niche market. [4]

13. Analyse why it is important for a business to get all the elements of the marketing mix right. [4]

14. Analyse why an established business may aim to sell a range of products at different stages of their life cycle. [4]

15. Analyse ONE example of a product for which a skimming pricing strategy may be appropriate and ONE example where penetration pricing may be more successful. [4]

16. Explain, with examples, THREE problems that a clothing business may experience when trying to sell products in another country. [6]

SECTION 2: Longer-answer questions

The pizza delivery company

Prakesh has managed to borrow the money to relaunch his traditional fast-food business, The Tikka Takeaway, in Bangalore, India, as a pizza restaurant and takeaway, including a home-delivery service. He has put together a menu, including 12 different pizza recipes in three different sizes, and he now needs to make as many people as possible aware of his new products and service. Due to overspending on the redecoration of his shop, however, Prakesh has had to set a low marketing budget.

1. Identify and explain TWO changes in Prakesh's marketing mix. [4]

2. Identify and explain TWO ways in which Prakesh's target market may change due to the switch from traditional food to pizzas. [4]

3. Analyse TWO possible pricing methods you would recommend Prakesh to consider for his pizzas when he launches the new business idea. [6]

4 Identify and explain THREE marketing methods you would recommend to Prakesh for the launch. [6]

5 Due to his local reputation and loyal customers, Prakesh does not want to change the name of his business. Do you agree with him? Justify your answer. [6]

The Maldives Reef holiday company

The Maldives Reef holiday company operates in a niche market. The target customers are high-income, young professionals, mainly from Europe, who are interested in combining taking a holiday with obtaining an advanced diving qualification. Guests are accommodated on one of the smallest, most exclusive resort islands, where all the chalets have their own private beach areas. The diving instructors are highly qualified and the company has good knowledge of the best underwater locations. The company spends very little on marketing, as most guests are regular travellers and recommendations come through word of mouth. Fiona, the marketing director, is keen to seek out new markets, due to a worldwide economic downturn. 'Maybe,' she says, 'we should explore a new market segment of more budget-conscious travellers, who still want to dive but are quite happy with basic accommodation and therefore a lower price'.

1 Explain the term 'niche market' in this case. [6]

2 Analyse how the unique selling point of the Maldives Reef holiday company enables high prices to be charged to current customers. [6]

3 Analyse ONE advantage and ONE disadvantage to the Maldives Reef holiday company of relying on the business from their loyal customers. [6]

4 To what extent do you agree with Fiona that the company should be looking for new markets? [6]

5 Suggest a market research strategy for Fiona to find out what budget-conscious customers want from a diving holiday. [6]

Zigzag: the school enterprise company

The Zigzag enterprise company at Good Start School in Livingstone, Zambia, has decided on two events to launch its enterprise this year: a school talent show and a doughnut sale during lunchtimes. They have carried out primary market research on pupils in school and have found out the following information about predicted sales.

- Talent show: at $5 they will sell 250 tickets, but if they drop the price to $3, they will sell 275 tickets.

- Doughnuts: at 50 cents they will sell 300 doughnuts, but if they drop the price to 30 cents, they will sell 500.

1 Identify and explain TWO possible reasons why Zigzag's market research may be inaccurate. [4]

2 Identify and explain TWO reasons why Zigzag's current target market may limit their success. [6]

3 Calculate the price elasticity of demand (PED) for each product, when the price is reduced, using the formula:

$$PED = \frac{\text{\% change in quantity demanded}}{\text{\% change in price}}$$ [6]

4 Using the information on price elasticity and the figures, recommend what price should be charged for each product. Explain your answer. [6]

5 The members of Zigzag have decided to try to extend their market to include selling wooden souvenirs to tourists in a local craft market. Analyse TWO ways in which their marketing strategy will need to change for these customers. [6]

6 Evaluate the extent to which personal selling in the craft market may lead to high sales of souvenirs for the Zigzag company. [6]

4 Operations management

4.1 Production of goods and services

4.1.1 The meaning of production

TOPIC AIMS

Students should be able to:
- understand how resources can be used and managed to help organisations achieve their objectives
- understand the difference between production and productivity
- identify factors that increase productivity.

A very productive system. In a Japanese sushi bar, the chef converts the rice, fish and vegetables into rice parcels which go round a moving belt for diners to choose from.

STUDY TIP

It is a common error to confuse increasing production with increasing productivity. Make sure you understand the difference between these two concepts.

ACTIVITY

Choose two businesses from the following: shoe manufacturer, hotel chain/hotel reception desk, cycle repair shop owner, hairdresser. Suggest ways each could increase productivity.

Inputs and outputs

Businesses convert inputs into more valuable outputs. This is referred to as adding value (see page 2). Production involves making resources more valuable. Figure 4.1.1.1 shows how various business inputs are made into more valuable outputs.

INPUTS

Information   Capital   Labour   Materials   Energy

↓

THE PRODUCTION PROCESS

↓

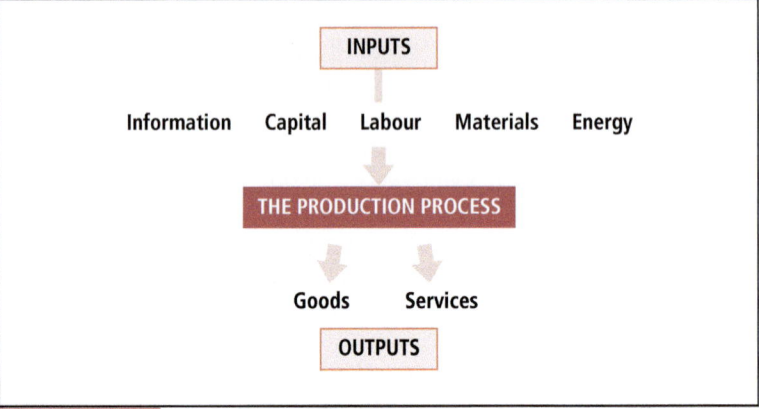

Goods   Services

OUTPUTS

Figure 4.1.1.1 The production process

A number of **operations** (organised work tasks) are usually carried out to add value when managing resources. Operations management is therefore the term that describes the process of managing these activities. An example is a Japanese sushi restaurant, where fish, rice and vegetables are brought into the restaurant as the main raw materials; other ingredients such as ginger and soy sauce will be added. Chefs then work with these materials to produce the sushi – parcels of rice containing the fish and vegetables. The chefs carry out operations such as taking the ingredients out of the stores, cutting up the fish and vegetables, rolling the rice parcels, and putting the prepared sushi on plates. The plates pass round a moving conveyor belt and customers choose which dishes they would like. The production process therefore involves converting the food materials into the finished sushi products.

Production and labour productivity

Production means making goods or services. **Productivity** refers to how effective resources are in producing goods. Productivity rises when resources are used well. The diners in the sushi bar receive quicker service than in an ordinary restaurant because they help themselves to food from the moving line produced by the chef – they do not have to wait to be served. More output is produced with given quantities of inputs. In a sushi restaurant, considerable output is achieved by a small staff.

The productivity of a company can be measured by the following calculation.

$$\text{Productivity} = \frac{\text{Quantity of output}}{\text{Quantity of inputs}}$$

Measurements are often carried out to measure the productivity of particular resource inputs. This is often the case with labour. For example, if a Toyota car plant produces 500 cars per hour with 1000 employees, then the labour productivity would be 0.5 cars per hour. (The figure indicates the amount produced by one worker.) If the number of cars increased to 600 per hour with the same number of workers, then labour productivity could be said to have risen to 0.6 cars per hour.

$$\textbf{Labour productivity} = \frac{500 \text{ cars per hour}}{1000 \text{ employees}} = 0.5 \text{ cars per hour}$$

There are a number of ways of increasing productivity. These include:

- organising work more efficiently (e.g. the layout of machines in a factory might be improved to reduce wasted time)
- using more productive resources (e.g. by using more modern machinery and equipment or training employees to work more efficiently)
- automation and computerisation: many factories today employ robots and automatic machinery (e.g. electronic eyes that check on the quantity of fluid in containers and stop the filling process when the containers are full)
- using approaches that motivate staff to work harder (e.g. offering bonuses, job rotation and job enrichment).

In some areas of work, particularly service jobs, it is not easy to increase productivity in a measurable way. Services often involve care and attention to customers. Examples are the work of dentists, doctors, teachers and accountants. In these cases, productivity should be measured not just by the quantity of work done, but also by its quality.

ACTIVITY

Identify four operations involved in each of the following.

1. Running a cinema.
2. Making a loaf of bread in a bakery.
3. Serving a customer with petrol at a filling station.

DID YOU KNOW?

Many service jobs are involved with leisure industries. The development of tourism in countries across the world has opened up opportunities for service jobs such as hotel receptionists, cleaners, restaurant workers, tour guides and sports instructors.

KEY POINTS

1. Businesses convert inputs into outputs through transforming resources.
2. Operations management is the process of managing resources in an efficient way.
3. Productivity is a measure of the quantity of output produced in relation to the input of resources.
4. Labour productivity measures output in relation to the number of employees (or labour hours) input in a particular period of time.
5. Productivity can be increased by improving the quality and the organisation of resources.

SUMMARY QUESTIONS

1. Explain how the production process involves converting inputs into finished outputs. Illustrate your answer with an example from a particular business. Show the various inputs and outputs, as well as the operations that take place in the business.

2. The following table shows the number of loaves baked per day in a bakery. The table shows that the number of loaves baked per day is increasing. What is happening to productivity?

Year	Number of loaves (per week)	Number of workers	Labour productivity (output per employee)
2012	10 000	20	
2013	12 000	25	
2014	21 000	30	

3. Using the examples of farming, construction and nursing, explain the difference between productivity and production. In which of these occupations would it be most difficult to measure productivity? Why?

107

4.1.2 Methods of production

TOPIC AIMS

Students should be able to:

- explain job, batch and flow production methods
- describe the main features of different production methods
- explain the main advantages of different methods
- select and justify methods appropriate to a given situation.

An example of job production. The fan of cables design on Angchuanzhou Bridge in Hong Kong was specified to help resist typhoon winds. At 1596 m it is also the longest bridge in the world.

DID YOU KNOW?

Today, a new idea has been developed – mass customisation. Using sophisticated computers, it is possible to quickly produce lots of items that have distinct features. In Japan, in particular, robot-controlled machinery can be programmed to make a specific product such as a car, for a specific customer, almost as quickly as a standard car.

Different methods of production

Some products are produced one at a time, with great attention to detail. Others are **mass-produced**, when hundreds of thousands of identical items flow off a production line. There are three main types of production methods, outlined below.

Job production

Job-produced items are produced individually to meet the requirements of a specific customer. They are typically expensive because of the amount of work needed to go into them. They may need to be altered if they do not meet the customer's specification the first time. The Angchuanzhou bridge that spans the mouth of the container port in Hong Kong is an example of **job production**. Like every bridge, it had to be designed and manufactured individually to meet local conditions – in this case, the length required and an ability to withstand typhoons.

Other examples of job production are designer-made clothes, suits and wedding dresses. The tailor will produce garments that are individually measured and designed to fit a particular customer. Job-produced items are sometimes produced on the premises of the producer: parts of a bridge may be constructed before being transported to the construction site. Shop and café signs are also job-produced, as are passenger ships and wedding cakes.

Batch production

In **batch production**, a number of identical, or similar, items are produced in a set or batch. The items need not be for any specific customer, but are made at regular intervals in specific quantities. Batch production involves work being passed from one stage to another. Each stage of production is highly planned.

We saw in 4.1.1 how a sushi restaurant is an example of high productivity. The process also illustrates batch production. A chef in a sushi restaurant makes a number of different types of sushi. For example, he or she may make a batch of 20 nigirizushi (hand-formed rice parcels with a fish topping). These will then be placed on the moving belt in the restaurant. The chef will then make 20 makizushi (circular rolls of rice surrounded by seaweed). The chef may then make 20 sweet dishes. The chef may then go on to produce another batch of 20 nigirizushi, and so on. Each time he places the fresh food on the belt. By producing batches, the chef can concentrate on one type of item at a time, while still supplying a steady supply of fresh food.

A key feature of batch production is that every now and then you have to stop the production process and change over to a new type of production using similar equipment. Many manufacturing and service organisations operate in this way. For example, in an electronics factory, the production line may be set to produce one type of electronic circuit board for the first two hours of the day. Then the machine may be reprogrammed to produce another type of circuit board for the next two hours, and so on.

Flow production

Flow production involves products or services passing down a **line of production**. The production process is a repeating one, with identical products going through the same sequence of operations; car production, chocolate bar manufacture and bottled drink manufacture are examples. Lifebuoy soap and cans of Coca-Cola are also produced in this way. Continuous flow involves producing for 24 hours a day, using automatic equipment in a standardised way. An oil refinery, for example, works on a continuous flow basis, with petrol being refined around the clock. While this production method may be ideal for the examples given here, a disadvantage is that there are many products that consumers prefer to be customised rather than mass-produced.

Figure 4.1.2.1 Providing a steady supply of sushi to the belt

Figure 4.1.2.2 Types of production

SUMMARY QUESTIONS

1 Think of three items that you or members of your family have purchased lately. Which are likely to have been produced by:
   - job production?
   - batch production?
   - flow production?

   Why do you think they were produced in the way you identified?

2 What would be the advantages and disadvantages of producing the following products by job production or flow production?
   - T-shirts
   - Suits
   - Running shoes

3 A confectionery company is producing a well-known chocolate bar for international markets. It needs to consider factors in different countries, such as languages, customer tastes, etc. How should it produce the bars? Explain your choice of method or methods.

ACTIVITY

The illustrations above show workers in several types of jobs. Identify an example of job production, flow production and batch production.

KEY POINTS

1 Different types of work have different methods of production.

2 Job production is suitable for products that need care and attention for each item.

3 Similar items produced in large quantities are more suited to batch production.

4 Identical products produced on a large scale benefit from line production.

5 New technology is changing these divisions.

109

4.1.3 Lean production

TOPIC AIMS

Students should be able to:
- identify and explain ways of implementing lean production methods.

Lean production means doing more with less. It is based on the idea that any use of resources that does not create value for the consumer is 'waste'. A lean company will make best use of resources by cutting out waste. Businesses hold inventories (stock) in order to convert these into finished goods to be sold. Holding inventory enables businesses to meet orders from customers. However, it is also costly to hold inventories so businesses seek to reduce their holdings through lean production.

CASE STUDY: The Toyota production system

A Toyota continuous-flow production line is designed to eliminate waste. Note the robots carrying out the production processes.

The Toyota production system was designed by the Toyota car company to cut waste and focus activity on the elements that add value for the customer. Through lean production, Toyota has cut the following seven wastes almost to zero.

1 **Overproduction**: producing goods before customers demand them. This leads to high storage costs and possible damage to items waiting to be sold.

2 **Waiting**: whenever goods are not moving or being processed, the waste of waiting occurs.

3 **Transporting**: transporting goods is a waste that adds no value to a product. Too much handling can also cause damage.

4 **Unnecessary inventory**: having too much inventory uses up space and gets in the way of productive activity.

5 **Motion**: employees involved in unnecessary bending, stretching and other body movements wastes time. It is also a health and safety risk.

6 **Over-processing**: using complex equipment to carry out simple tasks can be wasteful.

7 **Defects**: products that are poorly made have to be rejected, and time is wasted on inspecting for faults.

Questions

1 Identify an activity that you are involved in (e.g. queuing in a shop or a fast-food outlet, cooking food, making something). Identify examples of the 'seven wastes' that are associated with carrying out this activity. How could these wastes be eliminated?

2 Give examples of the ways in which Toyota is able to produce more with less.

STUDY TIP

Management likes lean methods because they reduce unit production costs. This will result in greater competitiveness and, hopefully, greater profits.

Acting lean

Japanese companies have been particularly associated with lean production. However, most other major companies are now using these techniques. The important thing is to identify those activities that add value for customers, and then try to cut out non-value-adding activities. There are some simple practical steps that can be taken to achieve this.

1 **Keeping work areas tidy and organised**. Time is not wasted on finding things or moving them around.

2 Just in time (JIT). JIT is another key element in the success of Japanese companies. Costs are cut simply by reducing the amount of goods and materials a firm holds in stock. Goods must be produced and delivered **just in time** to be sold, partly finished goods must be assembled just in time into finished goods, components to go into partly finished goods are prepared just in time, and materials are made into parts just in time. At the centre of a JIT system is the heartbeat of a factory: this is the speed at which the production line runs. A JIT system is sometimes termed an advanced manufacturing system. Figure 4.1.3.1 illustrates the process.

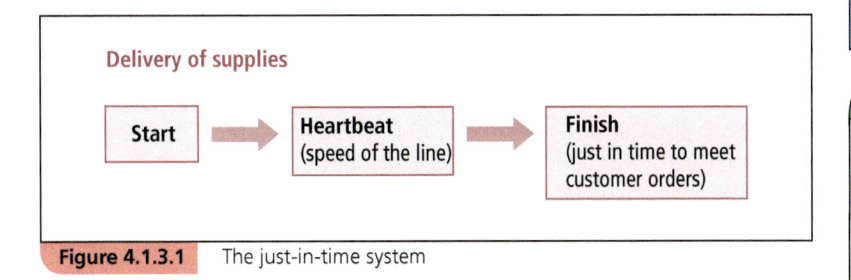

Delivery of supplies

Start → Heartbeat (speed of the line) → Finish (just in time to meet customer orders)

Figure 4.1.3.1 The just-in-time system

3 Kaizen. Another important part of the process is **kaizen**, or continuous improvement. Everybody in a company is given responsibility for identifying and suggesting ways of improving production. It does not matter how small the change is, provided that it cuts out waste. In this way, a better product or service is provided for the end-customer.

SUMMARY QUESTIONS

1 Copy and complete the paragraph below using the following words.

Lean / value-adding activities / just in time / waste / overproduction

Customer satisfaction can be increased by cutting out and eliminating _____. For example, this could involve eliminating _____ that occurs when products are made before customers have demanded them. The important thing is to concentrate on _____. The concept of _____ production was first developed in Japan by employees of the Toyota company. Another important idea stemming from Japan is that of _____ where products and parts are made to be delivered at the time they are required, but not before.

2 What are the benefits of creating a lean product (or service):
- for the product/service provider?
- for the customer/clients of the provider?

3 How do the processes of kaizen and just in time contribute to lean production?

DID YOU KNOW?

'Lean' can be applied to providing services as well as goods: a hairdresser could cut waste by identifying which activities they carry out that do not add value for customers. A government service (e.g. a hospital or school) could identify waste that could be cut out in order to provide a better service to users.

ACTIVITY

How could you apply some of the processes of lean production to doing some of your schoolwork, such as revising for an exam?

STUDY TIP

Ways to increase productivity include using internet broadband connections (faster than dial-up) or advanced factory robots that make fewer errors than human operators or more traditional machinery.

KEY POINTS

1 Lean production cuts out activities that do not create value for customers.

2 Any activity that provides benefits for customers is a value-adding activity.

3 Lean involves identifying and eliminating wastes. Toyota identified seven wastes that could be cut.

4 Lean applies to services as well as to manufactured products.

4.1.4 How technology has changed production methods

TOPIC AIMS

Students should be able to:

- understand the concept of productivity
- understand the concept of turning resource inputs into an output
- show awareness of methods of improving efficiency, e.g. automation, new technology
- show awareness of the impact of the implication of change for production methods and labour skills.

STUDY TIP

Improvements in efficiency reduce unit costs because resources are used more effectively.

DID YOU KNOW?

New technologies can be rapidly transferred around the world: a new automated factory system, such as a bottling or canning factory, can be set up wherever there is available land and labour. This makes it possible for large international firms to set up in low-cost locations, where government taxes and labour costs are low.

Efficiency

Inputs are people, money, raw materials and assets such as factories or offices. *Outputs* are goods and services. Efficiency involves turning inputs into outputs for maximum impact on productivity.

An organisation, or a process that an organisation carries out, can be more efficient and productive if it produces:

- the same output with fewer inputs
- more or better outputs from the same inputs.

An efficient organisation can provide its customers with better value for money and build a reputation for quality, which then leads to customer loyalty. Adopting new production methods often involves a substantial investment in new equipment – for example, the purchase of a new automatic production line. Although investment is costly, it should lead to increased profits in the long term.

Some people see new technology as providing a threat to jobs. For example, in agriculture, many farm workers have been replaced by tractors, and harvesting and sowing machines. However, in other industries, new technology has created work, or at least kept people in work. In the oil industry, for example, advanced technology enables oil to be drilled at greater depths. Workers may need to be retrained to work with the new equipment, but often their wages increase as the business prospers.

Methods to increase efficiency

A technique is a way of making something, using available resources such as human labour or machines. Technological change occurs when new techniques of production are applied. Technology has been a major driving force in enabling efficiency in the modern world. This is particularly true with the development of the internet and the use of computers in production. These are some of the computer-based innovations now used in industry.

- **Computer-aided design (CAD)** is a system that works like an electronic drawing board, allowing complex two- and three-dimensional shapes to be modelled quickly and accurately on screen, stored conveniently and copied when needed. Engineers in Nigeria design oil platforms using computers networked with qualified draughtsmen and draughtswomen in India. CAD has improved the reliability and speed with which complex structures such as aeroplanes, cars and bridges can be designed.
- **CADCAM (computer-aided design/computer-aided manufacturing)** refers to the use of data from a CAD system to drive machines as part of the manufacturing process. A bridge designer can design part of the structure on a computer and the design can be sent instantly to the factory computer, so that the parts can be cut to size.

- **CIM (computer-integrated manufacturing)** involves the computer-controlled manufacturing system driving machine tools. These tools, or robots, are multipurpose machines that can be programmed and reprogrammed to perform physical tasks. An industrial robot in a car factory may be programmed to paint and then reprogrammed to weld pieces together or to assemble parts.
- **Computer-based inventory control**. inventory-control systems are used in manufacturing and retailing to ensure the arrival of inventory just in time for purchase by the end-customer. For example, it is essential that retailers of fresh fish, vegetables or fruit, provide customers with the latest inventories. By ordering just the right levels needed, waste is minimised. For tinned and packaged goods, electronic barcodes make it possible to manage a computer-based inventory-control system.
- An **EPOS (electronic point-of-sale system)** works in the following way: items for sale carry barcodes. When new inventory arrives, the numbers are registered in the inventory system. At the checkout, the barcodes of sold items are scanned in. The cash till adds up and records the sales. The cash till automatically creates the bill, which is a record of transactions with an individual customer. The customer then pays and receives a record of their payment. At the same time, a record is made on the back-office system showing items sold. The back-office computer will then automatically reorder new inventory to replace the products that have been sold.

Other ways of improving efficiency include:

- changes in working methods (e.g. cutting out wasteful activities that take up time)
- total quality management – ensuring quality is focused on at every stage of production
- people simply working harder – perhaps because there is some form of bonus or other motivating factor.

Automation

Automation is the use of machines in a series of tasks. Each machine is linked to another, without human intervention. Computers can be programmed to start, finish, shut down and speed up operations, as well as detect flaws in a system, without human intervention. Investing in automation is costly, but will lead to high levels of accuracy at very low cost.

> **STUDY TIP**
>
> Changes in production methods produce benefits for a business, but may also generate problems, such as making employees redundant. The key to a successful business is managing the change.

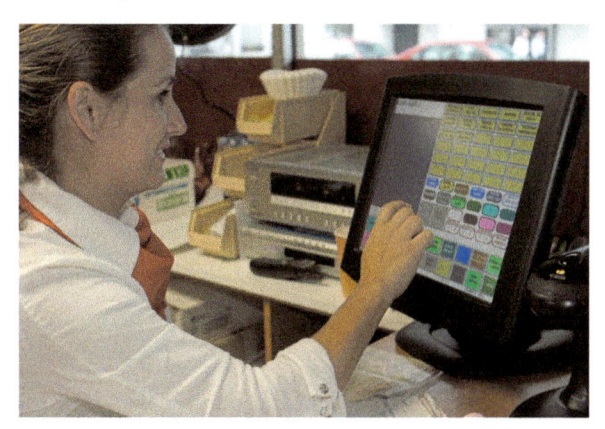

An EPOS system increases efficiency in a hotel, restaurant or supermarket by speeding up operations.

> **KEY POINTS**
>
> 1. In the modern world, new technology enables businesses to become more productive.
> 2. Computer-driven technologies have played a major part in increasing productivity across the globe.
> 3. New technologies can replace as well as create jobs.

> **SUMMARY QUESTIONS**
>
> 1. What is automation? Give an example of how automation has been used to improve manufacturing.
> 2. Give two examples of how efficiency can be increased in manufacturing.
> 3. How do computers improve efficiency in production?

4.2 Costs, scale of production and break-even analysis

4.2.1 Costs and classification of costs

TOPIC AIMS

Students should be able to:
- state and explain the cost structure of a business
- demonstrate understanding as to why the process of production generates costs
- classify costs into fixed and variable/direct/indirect
- identify examples of different types of costs using the fixed and variable classification.

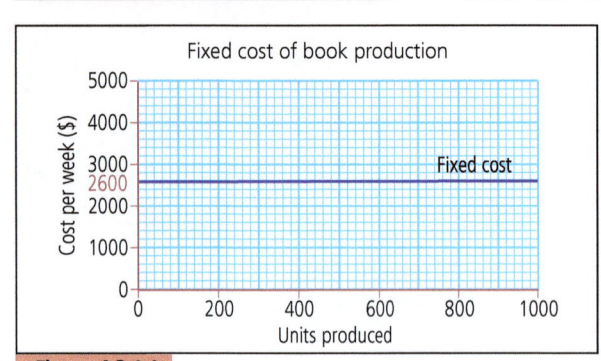

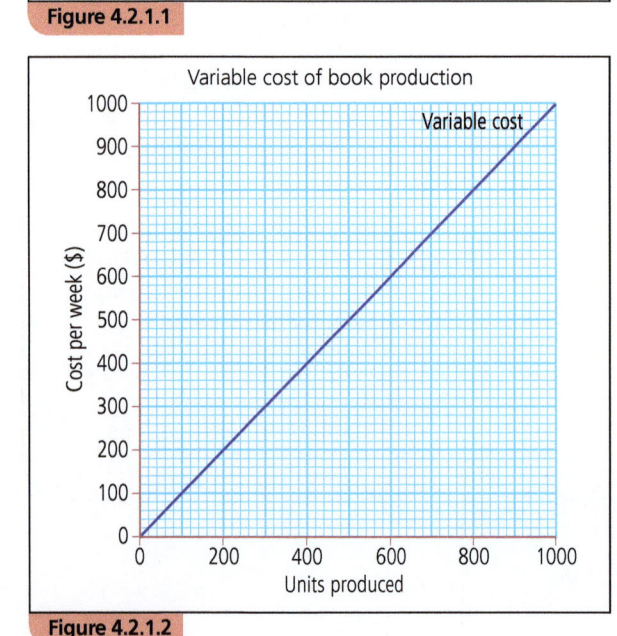

The importance of costs

All business production involves **cost**. For example, in book production, costs include the fee paid to the author, editor and designer, and, later in the process, the paper used for printing and the energy to drive the printing presses. In business, it is essential to keep costs of production as low as possible. Businesses with lower costs have an advantage over rivals.

Fixed and variable costs

To help managers decide how to produce and how much to produce, costs may be split into two types: fixed costs and variable costs.

Fixed costs do not increase as output increases – for example, rent, heating bills, mortgage repayments, rates and salaries. These costs remain the same whether the firm produces 0 units of output, 100 units of output or 10 000 units of output. They remain fixed because the business is obliged to pay them, regardless of how much it produces.

Fixed costs can be drawn as a straight line. For example, if a book publisher has three types of fixed costs – rent $500 per week, salaries $2000 per week and heating/air-conditioning bills $100 per week – then the fixed costs will be $2600 per week (Figure 4.2.1.1).

Variable costs increase as output increases. As output increases, more of these costs are incurred. For example, if you produce more books, you need more paper and more energy to run the machines for longer.

Variable cost starts at 0. It then rises, depending on the variable cost for producing each unit of production. For example, if the variable cost of producing 1 book is $1, then the variable cost of producing 2 books will be $2, 10 books = $10, 100 books = $100, 1000 books = $1000 and so on (Figure 4.2.1.2).

Total cost

The total cost of producing different levels of output is found by adding the fixed and variable costs. It simply involves combining the fixed and the variable cost curves at different levels of output. The total cost curve should therefore start at zero level of output. At this point, total cost is simply made up of fixed cost. Then the variable cost is added to the fixed cost for each level of output (Figure 4.2.1.3).

Figure 4.2.1.1

Figure 4.2.1.2

The **average cost** is the cost of producing a typical unit. This can be found for particular output levels, or numbers of the unit being produced. It is calculated by dividing the total cost of producing a specific volume of output by the number produced. It thus provides a measure of the cost of producing a single unit of production.

Total cost of production comprises the total fixed cost and the total variable cost of producing a given level of output. We can illustrate this point by using information from the graph (Figure 4.2.1.3).

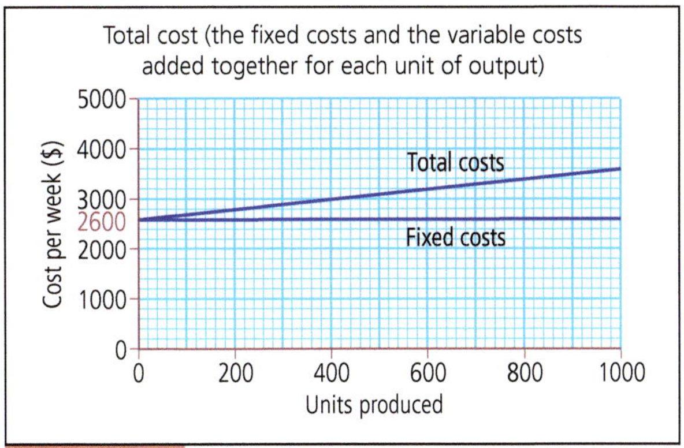

For example, the average cost of producing 600 units can be calculated in the following way:

Total cost of producing 600 units = $2600 (total fixed cost) + $600 (total variable cost at $1 per unit) = $3200.

$3200 divided by 600 units = $5.33 (the average cost).

You should be able to see, from the the same graph, that the average cost of producing 200 units would be $14 ($2800 divided by 200 units).

The example illustrates that, as companies expand production, they will initially be able to benefit from falling average cost per unit (up to a certain point). The point where average cost falls to its lowest point is referred to as the 'optimum output'.

Figure 4.2.1.3

STUDY TIP

When drawing a chart, remember to give the chart a title, label the axes and use sensible scales.

SUMMARY QUESTIONS

1. Which of the following describes variable costs, fixed costs and total costs?
   - Costs that do not change with the level of output that is produced.
   - All the costs of production.
   - Costs linked to the quantity produced.

2. A small taxi business has 10 taxis and employs taxi drivers to work for the firm. Explain which of the following would be included as fixed costs of running the taxi service and which would be the variable costs. Explain your answers.
   - The cost of renting the premises from which the business runs.
   - The petrol cost of each taxi journey (calculated per kilometre or mile).
   - The cost of maintaining a radio-controlled booking service in the office of the taxi business.

3. A business selling flowers has the following cost structure:
   - Rent per month: $300
   - Salaries per month: $1000
   - Cost per bunch of flowers prepared for sale: $1
   - Telephone (line rental, calls) per month: $100

   Illustrate this information in the form of a diagram showing the fixed costs per month. Draw another diagram to illustrate the variable costs per month.

ACTIVITY

Using the example of a local farm or small manufacturing business in your area, identify what items are likely to be the fixed costs of the business and what the variable costs will be.

KEY POINTS

1. Calculating costs is an important part of managing production.
2. Fixed costs do not alter with the number of units produced or sold.
3. Variable costs increase as production levels increase.
4. Total cost is the combination of fixed and variable cost at each level of output.

4.2.2 Scale of production

TOPIC AIMS

Students should be able to:
- explain the concepts of economies and diseconomies of scale
- understand the reasons why economies and diseconomies occur
- identify examples of economies and diseconomies of scale.

STUDY TIP

It is a common error to say that higher production leads to lower costs. It is very important to distinguish between total costs and the cost per unit (item). Economies of scale reduce unit costs.

Large greenhouses like these have been built in the Philippines for growing flowers. These are expensive to erect, but enable large-scale production at lower costs.

ACTIVITY

If your school were to double in size over the next 10 years, what economies of scale might the school be able to benefit from?

From a small start ...

Most of the giant businesses that we know today began on a small scale, as homemade efforts. Coca-Cola was originally brewed up on a kitchen stove, and many mechanical goods, like bicycles and tractors, were first hammered together in an inventor's backyard.

Many businesses prosper as they become larger. An advantage of growth is **economies of scale**. Economies of scale occur when large businesses produce larger outputs at lower unit costs.

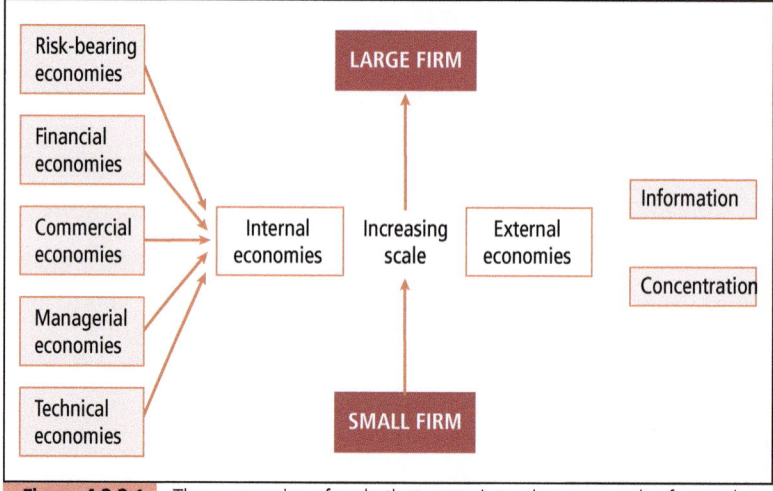

Figure 4.2.2.1 The economies of scale that come into play as a result of growth

It is helpful to distinguish between:
- internal economies of scale – that result from the growth of a business
- external economies of scale – that result from the growth of the industry of which the business is part.

Internal economies of scale

The most obvious benefit of growth is the ability to produce units of output more cheaply. In the Philippines, there has been an increase in fresh flower production using large-scale greenhouses. The greenhouses are expensive to set up: to benefit from large-scale economies, the structures need to be at least 1000 square metres in size. Once they have been installed, however, they enable growers to produce large quantities of flowers with fewer chemicals, water and fertiliser. Other economies from large-scale production are outlined below.

Labour and management economies

Large organisations can employ specialist staff, such as accountants and researchers, who can relieve general managers of responsibility for these areas.

Buying and selling economies

As firms grow larger, they can buy their inputs, such as raw materials or finished goods, in bulk. When you buy in bulk, you can negotiate discounts. The cost of transport per unit will be much lower with larger loads. Larger firms are also better able to organise the selling of their products. For example, if a business can sell all its output to one or a few buyers, the cost of making each sale will be considerably lower than if it deals with thousands of separate customers.

Financial economies

Large firms can borrow more cheaply than smaller ones. This is because they are usually regarded as a safer investment.

Risk-bearing economies

Large firms can spread risks over a number of products or markets. This is diversification. For example, Cadbury, the British chocolate manufacturer, produces a range of chocolate products that appeal to different people, including Dairy Milk and Creme Eggs. The company spreads its risk by operating in many countries across the globe.

Diseconomies of scale

There are some disadvantages to being large. These are **diseconomies of scale**. One of the most important disadvantages is managing an organisation that gets too big. An organisation that takes on too many activities may not have the resources to carry out all of them efficiently. It may be less able to react to market needs as quickly as a small organisation. Communications within a large organisation may also deteriorate because of the numbers of people involved.

External economies of scale

External economies of scale are those shared by a number of firms in the same industry in a particular area. Examples are explored below.

Economies of concentration

As firms within an industry grow larger, more numerous, special services (e.g. a skilled workforce) may develop. Businesses in that area may gain an improved reputation. Suppliers of parts and services may move to the same area. For example, there are many hairdressers in large cities. This may lead to the setting up of local businesses supplying hairdressing supplies, such as hair products, scissors, mirrors or basins.

Economies of information

Larger industries can set up special information services to benefit all companies. These might be a specialist research organisation jointly owned by a number of firms, or specialist magazines and publications about a particular industry.

Of course, external diseconomies of scale may also arise. These might include pollution and congestion in a particular area where too many similar businesses have set up, and too much competition, which drives down prices.

ACTIVITY

Working with a partner, decide whether the following are internal or external economies of scale. In each case, explain how the economies would drive down costs for a firm or firms in the industry.

- A fish-canning factory makes use of a new automated production line.
- A food-processing firm in Accra, Ghana, is able to sell all of its supplies to one supermarket chain.
- A firm develops new carbon-capture technology that will enable other companies to reduce their greenhouse gas emissions from production.

SUMMARY QUESTIONS

1 Define economies of scale. List and explain five major types of economy of scale that a large hotel might benefit from.

2 Huge sporting stadiums are required for major sporting events, such as the 2016 Olympic Games in Rio de Janeiro, the 2012 Games in London and the 2010 Commonwealth Games in Delhi. What diseconomies of scale might result from running such huge stadiums?

3 What are external economies of scale?

KEY POINTS

1 Economies of scale enable firms to produce more at lower cost per unit.

2 Economies of scale can be internal or external.

3 Firms can grow too large and become difficult to organise, so that unit costs go up; the result is diseconomies of scale.

4.2.3 Break-even analysis and cost-based decision making

TOPIC AIMS

Students should be able to:
- explain a simple break-even chart
- construct a simple break-even chart
- interpret a given chart and use it to analyse a situation
- show understanding of the limitations of a break-even chart.

An understanding of the cost of production helps a business to decide whether to produce additional units of output, depending on whether it can cover costs with revenue.

Break-even

Break-even is the point at which an organisation covers its costs with the money it makes through sales. If sales go beyond the break-even point, profits are made. If sales do not reach the break-even point, losses are made.

A **break-even chart** is prepared in advance to see how much the business needs to sell at a particular price. It is possible to make simple decisions using a break-even chart, e.g. by calculating the alternative break-even points.

Producing a break-even chart

A break-even chart shows the point at which a business breaks even, and the profits and losses it will make at various levels of activity. It is constructed by:

1. labelling the horizontal axis to show different levels of production (or sales)
2. labelling the vertical axis to represent the value of costs and the value of sales revenue
3. plotting fixed cost – this will be a straight horizontal line which starts at the value of all the fixed costs
4. plotting total costs – the total cost line is found by adding the fixed cost and the variable cost for each level of output
5. sales revenue is plotted by showing the total value of money received from selling the product – this is calculated by: Number of items sold x Price per unit.

STUDY TIP

Remember that the sales revenue line always starts at the origin; the total cost line starts from the point where the fixed costs intersect with the y axis.

ACTIVITY

Draw the break-even chart for each of the following businesses and calculate the break-even number of sales needed.

- A taxi driver who charges an average price of $10 per customer for a cost per trip of $5; the driver has fixed costs of $25 000 per year.
- A hairdresser who charges an average of $12.50 per customer for a cost per visit of $5; the hairdresser has fixed costs of $100 000 per year.

DID YOU KNOW?

Break-even for a period of time (e.g. a month) can be calculated by a simple formula:

$$\frac{\text{Average month's fixed costs}}{\text{Unit selling price} - \text{variable cost per unit}} = \text{Number of units needing to be sold to break even}$$

Limitations of the break-even chart

A break-even chart is only a rough guide. One of the problems is that it is not easy to estimate costs. Variable costs can change quickly – for example, if the price of labour or raw materials increases. The variable cost may also alter with the scale of production – the more that is produced, the lower the unit cost will be. However, break-even charts are helpful in indicating to business owners roughly how much they need to make or sell in order to break into profit.

CASE STUDY: Break-even for school textbooks

A business produces business studies textbooks which it sells directly to schools. The business has fixed costs of $80 000, made up of rent on its premises, salaries for staff and some other overhead costs. However many books it produces, it will therefore have this fixed cost to pay.

In book production, variable costs include the paper and card that go into the book; fixed costs might include the rental of the factory space.

It has been calculated that the variable cost of producing books is $8 per book. This $8 includes the cost of paper, ink and of running the printing presses. The business will sell the books for $12 each.

The managers have set out the information above in the form of a table, showing costs and sales revenue at three different levels of output.

	10,000 units ($)	20,000 units ($)	30,000 units ($)
Fixed costs	80 000	80 000	80 000
Variable cost = $8 per unit	80 000	160 000	240 000
Total costs	160 000	240 000	320 000
Sales revenue $12 per unit	120 000	240 000	360 000

When this information is shown in a chart form, it immediately becomes clear where the break-even point is.

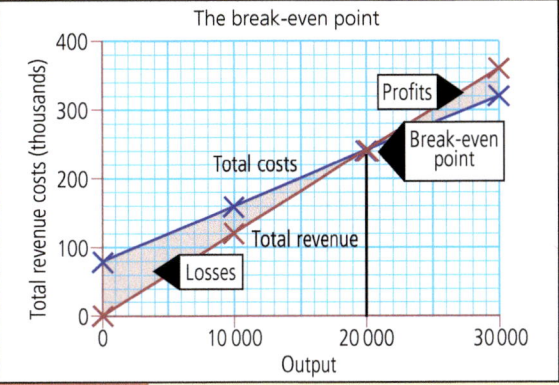

Figure 4.2.3.1

When 20 000 books are sold at $12 each, total sales revenues are $240 000. The total cost of producing these books is $240 000 ($80 000 of fixed costs and $160 000 of variable costs). If the firm is able to produce and sell higher levels, then its profits will increase. For example, if it can sell 30 000 units, its profit will be $40 000 (total cost $360 000 and total revenue $320 000).

Questions

1 How much profit, or loss, will the business make if it sells 10 000 books?

2 How much profit, or loss, will the business make if it sells 25 000 books?

SUMMARY QUESTIONS

1 What two figures are equal at the break-even point? Explain the meaning of fixed and variable costs? Which of these types of costs does a business need to cover to break even?

2 An ice-cream shop sells luxury ice creams at $5 each. Variable costs per ice cream are $3. The owners of the ice-cream shop have fixed costs of $5000 per month, including the lease. How many ice creams need to be sold to break even?

3 Seema Patel plans to set up a busy restaurant in a smart business location. This will immediately incur a fixed cost of $100 000 for the first year of trading. Market research indicates that a typical customer will pay $8 for a meal, and variable costs (such as cooking ingredients and the costs of serving customers) will amount to $3. How many customers will need to be served in the first year for Seema to break even? Show how you calculated this.

KEY POINTS

1 The break-even point is the point at which a business just covers its total costs with sales revenues.

2 The break-even point is expressed in terms of the quantity of items made or sold.

3 An alternative method for calculating break-even is to divide the total fixed cost by the contribution from selling each unit.

4.3 Achieving quality production

4.3.1 Quality

TOPIC AIMS

Students should be able to:
- explain the importance of quality control
- explain why quality control and quality assurance matter to a business.

Moving towards quality

Today, we use the term **quality** to mean 'producing a good or service to customer requirements'. There are three main steps that international companies have taken in moving towards quality: quality control, **quality assurance** and, more recently, **total quality management (TQM)**.

Quality control

Quality control has long been part of business practice. It involves inspectors checking finished goods, and detecting and cutting out components or final products that do not meet the required standard. It can involve considerable waste, as substandard products have to be scrapped.

Quality assurance

This is less wasteful than quality control. Quality assurance occurs both during and after production, and seeks to stop faults happening in the first place. Quality assurance aims to make sure that products are produced to the required standard. It is the responsibility of the workforce working in teams, rather than of inspectors.

Total quality management (TQM)

This is the most complete form of operations management. Everyone in the workplace is encouraged to think about quality in everything they do. Every employee places customers at the heart of the production process. Quality management is the process of managing quality at every stage within an organisation and in every aspect of operations within a company. It will be set out in clear documents, and employees in the company will be trained to operate using the highest quality standards.

Total quality management involves creating small groups of employees called **quality circles**. These employees meet regularly to discuss ways they can improve the quality of their work. They are encouraged to suggest new ideas to cut out waste. The result of fewer defects and getting it right first time may actually be a decrease in costs.

Figure 4.3.1.1 Three stages in the move towards quality

STUDY TIP

Quality control does not simply mean producing the best quality.

International quality standards

It is important for consumers that all products and services meet certain standards. A standard is a published document that sets out precise criteria, or rules, designed to be used consistently when producing a good or managing a process.

Various bodies have been set up by governments working with industries to set these standards. The world's first standards body was the British Standards Institution (BSI). The standards it set out are based on best practice and cover processes applicable to, for

DID YOU KNOW?

Today, there are standards bodies in all countries across the world. For example, Barbados in the Caribbean has its own Barbados National Standards Institution, BNSI.

example, manufacturing footballs, handling waste or meeting safety standards. BSI provides certificates to show that the standards have been met. BSI inspectors monitor companies to check that they are applying the standards.

Businesses worldwide seek to meet BSI standards. An engineering company in Kenya or Indonesia will seek BSI certification for its components and finished items, to show that their products meet a highly regarded international standard. This would then raise their company's reputation.

Modern quality standards are set at a number of levels. They relate to thousands of products, services and processes:

- internationally (e.g. ISO indicating standards agreed by bodies worldwide)
- in a particular part of the world (e.g. EN indicating standards agreed in Europe)
- national standards (e.g. BS indicating British standards).

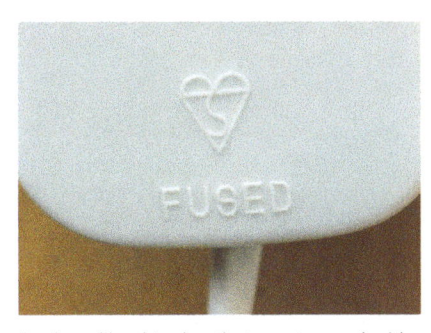

Products like this plug that are stamped with the BSI mark give consumers a reassurance of quality.

DID YOU KNOW?

The international governing body for football competitions, FIFA, licenses manufacturers to produce footballs. The balls must pass six tests – for weight, circumference, shape, loss of air pressure, water absorption and rebound. Manufacturers whose balls meet the standards can have the official marking stamped on their balls – 'FIFA APPROVED' or 'FIFA INSPECTED'.

ACTIVITY

Use the web page www.fifa.com and carry out a search for Football Test Criteria to find out more about the test criteria applied by FIFA.

SUMMARY QUESTIONS

1 Match the following terms with the definitions below.

Quality product / quality control / total quality management / standards / international standards
- Detecting and cutting out faults after they have happened.
- Creating a system that cuts out waste in every element of production.
- Published documents setting out criteria on which rules can be based about how to produce goods.
- A good that meets customer requirements.
- Agreed criteria for producing goods and services that are agreed across the world.

2 The British Standards Institute (BSI) works with industry specialists to identify best practice. BSI has over 30 000 standards. What would be the advantage to manufacturers in a small country, seeking to export goods, of applying BSI standards to production processes in their company?

3 A company currently has a system of quality control. It uses careful inspection at the end of its production line for motorcycle helmets to check for faults. Any rejects are discarded. Explain why this company might be better moving on to developing quality assurance or total quality management.

KEY POINTS

1 Customers expect to be provided with products and services that meet the required standards.

2 Quality control involves checking for quality at the end of the production line.

3 Quality assurance occurs both during and after production to check for faults.

4 Total quality management takes place at every stage of production. Quality circles suggest ways of cutting out waste.

4.4 Choosing locations

4.4.1 Factors influencing location and relocation

> **TOPIC AIMS**
>
> Students should be able to:
>
> - identify and explain factors relevant to the location decisions of: a) a manufacturing business or b) a service-based business
> - show awareness of factors that a business considers in determining in which country to locate itself
> - recommend and justify an appropriate location for a business in a given situation.

In recent years, many North American and European companies have set up operations in India and China, where a highly skilled labour force is available at a lower wage cost.

> **ACTIVITY**
>
> These are some of the factors that influence the location of a large supermarket:
>
> - plenty of land available, including car parking
> - ease of access to labour
> - close to transport links for supplies
> - near to customers.
>
> Produce a list showing the factors that might influence the location of:
>
> - a service business
> - a manufacturing business.

Location and relocation

An important consideration for a new business is **location** – that is, where to site it. Considerations involve being close to the market, or on sites where costs are low, perhaps because labour is plentiful and wages are cheap. Later on, a firm may choose to relocate, often because costs have become too high at the original location. In the first decade of the 21st century, many Western companies relocated manufacturing and other functions to India and South East Asia, where production costs were lower.

Distance to markets

Many businesses need to be located close to their market (i.e. their customers). Many manufacturing industries locate close to markets, particularly if they produce bulky or fragile items that are expensive to transport. Service industries, such as hairdressing, restaurants and entertainment, need to be near to customers. Other services, such as banking and insurance, sometimes need to be near to customers (although many transactions are now carried out online).

Availability of raw materials

Some manufacturing businesses use a lot of heavy, bulky raw materials to make their products, even though the end-product is smaller and lighter. For example, finished steel is a lot lighter than the ore, limestone and other materials of which it consists. If the raw materials are bulky and expensive to transport, it makes sense to locate near their source.

Transport costs

Two major influences on transport costs are the raw materials and how near the market is. These depend on whether the industry is 'bulk increasing' or 'bulk decreasing' (i.e. whether the goods become larger and heavier or smaller and lighter as they are assembled). Many businesses (e.g. hotels, factories) set up close to good transport links – for example, near a major road junction, rail station or airport.

Availability of land

Land costs vary considerably. Firms such as large automobile production plants that need a wide area to make their goods, or giant supermarkets that need a large selling area, will choose sites that are out of town where costs are lower.

Availability of labour

The right sorts of labour and skills are easier to find in some areas than others. If businesses want a large pool of cheap labour, they might set up in centres of population where there are not many employers. If they want skilled labour they will set up where they are most likely to find those skills. In recent years, many Western companies have set up call centres in India, where there are large numbers of highly educated people with information technology skills and where wage costs are relatively low.

Safety

Some industries (e.g. nuclear power stations, munitions factories and some chemical companies) will be wise to locate their premises well away from heavily populated areas, to avoid danger to the public.

Utilities

A business must consider five standard utilities: gas, electricity, water, disposal of waste and drainage. Industries such as food preparation and paper production use large quantities of water. Food processing creates waste and the cost of waste disposal will affect location.

Communications

Many businesses need a strong core of IT communications systems. It is therefore important to set up in areas where communications are clear and reliable. This might exclude some mountainous or highland areas, or countries where the links do not exist. Cities with excellent wireless and broadband facilities are a strong attraction for new businesses.

Regional factors

Locating in the same area as similar businesses, suppliers and markets may be considered an advantage. The quality of local schools, housing and leisure facilities can also help to encourage high-quality staff to join and stay with the business.

Government incentives and other legal factors

The government provides financial support to businesses to set up in some regions. These will usually be areas of higher unemployment. There are also legal factors such as not being able to locate industrial premises in residential areas.

Deciding in which country to locate

In the modern global economy, companies will consider a range of countries to locate in or to relocate to. Key considerations will be having access to larger markets, and the possibility of reducing costs in new locations. For example, many American IT-based companies have transferred jobs to India and China. American companies like Microsoft®, Accenture and IBM have set up offices employing thousands of people in large Indian cities, where there are a lot of highly skilled employees available at lower wages than in the United States. By setting up these new units, the US companies also benefit from having access to the new, huge, growing markets of India and China.

Another consideration that will be important for a business is the stability of the government and the exchange rate in the host country. If exchange rates fluctuate often, this causes difficulties in planning and predicting the value of sales and costs such as wages.

> **STUDY TIP**
>
> If a business relocates to another country, it will gain certain advantages, but it will also incur extra costs. For the move to make sense, the advantages must be expected to be greater than the costs.

KEY POINTS

1. Important location considerations for manufacturing companies are access to raw materials, good transport links, access to a workforce and to the market. Low costs are important.

2. Important considerations for some service industries are to be close to the market and to recruit skilled employees.

3. Important location considerations when choosing a country are costs, the quality of labour and the stability of government and the exchange rate.

SUMMARY QUESTIONS

1. Which three factors do you think are most important in locating the following? In each case, justify your answer.
   - Gold mining
   - Nuclear power plant
   - International call centre

2. What factors do you think a supermarket business should first consider before deciding to branch out into a new country?

3. Explain why a Japanese motor manufacturer like Toyota might want to set up a car plant in Western Europe.

Unit 4 — Practice questions

SECTION 1: Short-answer questions

1. Identify and explain TWO objectives of the production department. [4]
2. Using the example of a McDonald's burger, identify the inputs, production process and output. [3]
3. Identify and explain TWO ways in which productivity may be increased in a clothing factory. [4]
4. Calculate labour productivity in a factory that employs 200 workers and produces 500 shirts every hour. [3]
5. Identify and explain TWO differences between batch and flow production. [4]
6. Analyse TWO reasons why a car production line that produces the same model, but with each car altered according to customer orders, may be categorised as both flow and job production. [6]
7. Explain, with examples, economies of scale that may be enjoyed by a very large clothing company, such as Levi Strauss & Co. Jeans. [4]
8. Identify and explain TWO reasons why communication difficulties in a large organisation may lead to diseconomies of scale. [4]
9. Explain, using examples from a bread production factory, the following examples of waste in the context of lean production: [6]
   - defects
   - overproduction
   - waiting. [6]
10. Explain how just-in-time production methods could cut down the areas of waste you have identified in Question 9. [6]
11. Explain why it may be said that under kaizen 'everyone in the organisation has two jobs'. [4]
12. Identify and explain TWO differences between quality control and quality assurance. [4]
13. Analyse why quality assurance does not simply mean producing the best quality. [4]
14. Analyse why a total quality management approach may lead to lower costs as well as better quality. [4]
15. Analyse why labour costs may be fixed or variable in a production business. [4]
16. Identify and explain THREE factors that will be important when deciding the location of:
    - a vegetable canning factory
    - a firm of solicitors. [6]

SECTION 2: Longer-answer questions

Daisy Fresh Cleaning

Flora runs a successful business from her home in Islamabad, laundering and dry cleaning clothes for local customers and business people who stay in nearby international hotels. She has built up an excellent reputation due to the speed and quality of her service. Flora collects the clothes twice a day from the hotels and returns them within 12 hours, fully washed, or dry-cleaned, and ironed. She uses large industrial machines and makes sure that similar colours are washed together. All items are pressed individually. Delicate items, such as silk dresses and suits, are kept separate and treated with extra care. Flora is so busy that she is looking for new premises for her business.

1. Identify and explain TWO methods of production used by Flora. [4]
2. Identify and explain TWO ways in which the quality of Flora's service may be measured. [4]
3. State TWO examples of fixed costs and TWO examples of variable costs for Flora's business. [6]
4. Identify and explain THREE factors that Flora will need to take into account when looking for new premises. [6]
5. To what extent may a break-even chart help Flora decide on a suitable location? Explain your answer. [6]

Amrita's fair trade spices

Amrita runs a production company, based on the outskirts of Delhi, India. The company produces large packs of Indian spice mixes, in a range of flavours, mainly for the export market. The packs are bought in bulk by overseas companies who use them to give authentic flavour to Indian ready meals for the Western market. The spices come into the factory directly from the growers in their dried form, and are ground up together, depending on the mix required, then packaged and labelled. Amrita's monthly costs are as follows:

Factory rent: $1000

- Business rates: $200
- Power: $300
- Amrita's wage: $200
- Production workers' wages: $0.50 per pack
- Raw materials (herbs per pack): $3 (growers are paid a fair-trade price, which is 50 per cent higher than the usual market price)
- Packaging and labelling per pack: $1.

The packs sell for an average price of $10, on the wholesale market.

1 Explain the term 'fixed costs' and calculate Amrita's total fixed costs. [3]
2 Explain the term 'variable costs' and calculate the variable cost per pack of herbs. [3]
3 Analyse ONE advantage and ONE disadvantage to Amrita's company of the fair-trade price paid to herb growers. [6]
4 Using graph paper, draw a break-even chart and work out the break-even monthly sales for Amrita's business. [6]
5 Evaluate the advantages and limitations of the use of break-even analysis to plan in a business like Amrita's. [6]

The market research call centre

Jim runs a telephone market research company based in the UK, on the outskirts of Manchester. He employs 100 staff at the call centre. Their job is to contact consumers by telephone and ask their opinions on everything from views on new products to which party they will vote for in the parliamentary elections. He is paid by the companies who employ him to carry out this research and produce reports. Jim would like to expand the call centre, but land is expensive and staff wages are rising by the day. He also finds that his staff productivity rate is very variable, as staff change jobs and leave the company frequently, and some workers are often late or unwell. Jim is investigating the possibility of moving the call-centre part of his business to India.

1 Identify and explain TWO possible ways that Jim may measure his staff productivity. [4]
2 Identify and explain TWO reasons why staff absence and frequent replacement may lead to low productivity. [4]
3 Identify and explain THREE factors that Jim will need to take into account if he is relocating his call centre to India. [4]
4 Evaluate the view that 'relocating to India will save money on land and labour costs'. [6]
5 Evaluate whether the call-centre move to India will benefit Jim's business customers. [6]

5 Financing business activity

5.1 Business finance: needs and sources

5.1.1 The need for finance

TOPIC AIMS

Students should be able to:
- identify the main need for finance
- understand why a business needs finance.

Setting up an office requires finance for capital items such as office machinery, as well as staff salaries and rental charges.

STUDY TIP

Salary costs are included in the start-up costs of a business, because they are not related to any specific level of output. Thus salaries are fixed costs, but wages are usually variable costs (the number of employees is directly linked to the level of output).

What is business finance?

Finance is a sum of money for use in a business, which is set aside for a particular purpose. The main purpose for finance in a business is:

1 setting up the business
2 running the business on a day-to-day basis
3 expanding the business.

CASE STUDY | **Sanjay's market research**

Setting up a new business is very costly. This is illustrated by the case of Sanjay, who has decided to set up a small market research business in a country in South East Asia. He has made out a list of payments that he will need to make just to set up in business. Costs are given in US dollars.

Start up costs	US$
Rental of 290 sq foot for the first 6 months (he has to pay 6 months in advance)	24 000
New office furniture and fittings	25 000
Laptops (Apple Macintosh x 4)	4000
Printer (LaserJet x 1)	400
Fax machine	400
Telephones (2)	100
Electricity deposit	150
Telephone/fax connection (5 lines @ $20)	100
Internet access	50
Legal fees	500
Staff salaries for the first month (2 x $1000)	2000
Total start-up costs	**56 700**

You can see from the table that the start-up period for any new business is costly. When businesses start up they have to pay in advance for items like office rent. They will also often have to pay a deposit to cover things like damage and breakages.

Additional costs will include installing services such as telephone and electricity. Other start-up costs include capital items: these are durable items that remain in the business for several years, such as furniture and computer equipment. In a manufacturing company, capital items would include the machinery. Where a business buys buildings directly, these would be included in the start-up costs.

Sanjay and other new entrepreneurs need to have access to finance to see them through this difficult start-up phase. Some of this finance may come from Sanjay's own savings, and some from family loans. However, he will still need to acquire finance from other sources.

Questions

1 What are the main costs of setting up a business?

2 What sources of finance could Sanjay have used to finance the start-up of his business?

3 What capital items did Sanjay require? Can you suggest a way of financing the purchase or hire of these?

Day-to-day running of the business

Once a business is up and running it will need to have funds to cover day-to-day costs. These will include items like staff wages, costs of supplies and raw materials, and bills that will need to be paid from the beginning. For most businesses, therefore, costs in the first 12 months are normally higher than revenues. The business is unlikely to make a profit in this early period.

Expanding (growing) the business

At some stage, many businesses choose to expand or change direction. For example, Sanjay may set up other offices in different cities in his country, or in other countries.

It is often easier to acquire capital to expand than to start up: once a business has built up a reputation and has a steady stream of income, it becomes easier to raise funds from lenders.

Expanding businesses can also raise funds through asset-based finance: the borrower borrows funds on the understanding that if they fail to make repayments, the lender can take over particular assets (the items that the business owns that have value, such as buildings, vehicles or machinery). This is known as offering **security** for a loan.

SUMMARY QUESTIONS

1 What is finance? Why is it important in starting up a new business?

2 Yin Qiang is just about to start up an exporting business, selling rice from China to wholesalers in Europe. He is seeking to borrow funds from his bank. He has calculated that he will need US$10 000 to start up the business. He has told the bank that this is the only capital that he will require, because once the business has started, he will be able to finance all further funding requirements from profits made by the business. Why might the bank be reluctant to give him the start-up capital he has requested?

3 Explain the difference between start-up costs and day-to-day running costs of a business.

DID YOU KNOW?

Many start-up enterprises fail to take into account all the costs necessary to set up. Costs such as inventory, staff, rent, computers, phones, taxes and legal fees should all be listed. Underestimating the amount of finance required can lead to the business failing.

ACTIVITY

Identify a business that has recently set up in your local area. This could be an agricultural business or a retailing business. Working with your teacher, identify the main starting costs for the business. Estimate what some of these costs might amount to. For example, wage costs will be based on typical wages in that type of business. Look at newspaper advertisements to gain an idea of costs of hiring premises and rents.

KEY POINTS

1 Finance is a sum of money that a business requires for specific purposes, mainly to start up, for day-to-day activities and for expansion.

2 Start-up costs are high; a business will need to take care to list the different costs before seeking funding.

3 Businesses take time to break into profit. They need funds to cover day-to-day running activities, particularly in the early days.

4 A business that expands will normally require additional sources of finance.

5.1.2 Major sources of finance

TOPIC AIMS

Students should be able to:
- understand the difference between short-term and long-term capital needs
- understand the importance of microfinance.

Capital needs

Businesses need finance for both short- and long-term purposes. In the short term, finance is required to make regular payments: wages, costs of supplies, electricity and utility bills. These short-term funds are called **working capital**. They may also be needed to bridge the gap between, for example, buying ingredients or components, and the eventual payment for the finished goods that the business aims to sell.

In the long term, finance is required to purchase the major assets on which the business is based: land, buildings, machinery and other permanent assets.

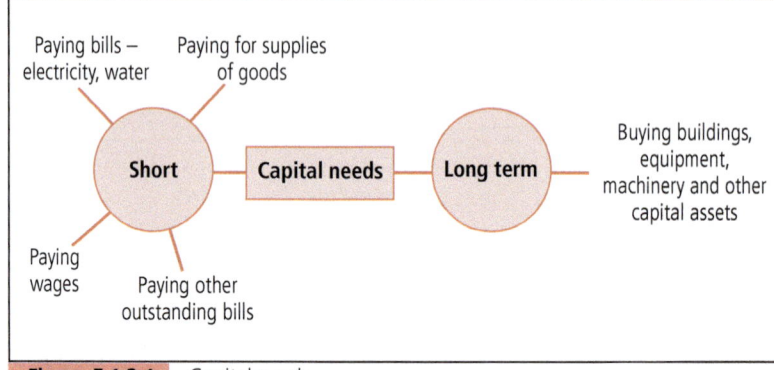

STUDY TIP

Make sure you understand the different sources of funds that can be used for short- and long-term capital needs. A business would not finance the purchase of a factory with a bank overdraft.

Figure 5.1.2.1 Capital needs

ACTIVITY

Golden Screen (GSC) is the largest cinema chain in Malaysia. Typical Golden Screen cinemas are located in shopping malls and offer a multi-screen formula. Altogether in Malaysia there are 28 separate cinemas belonging to GSC with a total of 238 screens. The cinemas provide a computerised ticketing service and online booking. Identify the long-term and short-term capital requirements that would have been needed to set up and run this cinema chain.

CASE STUDY | Microfinance in Pakistan

Microfinance enables the poor to become independent by using small sums of finance to get started in business.

Microfinance (microcredit) is an important way of providing finance to poorer members of society so that they can set up and run their own businesses. In Pakistan the government uses its Poverty Alleviation Fund (PPAF) to provide financial support to microfinance banks. These banks then provide finance to people who previously did not have bank accounts and enable them to set up independent businesses. Many of the beneficiaries are women. Finance is provided for all sorts of initiatives, e.g.

opening a small shop, setting up a textile business, developing innovative ideas. A good example of a microfinance bank is Apna Microfinance Bank Ltd, which provides loans to small farmers, e.g. to buy seed. The emphasis is on giving a 'hand up' rather than a 'hand out'. The government in Pakistan estimates that there are 25–30 million potential customers for microfinance. Its target is to provide microfinance to 10 million customers by 2015.

Questions

1 Explain why poor people in Pakistan might benefit from microfinance.

2 How is the concept of providing a 'hand up' likely to benefit the economy of Pakistan?

There are a number of major sources of finance that a business can use to meet its capital needs.

1 **Owner's funds**. The owners of a business provide important finance. An owner investing capital in a business gives lenders more confidence in it. Additional **owner's funds (capital)** come from ongoing profits ploughed back into the business.

2 **Loans**. The bank provides the loan and the borrower repays the capital over time, usually in monthly instalments with interest. Loans are typically taken out over a period of years rather than months. It is more difficult to secure a business loan from a bank at the start-up stage.

3 **Mortgage**. A **mortgage** is a method of long-term finance: it is a loan for the purchase of property that is secured on the property. If the borrower fails to make repayments, the lender can take them to court and, if necessary, take over ownership of the property. The size of the mortgage depends on the value of the property and how much is borrowed.

4 **Short-term finance**. Trade credit is an important form of short-term finance. The supplier does not expect immediate payment for goods or services. There is a period of trade credit – for example, one month, three months or longer. Many small businesses use a credit card for short-term bills. (Credit cards are not available in all countries.) Payment is made for goods with a credit card provided by a finance company. The business can then pay the credit card company at the end of the month, or later. The longer the business takes to repay the credit, the more interest they will have to pay. Another form of short-term finance is an overdraft (see page 130).

5 **Microfinance**. For some very small businesses, particularly in rural areas, it is almost impossible to get credit. Professor Mohammad Yunus started the Grameen Bank in Bangladesh. This is called microcredit and provides small amounts of funds to set up microbusinesses, to help people who would otherwise have no means of earning an income.

KEY POINTS

1 Businesses need short-term finance to provide working capital.

2 Typical sources of short-term finance include trade credit and credit card payments.

3 Businesses need long-term finance for substantial capital expenditures.

4 Long-term finance may be in the form of a mortgage to help finance property purchases.

SUMMARY QUESTIONS

1 What is working capital? Give two examples of sources of funds for working capital.

2 Businesses have short- and long-term capital needs. Provide three examples of fund sources that could be used to meet short-term capital needs, and three examples of types of finance that could be used to meet long-term needs.

3 Explain the main difference between:
- a mortgage and a loan
- trade credit and credit card finance.

5.1.3 Sources of internal and external finance

TOPIC AIMS

Students should be able to:

- identify internal and external sources of finance available to a business
- understand the difference between internal sources of capital and external sources
- show knowledge of the different sources available to a business
- understand the impact on a business of different sources of finance
- show awareness of the possible impact of debt capital compared to owner's funds.

The world's smallest car, the Tata Nano, required internal and external financing.

ACTIVITY

Identify a local business that you are familiar with. Assume that the business needs finance quickly. What items does the business have that it could sell and then lease back? What other sources of finance could it use to raise capital?

Finance

Millions of businesses have been set up worldwide during the last 10 years. None of them would have progressed beyond the ideas stage if they had not been able to get hold of a basic ingredient of business – finance!

A company that has hit headlines in recent years is India's Tata Motors. This is a public company (see page 22). In 2009, the company launched the world's smallest and cheapest car, the Tata Nano, priced at about US$2000. Two of the principal sources of finance to build the car were:

- selling shares to shareholders. The shareholders are the owners of the Tata corporation, and so part of the business. This capital is therefore internal capital, raised inside the business
- borrowing from the banks. Tata borrowed considerable sums of money in loans to build the production plant to manufacture the cars. This is external finance, raised outside the business.

Internal finance

We have seen that internal finance is the capital provided by the owners. A sole trader business provides internal finance from a single owner. Sole traders frequently expand by taking in partners who bring in more capital to the business.

Companies raise capital by selling shares. The shareholder buys shares and so provides capital for the business. Another source of internal finance for a business is the profit that it generates.

Businesses can also raise finance by selling some of their assets, such as a piece of land, a factory or a machine. Sometimes they do this and then lease (hire) the item they have sold from the buyer. They lose the asset, but gain cash to run the business.

External finance

The following table summarises the several sources of external finance available to a business.

Source or finance	Explanation
Trade credit	The time between receiving the good or service and having to pay for it.
Overdraft	Most frequently used form of short-term finance, used to ease cash-flow problems. Arrangements are made between the customer and the bank on an agreed drawing limit on a current account. Interest is calculated on the level of the overdraft on a daily basis.
Leasing and hire purchase	Major banks have links with finance houses which provide a variety of schemes so that the customer receives goods and makes payments over time. Goods on hire purchase remain the property of the finance company until all the payments have been made. Leasing enables a company to use an asset without having to pay for it. The lessee uses the asset and makes regular payments to the owner, the lessor.

Loan	Sums of money typically lent for a specific purpose (e.g. to buy an asset). Interest is charged on the amount owed.
Mortgages	Loan secured on property.
Government grant	Important source of finance for many businesses: the government provides finance for the business for particular purposes (e.g. to update machinery).
Venture capital	Venture capital companies provide finance in return for a shareholding in the organisation, and some control.

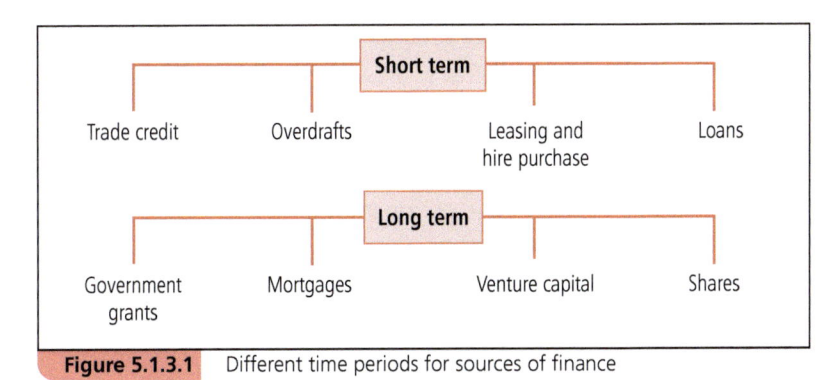

Short term: Trade credit, Overdrafts, Leasing and hire purchase, Loans

Long term: Government grants, Mortgages, Venture capital, Shares

Figure 5.1.3.1 Different time periods for sources of finance

The ratio of external to internal finance

When a business raises internal finance, it owes money to the owners. When it makes a profit, it can give the owners a good return on their investment by paying a high dividend to shareholders; in poor years it can limit the amount it pays.

However, a business is legally bound to pay providers of external finance. For example, with a loan or mortgage, it is required by law to make repayments. Similarly, it must pay for goods received on credit and money borrowed on a credit card.

A business must therefore maintain a good balance between finance raised internally and externally. If it raises too much capital externally, it may build debts for itself that it is unable to pay back in years when profits are low.

The ratio between capital raised internally (owner's funds) and capital raised externally (external finance) is called the **gearing ratio**.

If a high percentage of finance is borrowed, this is referred to as a high gearing ratio.

SUMMARY QUESTIONS

1. What is the difference between internal and external sources of finance? Give an example of who might provide these funds.
2. What sources of finance would you recommend when businesses have the following needs for funds, giving reasons for your choices?
   - A start-up business wishes to have 20 new computers available for use.
   - A farmer requires seeds and fertiliser, which he will pay for at harvest time.
3. What are the risks of high gearing?

STUDY TIP

A company with a high gearing ratio relies heavily on borrowed capital to finance its activities. It is taking a financial risk, as it has to make a return on this capital which is greater than the rate of interest on the loans. If the gearing ratio is very low, it often means that a business is short of capital, because it does not borrow money. So too high or low a gearing ratio can be 'bad'.

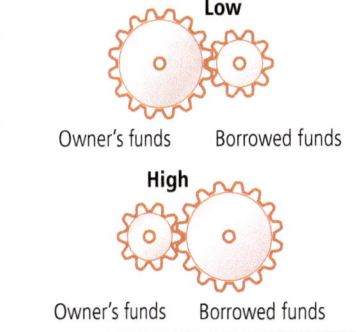

Low: Owner's funds, Borrowed funds
High: Owner's funds, Borrowed funds

Figure 5.1.3.2 The higher the percentage of finance that is borrowed (i.e. the higher the gearing), the bigger the risk that the company will not be able to pay the interest in years when profits are low.

KEY POINTS

1. Internal finance is raised within a business. It may be owner's capital or profits. In a company it will be share capital.
2. External capital is raised outside the business; sources may be mortgages, loans or hire purchase.
3. The gearing ratio describes the relationship between internal and external capital.
4. Where profits fluctuate, it is risky to have a high gearing ratio.

5.1.4 How to choose finance

TOPIC AIMS

Students should be able to:

- explain the basis upon which the choice of finance is made
- understand the factors to be considered in determining an appropriate source of finance
- show appreciation of the significance of size of the business, capital need, length of time or risk
- recommend and justify an appropriate method(s) of finance in a given situation.

Large international businesses like Toyota are able to raise capital from shareholders, as well as borrow money at preferential rates of interest.

Choosing a source of finance

In seeking finance, businesses need to consider the following factors.

- **The sum required**. The amount of capital required can range from just a few dollars to pay an outstanding bill, to a huge investment in a new factory. When a business requires a large sum of money, it will have to borrow from a large financial institution, or ask shareholders to provide more share capital.
- **The cost of borrowing**. Most sources of investment require interest payments, or that the lender receives a share of future profits.
- **Risk**. The more risk the lender is taking, the more interest payment they will expect. Some forms of borrowing, such as from a credit card company, can be very expensive.
- **Permanent or temporary**. Some forms of financing are permanent (e.g. when a company sells shares, it does not have to repay the money to the shareholders). Other types of borrowing are for a fixed period (e.g. a 25-year mortgage, a 3-year loan).
- **The size of the business**. Large businesses usually have access to a wider range of sources of finance. They can also often borrow at lower interest rates because their custom is valued more by the lender than the custom of a small business.
- **Influence and control**. Some lenders, such as venture capitalists and banks, will only provide capital in return for some input into the running of the business.
- **Advice**. Some providers of capital offer advice in addition to the capital. This can be particularly helpful for a business person, although they may have to pay for the advice.

Matching

Businesses need to match their need for finance with a suitable source. We have seen that key points to consider are:

- Should we raise finance internally or externally? If the business relies on external finance, it can build debts which are difficult to meet when cash flow is low.
- Should we raise finance for a short or long period? The longer the period that capital is raised, the higher the interest rate is likely to be.
- When are we going to be able to repay? If a business is unable to repay borrowings in the short term, it should seek longer-term finance.
- Are we willing to lose some of the control of our business? If a business raises finance from borrowing, then it risks losing some control of what it does to outsiders.

The idea of matching is best illustrated by looking at two examples.

1 A food shop is just about to open up. The shopkeeper has bought the premises and the fittings, but now needs to purchase food to sell (an inventory). She needs a fast injection of cash to make these purchases, knowing that she will be able to make payments once the inventory has been sold.

Possible solutions:

- She could take out an overdraft with her bank to pay for the inventory. She would only have to pay interest for each day that she is overdrawn. However, the bank may not grant her an overdraft if she does not have enough money coming into her bank account.
- She could pay using her credit card. Many small businesses finance cash purchases in this way. However, the interest charged on outstanding credit on credit cards is high.
- She could buy inventory by taking trade credit. The supplier would give her credit until a set date. However, this might limit her suppliers, so that she loses some control of her business.

2 A large international business wishes to set up a new factory in an overseas market. How could it raise the capital?

Possible solutions:

- Funds could be raised internally by selling more shares in the business. A relatively cheap way of doing this would be to invite existing shareholders to buy more shares. It would be much more expensive to advertise the shares for sale to a wider public.
- The business could borrow money in the form of loans from investors. It would take time to attract investors, however, and they may want a stake in the business.
- The business could create a joint venture with a partner in the overseas market. The factory would then become part of a new business that would be jointly owned by the two partners.
- The business might be able to receive a grant and tax breaks from the host country.

SUMMARY QUESTIONS

1. What are the main considerations when choosing a suitable form of finance?
2. What forms of short-term finance would you recommend to a business that continually finds that it is short of cash at the end of each month?
3. A business has a seasonal sales pattern. For the first 3 months of the year, its sales revenues are high and easily cover costs. For the next 6 months, revenues fluctuate: sometimes they are higher than costs; at other times they are lower. In the final 3 months, sales revenues are always below costs. What sources of finance would you recommend that the company employs in each of these periods?

STUDY TIP

Students often think that it is easy for a business to raise extra capital by issuing more shares. For a small unincorporated business this is not an option. Even for large companies it may not be easy if potential shareholders have doubts about the future of a company.

ACTIVITY

Look in local and national newspapers to find a story about a business that is expanding. Suggest suitable sources of finance that would finance the expansion.

KEY POINTS

1. Businesses need to consider several factors when choosing sources of finance.
2. The greater the loan, and the longer the loan period, the greater the likely rate of interest.
3. Large businesses generally have access to a wider range of sources at lower cost.
4. Taking outside finance into a business risks losing some control over decision making.
5. The need for finance needs to be matched to the sources available.

5.2 Financial information and decision making

5.2.1 Cash and cash-flow forecasts

TOPIC AIMS

Students should be able to:
- understand why cash is important to a business
- understand the concept of a cash-flow forecast
- show awareness of the importance of cash-flow forecasts
- construct and interpret a cash-flow forecast
- understand the importance of timing in cash-flow forecasting.

Any type of business needs cash to keep running. For example, a street vendor needs cash to purchase new inventories of fruit to sell and to service their vending cart. Without this cash, their business would close.

STUDY TIP

It is a common mistake to assume that sales and cash are the same. If a business sells on credit, it has to wait for the trade receivables to pay cash. This then affects the cash flow of the business.

The importance of cash

Businesses need to have a steady flow of **cash** to survive. Without cash, a business cannot make payments and would soon have to close.

Businesses use a **cash-flow forecast** chart to keep a record of the movement of cash they expect to have coming in and going out. Receipts represent cash flowing into the business; payments represent cash flowing out of the business. The balance is the amount of cash that the business will have at a particular moment in time (see case study, *Pritesh*, opposite).

CASE STUDY | Calculating cash flow for Tarun

Tarun owns a small sole-trader business as a street vendor of fresh fruit. At the end of December, he has a cash balance of 1000 rupees. His only outgoing is the purchase of fresh fruit from gardens at the edge of the city. He makes purchases of fresh fruit costing 5000 rupees a month. He then transports the fruit to his vending stall in the city centre. This costs him a further 1000 rupees a month. He has forecast that the value of his sales receipts will be as follows: January 8000 rupees, February 7000 rupees, March 6000 rupees, April 7000 rupees, May 10 000 rupees, June 11 000 rupees.

Questions

1 Set out a cash-flow statement for Tarun's business.

2 In which month was his cash balance lowest?

From time to time businesses are faced with cash-flow problems where they do not have enough cash in the business in the short term to meet pressing liabilities (i.e. debts that must be paid quickly). To resolve short-term cash-flow difficulties a business can:

- increase its own borrowing (take out new loans)
- delay paying debts that they owe
- ask trade receivables (people that owe the business money) to pay up more quickly.

You can see that each of these measures will provide the business with more cash to finance day-to-day cash needs.

CASE STUDY | Pritesh

Pritesh is the owner of a small clothes shop selling T-shirts and jeans. His business has been in existence for 3 years, and he finds it quite easy to predict the income (receipts) coming into the business and the expenses (payments). He has set out a chart to illustrate payment and receipts for the first 6 months of the year.

All figures in dollars	Jan	Feb	Mar	Apr	May	Jun
Balance B/F	1000	2000	1750	1750	1250	750

Income

	Jan	Feb	Mar	Apr	May	Jun
Sales	3000	2250	2500	2500	2000	2000
Total receipts	3000	2250	2500	2500	2000	2000
Total cash available	4000	4250	4250	4250	3250	2750

Expenses

	Jan	Feb	Mar	Apr	May	Jun
Purchases	1000	1250	1250	1500	1250	1250
Wages	1000	1250	1250	1500	1250	1250
Total payments	2000	2500	2500	3000	2500	2500
Balance C/F	2000	1750	1750	1250	750	250

To understand how the chart is set out, look at the column for January. The first item that appears is Balance B/F. B/F stands for brought forward. So $1000 is the sum of cash that the business had at the end of December in the previous year.

The next heading is **Income**. Pritesh has only one type of income: sales of clothes. In January he sold $3000 of clothes for cash. Total receipts (income) for January are therefore $3000. This should be added to the cash that was brought forward from December.

If we add $3000 (cash receipts) to $1000 (cash brought forward), we can see that the total cash available to the business in January is $4000.

This cash can be used to make payments. Pritesh makes two types of payments:

- purchases of clothes that he buys to resell – he pays $1000 for these
- wages – he has to pay out wages of $1000.

So his total payments amount to $2000 ($1000 purchases + $1000 wages).

Remember that in January Pritesh expects to have total cash available of $4000. If he has to pay $2000 out of this for expenses, his balance at the end of the month will be $2000. This is shown in the bottom left-hand corner of the chart as $2000 Balance C/F. C/F means that this sum will be carried forward into February.

The same process can be carried out for each month of the forecast.

The closing balance figure is very important. If it is negative (i.e. if the business has no cash of its own and has to borrow to finance the shortfall), the business cannot automatically meet its debts and could be in trouble.

Questions

1. Working with a partner, take it in turns to explain each of the columns to each other.
2. When does Pritesh have least cash available?
3. Why is timing important in working out cash flows to the business?

SUMMARY QUESTIONS

1. What is the purpose of the cash-flow statement?
2. Define the following terms.
   Opening balance / closing balance / income / expenses / receipts / sales
3. Why is timing so important in managing cash flow in a business? What are the dangers of not having enough cash to meet outgoings?

KEY POINTS

1. Failure to manage cash flow is one of the main reasons why businesses fail.
2. Businesses need to check their cash flow on a regular basis.
3. A cash-flow forecast estimates the incoming and outgoing of cash to a business.
4. Income in the form of receipts needs to be greater than outgoings in the form of spending.

5.3 Income statements

5.3.1 Profit

TOPIC AIMS

Students should be able to:
- explain the concept of profit
- show understanding of why profit matters to a private sector business
- show an awareness of the difference between retained and distributed profit.

Profit

A private sector business exists to make money for the owners. The money they are interested in is not the money that the company makes from sales, but the money that ends up in their pocket, purse or bank account – in other words, the **profit**. Profit is the final amount of money that a business makes, once all the costs have been subtracted from sales **revenue**. Profit is the reward that a business owner receives for taking a business risk. Profit also provides a source of finance.

The notes that follow explain how the end profit figure is reached.

Gross profit

The **gross profit** of a business is the profit less all the costs of the things that it had to do to earn that profit. For example, a firm selling computers might buy them for $400 and sell them for $600. It sells 10 computers per day. To work out the daily gross profit, we would need to do the following:

1 Work out sales revenue: 10 computers x $600 = $6000

2 Subtract the costs: 10 computers x $400 = $4000

Daily gross profit = Revenue − Costs incurred in making that revenue
$2000 = $6000 − $4000

Calculating gross profit

Gross profit is a good indicator of the efficiency of the selling activities of a business. A trading business buys in goods which it then sells to the customer for a higher price. **Cost of sales** can be reduced by buying from a cheaper supplier or by arranging discounts for bulk buying. It is then important to price the items in such a way as to make a healthy gross profit from selling activities.

Gross profit = Revenue − Cost of sales

Profit

If the business wants a clearer indication of how much profit it is making, it will calculate its **profit**, by deducting the overhead costs from the gross profit. These are indirect costs, such as the rent of the building, the salaries of the senior directors, interest payments on loans, and heating and lighting.

Profit = Gross profit − All expenses associated with the normal running of a business

ACTIVITY

A business has calculated that its annual overhead costs amount to $100 000. The business consists of three separate teams. Their revenue and cost figures are shown in the table below.

Team A	Team B	Team C
Revenue $50 000	Revenue $200 000	Revenue $150 000
Cost of sales $10 000	Cost of sales $100 000	Cost of sales $100 000

1. Calculate the gross profit of each of the teams.
2. Calculate the gross profit of the business as a whole.

Retained and distributed profit

A business has a choice about what to do with its profit. One alternative is to retain, or keep back, as much profit as possible in the business. This *retained profit* can be used to expand and improve the business. This will help the business to become more competitive, by giving customers better value for money.

The alternative is to distribute the profit to the owners. Owners will want to receive some of the profit in the form of a **dividend**. If they do not receive what they consider to be a good dividend, they might sell their shares.

Retained profit is therefore the profit left over after the shareholders have been paid their dividends.

SUMMARY QUESTIONS

1. Two students are having an argument about what they understand profit to be. Thaksin says that profit is the sum of money that a business makes when you add together all the sales it makes in a given period of time. Meena disagrees; she thinks that profit is the difference between sales revenues and all the costs that a business incurs in making those sales.

   Which of these students do you agree with, and why?

2. What problems would arise from a business:
   - retaining all its profit in a given year?
   - distributing all its profits in a given year?

3. Which of the following would you expect to be higher in a profitable business? Explain why.
   - Profit or gross profit?
   - Sales revenues or direct costs?

ACTIVITY

A business manufactures perfume which it sells at $10 per bottle. It sells 1000 bottles in a month. Its manufacturing cost per bottle is $1. Calculate the gross profit of the business per month.

STUDY TIP

Remember that profit is not the same as cash. You need to be able to explain why this is the case.

KEY POINTS

1. Profit is the final amount remaining after all costs have been paid from revenue.
2. Revenue is the money charged to customers for buying goods and services.
3. Costs are the total money it takes to provide products or services.
4. Gross profit is the difference between revenue and the cost of sales.
5. Profit is the true profit when overheads are deducted from gross profit.

5.3.2 The function of profit

TOPIC AIMS

Students should be able to:
- explain the importance of profit as a reward for enterprise and risk taking
- show awareness of why cash and profit differ.

Profit is a reward for owners of a business. It also provides an important source of investment funds. With profit, a business is able to buy more inventory, buy machinery and buildings, train its staff to higher standards and engage in other improvement activities.

Profit is also important for the business owners. In setting up and running it, the owners are taking a risk with their money. They make nothing if the business does not generate a profit. There would be little point in starting a business if there were no opportunity to make a profit.

If a business fails to make a profit for a long period, it will probably have to close down. This could be disastrous for employees, suppliers and the local community.

Hiroshi Yamauchi, who transformed Nintendo – in 2009 he was Japan's richest man

CASE STUDY | Nintendo

Hiroshi Yamauchi transformed Nintendo from being a maker of card games into a multibillion dollar video-game giant. Even during the global economic recession in 2008/9, the company made record profits. For the financial year ending 21 March 2009, the company profit was 279.1bn yen (95 yen = US$1). The company was able to weather the economic crisis better than its rivals, mainly due to the success of its Wii console. This sold 10.17 million in 2008/9, and its portable DS device made over 9.95 million sales. Nintendo announced these profits at a time when its main rivals, Sony (maker of the PlayStation systems) and Microsoft (which produces the Xbox consoles), were making job cuts.

Questions

1 Why do you think that Nintendo was able to make such large profits?

2 Hiroshi Yamauchi owns 10 per cent of the shares in Nintendo. He became Japan's richest man in 2008/9. How has he been able to benefit from being an entrepreneur? Do you think that entrepreneurs like Hiroshi Yamauchi deserve the rewards that they receive?

ACTIVITY

Study the headlines in the financial pages of a newspaper. Find out a headline related to a company making a profit. Does the paper suggest that the profit is large or small? How has the profit been made? Does it state how much of the profit will be distributed to shareholders?

DID YOU KNOW?

A business should hold enough cash to service its regular day-to-day needs and unforeseen cash requirements. Too much cash, however, is money that is not being used profitably. Cash that simply sits in the tills does not earn any interest.

The difference between cash and profit

It is very important to understand the difference between cash and profit. A business needs both. Cash is the money that a business has in its tills and its bank accounts at a particular moment in time. Cash is required to pay bills. It is needed when trade payables (people to whom the business owes money) demand payment. If trade payables are not paid, they can take the business to court. The court can decide that a business should be closed down and its assets sold off to pay pressing debts. So it is essential to have cash.

However, cash is not profit. Cash is simply money that is available to the business. It might come from profit, but it could just as easily be borrowed from someone else.

Profit is earned from running a business well. A business earns a profit when the money that it makes from sales revenue is higher than the cost of running the business. Profit is earned over a period of time.

Profit as a reward

People who put money into a business – that is, shareholders – take a risk. They could invest in other things, such as lending money to the government. They may make less money from holding shares than they would lending to the government. Buying shares in a company therefore needs to be rewarded. Profit acts as an incentive to take risks. The greater the chance of making a profit, the more likely that people will be willing to take a risk.

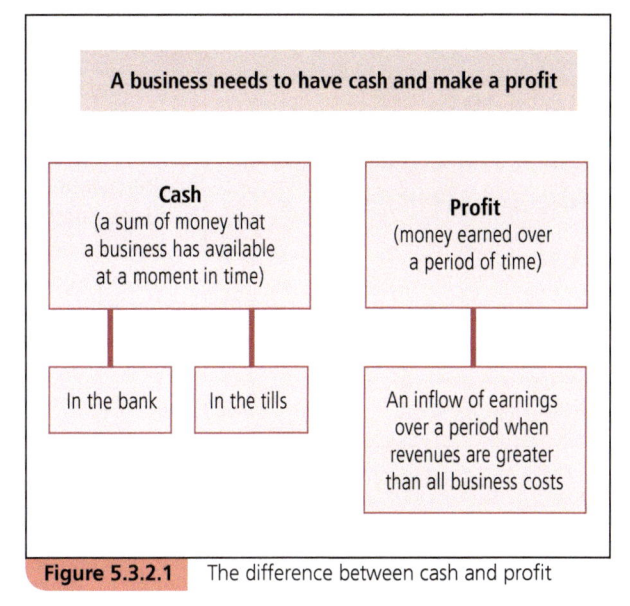

A business needs to have cash and make a profit

Cash (a sum of money that a business has available at a moment in time)
- In the bank
- In the tills

Profit (money earned over a period of time)
- An inflow of earnings over a period when revenues are greater than all business costs

Figure 5.3.2.1 The difference between cash and profit

DID YOU KNOW?

There are two types of shares: *ordinary* for investors prepared to take a higher risk, and *preference*, with a smaller risk. When a company distributes its profits, preference shareholders, as its name suggests, are paid before ordinary shareholders.

STUDY TIP

A business ceases to trade when it runs out of cash. It can survive in the short term, however, even if it makes losses.

SUMMARY QUESTIONS

1. Which of the following refers to cash, and which to profit?
   - It is a sum of money that exists at a given moment in time.
   - It is earned by a business over a period of time.
   - It is held in the bank or the tills.
   - It needs to be available to pay off debts.
   - It is the difference between revenues and costs.
2. Who receives the distributed profit of a business in:
   - a sole-trader business?
   - a company?
3. What problems might arise when:
   - a business makes a large profit but has no cash?
   - a business has a large amount of cash but does not make a profit?

KEY POINTS

1. Profit is a reward for taking a risk. Shareholders take risks, as do the other owners of a business.
2. A business needs to make a profit over a period of time. This profit can be ploughed into improving the business.
3. A business also needs to have cash to cover day-to-day costs and to meet pressing bills.
4. Businesses need to make a profit and at the same time have an appropriate cash balance.

5.3.3 Income statements

TOPIC AIMS

Students should be able to:
- understand the main elements of an income statement
- interpret a simple income statement
- use income statements as an aid to decision making.

Business owners need to know what their costs are, and what money is coming in. The financial statement that helps them to do this is called an income statement. This account shows owners how well the business is being run. It is also helpful if the owner needs new funds, such as a bank loan, because it gives an idea of how big a risk a lender will be taking. *Actual income statements* can be produced at the end of a trading period. This might be each year, or over a much shorter period, such as one month.

Businesses can also create *forecast income statements* to show how much they expect to make in a future period.

An actual income statement shows how much a firm has earned from selling its product or service, and how much it has paid out in costs. The difference between revenue and costs is the profit earned.

A typical income statement will look like the following.

	$ million
Revenue	1000
less Cost of goods sold	(400)
Gross profit	600
less Overhead costs	(200)
Trading/operating profit	400
Profit for shareholders (dividends paid)	(150)
Retained profit	250

Reading the income statement

In the account shown above, the firm has sold $1000 million worth of goods. All the expenditures involved in making these sales accounted for $400 million.

So if a chain of bookshops had paid $400 million for all the books that it sold in a year, and sold these books for $1000 million, this would give a gross profit of $600 million.

It is then necessary to take off the $200 million in overheads that it cost to run the bookshops during the year: rent, salaries, advertising, and so on. The bookshop thus makes a trading profit of $400 million.

It then needs to decide how to share this $400 million between the shareholders and retain profit to improve the business. In this case, the business distributed $150 million to shareholders and retained $250 million.

An income statement gives an immediate indication of how well a business has done over a period of time. If an investor has put money into the business, they will want to see that revenue more than covers costs. If the cost of sales is almost as high as the sales revenue figure, the business will not have much scope for making a profit.

DID YOU KNOW?

An easy way to read an account is to put negative (minus) numbers in brackets to show that they are deducted.

STUDY TIP

In the income statement, trading profit applies to companies that buy and sell goods (i.e. shops and other retailers). Operating profit is used for manufacturing companies that make goods, sometimes to sell to final consumers, sometimes to retailers.

Cooking Pots

Cooking Pots is a public limited company that sells cooking containers to the catering industry. It has set out its income statement for 2013.

Income statement for Cooking Pots for year ended 31 December 2013

	$m
Revenue	?
Cost of sales	(700)
Gross profit	300
Overheads	(?)
Profit	100

Questions

1 Why is it important for Cooking Pots to make a profit? Give two reasons.

2 Some of the figures are missing in the table. Calculate what they should be.

ACTIVITY

A small business has an annual sales revenue of $150 000. It has a number of overhead costs, including $3000 for insurance, $80 000 for staff salaries, $2000 interest on loans and energy bills of $5000. During the year it has sold $50 000 worth of inventory.

Set out the income statement for this business for the year's trading.

It is also important to look at the overheads in relation to revenue. If overheads cut into profits, it might be sensible for the business to move to a cheaper location, or to look at other ways of reducing overheads (e.g. cutting energy bills or staff salaries).

SUMMARY QUESTIONS

1 Ping Yung has kept records of the revenue and costs involved in running his bicycle shop.
   - Purchases of bicycles to resell: $80 000
   - Energy costs of running the business: $10 000
   - Advertising: $2000
   - Wages: $10 000
   - Revenue from sales of bicycles: $150 000
   - Rent on premises: $10 000

   Can you organise these figures into an income statement for him?

2 Explain the difference between the following terms.
   - Revenue and cost of sales
   - Gross profit and profit

3 Seema Singh is puzzled by the way that entries are presented in her income statement. Her accountant has set it out using the following figures.

	$
Revenue	2000
Cost of sales	(1000)

   Explain why the accountant has put the cost of sales figure in brackets.

KEY POINTS

1 The income statement account shows how a business has generated a profit or loss in a particular period of trading.

2 The top part of the statement shows the revenue a business has made and the costs involved in making the revenue. The difference is 'gross profit'.

3 The statement then goes on to deduct the overhead costs of running the business to arrive at profit.

4 Some of the profit will be retained in the business. The remainder can be distributed to the owners of the business.

141

5.4 Balance sheets

5.4.1 Main elements of the balance sheet

TOPIC AIMS

Students should be able to:
- understand the main elements of a balance sheet
- understand the difference between assets and liabilities
- interpret a balance sheet and deduce simple conclusions, such as determining how a business is financing its activities and what assets it owns.

ACTIVITY

Choose a business that you are familiar with, such as a local factory or large shop. Make a list of the types of non-current assets and current assets that the business will have. For example, a non-current asset for a newspaper business might be the computers journalists use to write their stories on. A restaurant's non-current assets might include the tables and chairs, as well as the oven.

STUDY TIP

Stakeholders find the data in a balance sheet very valuable. Banks will look at the financial stability of the business; suppliers might assess the probability of being paid what they are owed.

Balance sheets

A **balance sheet** is a statement showing the financial health of a business at a particular moment in time. It is usually drawn up at the end of the financial year, but can also be created at other times (e.g. halfway through the year).

Assets and liabilities

Information in a balance sheet enables you to compare immediately how much a business owns and how much it owes to lenders (e.g. banks).

Assets are items that are owned by a business. There are two main types of assets: *non-current* assets and *current* assets. Non-current assets are items used continuously by the business, such as buildings, machinery and vehicles. Current assets are also owned by the business, but they are more easily turned into cash (and include cash).

The three main types of current assets are:
- inventory waiting to be sold by the business
- trade receivables – money owed to the business by credit customers
- cash.

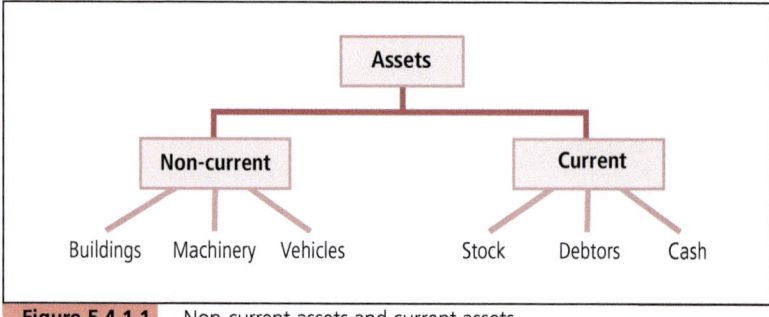

Figure 5.4.1.1 Non-current assets and current assets

Liability is money that a business owes. It is the money that the business is responsible for paying to others. **Non-current** liabilities are debts that a business has to pay over a number of years. Some of them may be very long-term, such as repayment of a 25-year mortgage. Short-term liabilities are debts that a business has to pay in less than a year.

The assets and liabilities can now be shown in a balance sheet. Figure 5.4.1.2 shows the balance sheet for Fresh Sandwiches, a company that manufactures and supplies fresh sandwiches to small retail outlets.

Non-current assets amounted to $100 000. This figure represents the value of the small kitchen that is owned by Fresh Sandwiches, and the work benches and kitchen tools it owns.

The **current assets** are $110 000. These include inventory consisting of filling ingredients to be made up into sandwiches (e.g. inventories of fresh meat and other ingredients that might need to be kept refrigerated). These are worth $50 000.

Balance Sheet for Fresh Sandwiches at 31 December 2013			
			$000s
Assets that are tied up	→	Non-current assets	100
Assets that can quickly be turned into cash	→	Current assets:	
		Inventories	50
		Trade receivables	50
		Cash	10
			210
		Share capital	140
		Profit	20
Loans that must be repaid in over a year	→	Non-current liabilities	20
Debts or loans that must be paid quickly	→	Current liabilities	30
			210

Figure 5.4.1.2 A balance sheet

Trade receivables are calculated as $50 000. This is the total sum owed by retailers who have bought sandwiches on credit. Additionally, Fresh Sandwiches holds $10 000 in cash (some of this will be held at the bank).

When the values of the non-current assets and current assets are added together ($100 000 (non-current) + $50 000 (inventory) + $50 000 (trade receivables) + $10 000 cash), this gives a figure for **total assets** of $210 000.

The next section of the balance sheet shows the value of the owners' interest in the business (how much the owners have put into the business), and consists of share capital ($140 000) and the profit that has been accumulated in the business over time ($20 000).

The final section of the balance sheet shows the two types of liability. First we have the non-current liabilities of $20 000.

Finally, current liabilities ($30 000) represent the sum of money that Fresh Sandwiches owes that needs to be paid back in the short term. For example, it may have bought its meat and bread on credit.

Setting out the balance sheet in this way helps us to illustrate what is termed the accounting equation, i.e. that the value of the assets of a business (non-current assets + current assets; $100 000 + $110 000) is equal to the owner's capital ($160 000) + liabilities ($50 000).

Assets ($000) = Owner's capital ($000) + Liabilities ($000)
100 + 110 = 160   + 20 + 30

Another way of looking at the accounting equation is to state that:

Assets minus liabilities = value of the owner's capital.
    210 − 50   = 160

Reading the balance sheet tells you important information about the assets and liabilities of Fresh Sandwiches and how the business is financed.

KEY POINTS

1. A balance sheet sets out the assets and liabilities of a business at a particular moment in time.
2. Non-current assets stay in the business and help it to generate wealth. Current assets are used in the process of production.
3. Non-current liabilities are debts owing in a period of more than one year. Current liabilities are debts owing in under a year.
4. The balance sheet consists of three sections:
   i. Assets
   ii. Owner's interest
   iii. Liabilities
5. The accounting equation shows that assets minus liabilities = owner's interest.

SUMMARY QUESTIONS

1. Which of the following are non-current and which are current assets of a business?

   Inventory / machinery / factory buildings / trade receivables / vehicles / cash

2. A business has the following assets and liabilities:
   - Non-current assets: $100 000
   - Current liabilities: $20 000
   - Current assets: $30 000
   - Non-current liabilities: $30 000

   Assuming the accumulated profit is $10 000, work out the figure for share capital. Also show how you would present the accounting equation in this instance.

3. A food-processing company manufactures canned fruit using a modern production line. It then sells the cans to large supermarket chains. What items would you expect to appear in the balance sheet for the company?

5.5 Analysis of accounts

5.5.1 Financial statements

TOPIC AIMS

Students should be able to:

- understand gross profit and profit, return on capital employed (ROCE)
- understand alternative ways that businesses can judge their success (e.g. ROCE, market share)
- interpret the performance of a business by using simple accounting ratios (return on capital, gross profit margin and profit margin)
- use accounting ratios, make evaluative comments on the success and performance of a business
- use a balance sheet to aid decision making.

Profit and profit margin

The account below shows the profit calculation for The Honey Shop, a specialist retailer of honey in a major city. It shows how much was spent on buying honey (purchases) and the total revenue received from selling that honey (sales). It also shows the expenses of running the business.

Income statement for The Honey Shop for the year ended 31 December 2013

	$	$
Revenue		30 000
Cost of sales (purchases)		(15 000)
Gross profit		15 000
Less Expenses		
Electricity	500	
Insurance	300	
Wages	4200	(5000)
Profit		10 000

Summarising the account we can see that:
Revenue = $30 000
Gross profit = $15 000
Profit = $10 000

From these figures we can make calculations which indicate how well the business is being run. It is important to find out how much profit the company is making for every $1 of sales.

The *gross profit margin* shows how much gross profit is made for each $1 of revenue.

The *profit margin* shows how much profit the business makes for each $1 of revenue.

The calculation is easy:

$$\text{Gross profit margin} = \frac{\text{Gross profit}}{\text{Revenue}}$$

$$\text{Profit margin} = \frac{\text{Profit}}{\text{Revenue}}$$

For example, for The Honey Shop:

$$\text{Gross profit margin} = \frac{15\,000}{30\,000} = \frac{1}{2} = 50 \text{ cents profit for every } \$1 \text{ of revenue}$$

$$\text{Profit margin} = \frac{10\,000}{30\,000} = \frac{1}{3} = 33.3 \text{ cents profit for every } \$1 \text{ of revenue}$$

Profit margins are often expressed as a percentage.

When gross profit margins for a business fall, this tends to indicate that either:

- the firm's prices are wrong: prices are either too high or too low
- the firm is paying too much for the items that it is buying for resale
- some of the items the firm is selling are being damaged or stolen.

STUDY TIP

It is a common mistake to think that profit and profit margin mean the same thing. Make sure that you understand the difference.

When profit margins fall, this tends to indicate that:

- the cost of one or more of the overhead costs has risen. The firm will need to look at ways of cutting these costs or of raising its own prices.

> **ACTIVITY**
>
> The income statement shown below is for a small clothes shop. Examine the account and then calculate the gross profit margin and the profit margin for the business.
>
> **Fashion Clothes Ltd income statement for year ended 31 December 2013**
>
> | | $ | $ |
> |---|---|---|
> | Revenue | | 150 000 |
> | Cost of sales | | (50 000) |
> | Gross profit | | ? |
> | less Expenses | | |
> | Rent and business rates | (15 000) | |
> | Advertising | (1 000) | |
> | Wages and salaries | (28 000) | |
> | Administration | (2 000) | |
> | Interest | (1 000) | |
> | Legal fees | (3 000) | (?) |
> | Profit | | ? |

> **DID YOU KNOW?**
>
> When you see the term 'profit' or 'profit margin' on its own this refers to the profit of the business, i.e. the end profit after cost of sales and expenses have been deducted from the revenue.

Return on capital employed

Comparing how well businesses are being run

It is always helpful to know how well a business is being run. Comparisons can be made with previous years' performance and the performance of similar companies. This is easier if the companies are the same size or in a similar industry.

One way of comparing businesses is to look at market share. This is the percentage of sales in a particular market that a particular business makes.

However, another useful comparison can be made using financial information. A good indicator of business performance is **return on capital employed (ROCE)**. ROCE is a calculation of how much profit a business makes as a percentage of the amount of money used.

$$ROCE = \frac{Profit \times 100}{Capital\ employed}$$

As noted above, to illustrate this point it is helpful to compare two businesses of similar size operating in the same market.

Firm A uses $100 000 worth of capital and generates a profit of $10 000. Firm B also uses $100 000 of capital and generates a profit of $5000.

Firm A's ROCE is $\frac{10\,000 \times 100}{100\,000} = 10\%$

Firm B's ROCE is $\frac{5000 \times 100}{100\,000} = 5\%$

CONTINUED

5.5.2 Financial statements (continued)

> **STUDY TIP**
>
> Ratios are more useful than absolute figures. When calculating ratios, think about whether a high figure is better than a low figure. For example, a high ROCE is better than a low figure, but a low gearing ratio (non-current liabilities expressed as a percentage of capital) is probably better than a high one.

> **ACTIVITY**
>
> The following table shows the profit and capital employed by three businesses.
>
> | Business | Capital employed ($) | Profit ($) |
> | --- | --- | --- |
> | Fresh vegetable store | 15 000 | 5000 |
> | New vegetable store | 14 000 | 7000 |
> | Traditional vegetable store | 16 000 | 4000 |
>
> Which business is using its capital best to generate profits?

Interpreting figures from the balance sheet

The balance sheet shows the financial affairs of the business at a specified moment in time. It provides information concerning:

- the nature and value of assets employed in the business
- the nature and value of liabilities to others
- how the business has been funded.

The outline format of a balance sheet is:

	$
Assets	50 000
Capital	30 000
Liabilities	20 000
	50 000

The net assets of the business (total assets less total liabilities) represents the owner's investment in the business (capital).

Assets are presented according to their **liquidity** (how easily they can be turned into cash), starting with the least liquid items:

- Non-current assets
- Current assets.

Liabilities, too, are presented starting with the least liquid:

- Non-current liabilities
- Current liabilities.

> **DID YOU KNOW?**
>
> Some accounting terms have changed in recent years to ensure international consistency. These up-to-date terms have been used in this book. However, you may still come across older terminology as follows:
>
> - *Trading and profit and loss account*, now called an income statement
> - *Stock* usually referred to as inventory in financial documents and statements
> - *Fixed assets* are now called non-current assets
> - *Long-term liabilities* are now called non-current liabilities
> - *Net profit* is now called profit
> - *Creditors* are now referred to as trade payables
> - *Debtors* are now referred to as trade receivables
> - *Final accounts* are now called financial statements

> **KEY POINTS**
>
> 1. The income statement shows how profit is reached.
> 2. From the income statement, profit calculations can be made for each $1 of revenue. These calculations give profit margins.
> 3. Comparing the profit with the amount of capital used gives ROCE, an indicator of how well the capital is being used.
> 4. The balance sheet can indicate the value of a business's assets and liabilities and how the net assets are financed.

CASE STUDY | Pina Mistry's balance sheet

Study the balance sheet below and answer the questions that follow.

Balance Sheet for Pina Mistry at 31 December 2013

	$000s	$000s
Non-current assets		
Land and buildings	300	
Motor vehicles	10	
		310
Current assets		
Inventory	60	
Trade receivables	5	
Cash	5	
		70
		380
Owner's capital	270	
Profit	30	
		300
Non-current liabilities		30
Current liabilities		50
		380

Questions

1 What types of assets does the business have?
2 What is the value of:
 • the non-current assets?
 • the current assets?
 • all of the assets?
3 What is the difference between current liabilities and non-current liabilities?
4 What does 'net current assets' mean? Why is it important for this to be a positive rather than a negative figure?
5 How would you measure the return on capital employed in a business?
6 What does 'total net assets' mean? What is the value of total net assets in this business?
7 Explain how the net assets of this business are financed.

SUMMARY QUESTIONS

1 The following table gives financial information about two businesses.

Business	Revenue ($)	Gross profit ($)	Profit ($)	Capital employed ($)
Engineering Supplies	240 000	60 000	30 000	300 000
Superior Engineering	300 000	75 000	30 000	200 000

Which of the businesses is the most profitable? Which has the highest return on capital employed?

2 Define the following terms.
 • Asset
 • Liability
 • Net current assets
 • Net assets
 • Financed by

147

5.5.3 Working capital

TOPIC AIMS

Students should be able to:
- identify and calculate working capital
- understand the concept and importance of working capital
- understand the concept of liquidity
- understand simple accounting ratios – current and acid test ratio.

Clothes shops need to have plenty of working capital to finance the purchase of new inventory and to pay wages and other bills. Inventory therefore needs to be sold quickly to generate more cash.

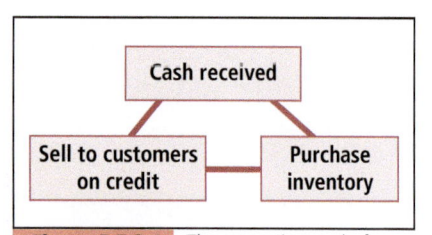

Figure 5.5.3.1 The operating cycle for a trading company

STUDY TIP

Liquidity can be more important than profitability in the short term.

The operating cycle

Every business has an operating cycle. For a manufacturing business, this starts with the purchase of materials, which are then made into a product. The cycle finishes with the receipt of cash from customers.

In a trading company (e.g. a wholesaler), the cycle involves the purchase of inventory, selling the goods on to customers, usually on credit, and then, after a short period, receiving a cash payment.

Incurring liabilities

In both of these operating cycles (for manufacturing and trading companies), a business will create liabilities. For example:

- the manufacturing company will buy raw materials and supplies on credit
- the trading company will buy inventories of goods on credit to resell.

Current liabilities are debts that the company must pay within a year.

The importance of current assets

In order to meet these ongoing liabilities, such as pressing payments or wages, a business will need to have access to cash and other **liquid assets**. These are assets that can be turned quickly into cash to make payments. These assets are also referred to as *current* assets. They are ranked in order of liquidity:

1. Inventories (least liquid)
2. Trade receivables
3. Cash (most liquid).

Current assets – current liabilities

The amount of working capital in a business is calculated by subtracting current (short-term) liabilities from current assets:

Working capital = Current assets – Current liabilities

Working capital is also commonly set out as a **ratio**. The ratio will show how many dollars of current assets a business has for each dollar of current liabilities.

The ratio should be at least: 1:1.

Ideally, it should be between 1.5:1 and 2:1.

The middle part of a balance sheet

You can read the working capital ratio from the middle part of a balance sheet.

For example, in 5.4.1 we set out the balance sheet for Fresh Sandwiches. The middle part was set out in the following way:

Current assets:	Inventories	50
	Trade receivables	50
	Cash	10
		110
Current liabilities:		**30**

In this case, the working capital ratio is 110:30, which can be simplified to 3.66:1.

In other words, the company had $3.66 of short-term assets for every $1 worth of short-term liabilities.

The acid test (quick) ratio

Businesses also use another ratio to check whether they have enough working capital. This is the **acid test ratio**.

This liquidity ratio does not include inventory. This is because if a business has to sell its inventory in a hurry, it will normally have to sell at a loss.

The acid test ratio is therefore: Trade receivables + Cash:Current liabilities.

In the example we showed for Fresh Sandwiches, this is: 50 + 10:30, which is 2:1.

This shows that for every $1 of liabilities that the business has, it has $2 of assets that can be turned quickly into cash.

The quick ratio should be at least 1:1.

Liquidity ratios only have a limited use. The balance sheet of a company is created on a particular day of the year, but the value of current assets and current liabilities changes every day as payments are made, new inventory ordered and new liabilities incurred. It is important, however, to have liquid assets, particularly in the form of cash. For example, a clothes shop will need working capital to pay for its inventory. To get this, it must make sure it stocks items that sell well, to keep the cash turning over in the business.

> **DID YOU KNOW?**
>
> A ratio is a comparison of the size of one number to another. For example, in 2009 it was announced that the size of the profits of the computer firm Apple Inc. were twice those of the industry average. This would be represented as:
>
> Apple profits : Industry average profits
>
> 2 : 1

> **KEY POINTS**
>
> 1. Liquidity ratios are important in indicating whether a business will be able to pay its bills.
> 2. The current ratio is the most widely used liquidity ratio. This measures the ratio of current assets to current liabilities. It should be at least 1:1.
> 3. The acid test ratio does not include inventory; inventory is difficult to sell quickly at the full price.
> 4. Liquidity ratios change from day to day; it is best to look at these over a period of time rather than on a single day.

SUMMARY QUESTIONS

1. The following table shows the current assets and current liabilities of three businesses. Work out the current ratio and acid test ratio for each of the businesses. Which of the businesses has the best working capital position?

Name of business	Current assets (Inventory + trade receivables + cash) $	Inventory $	Current liabilities $
Shankar Kumar (shawl merchant)	40 000	30 000	10 000
Shi Fang Fang (photography)	100 000	80 000	70 000
Peter Burden (cake shop)	50 000	20 000	30 000

2. At the end of the year, a business has non-current assets of $200 000, inventory worth $80 000, trade receivables of $60 000, cash of $20 000 and current liabilities of $100 000. What is its working capital ratio? What is its quick ratio?

3. Why does a business need to have working capital? What are the dangers of having:
   - too little working capital?
   - too much working capital?

5.5.4 Users of accounts

TOPIC AIMS

Students should be able to:

- understand what users can gain from analysing accounts
- show awareness of the different users of accounts
- show knowledge of what users might look for in the accounts of a business
- show how users such as lenders (e.g. a bank) might use accounts as the basis upon which to make decisions.

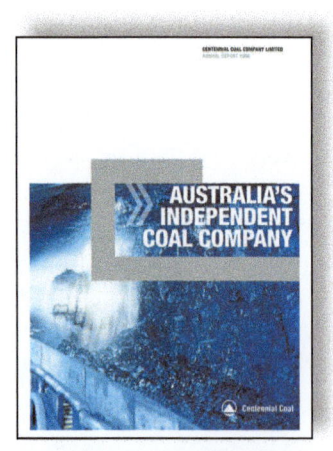

The front cover of the annual report produced by an Australian mining company, Centennial Coal, containing financial statements such as the income statement and the balance sheet.

ACTIVITY

Send a request to the head office of a major company in your country for a copy of the annual report to shareholders. Look at the income statement in the report. What use do you think shareholders, lenders, employees and tax collectors could make of this statement?

'Who reads the accounts?'

Different groups of people read company accounts. The information provides important useful details. The accounts give a picture of the past and present position of a business and some idea of its future prospects.

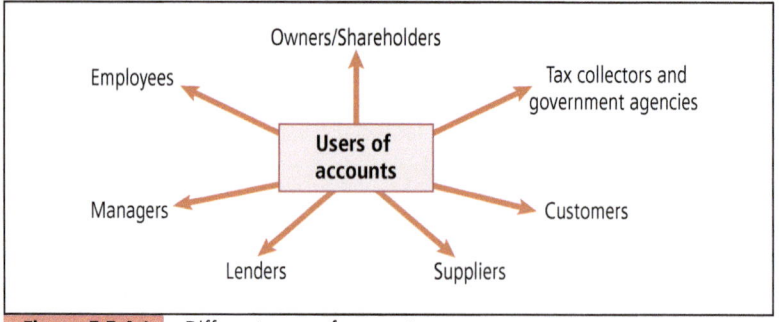

Figure 5.5.4.1 Different users of accounts

Owners/shareholders

In a small business, the owners may be a sole trader or group of partners. In companies, the owners are the shareholders. As the principal risk takers, owners want to know that their investment in the business is being looked after. They can always decide to take their money out and invest elsewhere. To help them decide, they will be interested in:

- profitability (from the income statement) – is the business making enough profit?
- liquidity – does the business have enough cash to meet pressing bills and debts?
- the financial position of the business (from the balance sheet) – what is the state of the business's assets and liabilities?

Lenders

Lenders want to know that the business is able to pay interest and eventually repay any loans. Banks will ask to see the accounts of a business to check whether they should risk lending to the business. They will want to look at figures for past profits, and also budgeted figures for future profits. They will want to check that a business has enough income to cover outgoing expenditures. In particular, lenders will be interested in the cash-flow position of a business. This relates to the timing of incomings and outgoings of cash.

Managers

Managers need to check on the profitability of their business, whether it has enough cash and whether it is investing in suitable assets.

Suppliers

Before they make supplies available on credit terms, suppliers will want their customers' accounts to indicate whether or not the business is financially sound, and whether it generates enough cash to pay for supplies.

Customers

Customers who have a long-term relationship with a company will want to make sure that the business is financially sound enough to keep supplying them. If the business they buy from is making excessive profits, this might suggest that they are being charged too much.

Employees

Employees are concerned about job security. They will want to make sure that their company can pay its debts and is profitable enough to pay the wages.

Tax collectors

The government collects a number of different taxes from businesses. One of the most important of these is a tax on profits. This should be shown in the income statement. Businesses also are likely to have to pay sales taxes – often in the form of a tax on value added by the business.

The government also uses business accounts to create national statistics, which can help it plan its national economic policy.

Annual reports

Small businesses, such as sole traders and partnerships, are expected to produce accounting information for the government tax collection department.

Companies are expected to produce an annual report. Public companies produce an annual report for shareholders. This annual report contains a statement from the chairperson of the company, giving a review of how the company has performed in the previous year and its plans for the coming year. The income statement and the balance sheet will be presented, along with another chart which shows the cash position of the business.

STUDY TIP

Think about how useful the accounts of a business are to the different stakeholders. Accounts do not always tell you everything you want to know. An income statement account does not tell you the capital of a business; a balance sheet does not tell you how much profit a business has made. Neither statement will tell you how successful a business is going to be in the future!

KEY POINTS

1. Users of accounts are groups and individuals that read accounts for specific purposes.
2. Shareholders (and other owners) use a business's accounts to check on the safety of their investment.
3. Other users of accounts include employees, managers, suppliers, customers, tax authorities and lenders; the accounts provide useful information on which to base important decisions.

SUMMARY QUESTIONS

1. What information will shareholders try to find in a company report?
2. Choose a well-known company that operates in your country. Identify five different groups of people in your country who would use the accounts of this business to find out financial information about the business. What information would they be looking at? How would this be of use to them?
3. What sorts of decisions do the following groups make that result from reading accounts and other information?
   - Lenders
   - Suppliers
   - Shareholders

Unit 5 — Practice questions

SECTION 1: Short-answer questions

1. Explain the purpose of a cash-flow forecast. [4]

2. Using the example of a bakery stall, explain why it is important to have cash available on a daily basis. [3]

3. Identify and explain TWO reasons why a new business may face higher payments than receipts in the first few months of trading. [4]

4. Explain how a small business owner may use a credit card to help with short-term cash shortages. [3]

5. State the formula for working out profit at the end of a trading year. [2]

6. Analyse TWO reasons why a business that has cash to pay for things on a daily basis may not make a profit at the end of the year. [6]

7. Explain, with examples from a small local business, the difference between gross profit and profit. [4]

8. Explain why major shareholders may face a difficult decision over the amount of profit to be retained by a firm. [4]

9. Explain how the following figures are calculated on an income statement:
   - trading/operating profit
   - retained profit. [4]

10. Identify and explain TWO reasons why profit is 'an important reward to business owners'. [4]

11. Explain why a successful business needs to retain profit as well as pay it out to shareholders. [4]

12. Explain, with examples, TWO differences between non-current and current assets in a business. [4]

13. Analyse why a prospective lender to a business will be interested in its balance sheet. [4]

14. Using the example of a clothes shop, analyse why the acid test ratio is a better test of liquidity than the current ratio. [4]

15. A business owner has published the following financial information for the past two years:

	2012 ($)	2013 ($)
Revenue	100 000	110 000
Cost of sales	40 000	50 000
Gross profit	?	?
Overheads	20 000	25 000
Profit	?	?

Calculate the missing figures and the gross profit and profit margins for each year. [8]

16. Analyse whether this business has been more successful in 2013 than in 2012. [6]

SECTION 2: Longer-answer questions

Blooms – Flowers for all Occasions

Grace's flower display business is based in Gaborone, Botswana. She supplies arrangements for special occasions such as festivals and weddings, and also has contracts with many of the local hotels. Demand is seasonal, but as she has been operating for five years, it is reasonably predictable. Grace employs one trainee assistant, but she does much of the artistic work herself. Grace holds a large inventory of flowers and plants on a daily basis, but she needs to make sure that she matches supply with demand as far as possible because of the short life of cut flowers. Grace's financial documents are shown overleaf.

Cash-flow forecast for the first half of next year

All figures in dollars	January	February	March	April	May	June
Balance brought forward	1000					
Income						
Revenue	1500	1000	3000	4000	5000	4000
Total receipts	1500	1000				
Total cash available	2500	1350				
Outgoings						
Rent	400	400	400	400	400	400
Purchases (average 50% of sales figure)	750	500				
Wages	1500	1500	1500	1500	1500	1500
Total payments	2650					
Balance carried forward	(150)					

Income statement for Blooms 2013

All figures in dollars	$
Revenue	48 000
Cost of sales	(24 000)
Gross profit	
Overheads	(20 000)
Profit	

Figures taken from the balance sheet for Blooms 2013:

- Current assets: $10 000
- Inventory: $6000
- Current liabilities: $8000

Use the financial information above to answer the following questions.

1 Fill in the missing figures for Grace's cash-flow forecast. [4]
2 Identify TWO months where Grace is forecasting a cash-flow problem. [2]
3 Do you agree that the bank should lend Grace the money to solve her cash-flow problem? Explain your answer. [5]
4 Identify and explain TWO ways in which Grace could improve her cash flow in the months when she may face problems. [4]
5 Calculate and fill in the gross profit and profit figures on Grace's income statement. [4]
6 Calculate the gross profit margin and the profit margin using the figures from Grace's income statement. [4]
7 Calculate the new margins if Grace's supplier increases the price of the flowers and plants she sells to Blooms by 10 per cent. [6]
8 Explain the following terms, with examples from the Blooms business:
- current assets
- inventory
- current liabilities. [6]
9 Calculate Grace's net current assets. [2]
10 Calculate Grace's current ratio. [3]
11 Calculate Grace's acid test ratio. [4]
12 Analyse your answers to Questions 9 and 10. What does this show about the liquidity of Grace's business? [4]
13 To what extent might the acid test ratio be a more accurate measure of liquidity for this type of business? Justify your answer. [6]
14 Explain why the following stakeholders will be interested in the accounts of Grace's business:
- her suppliers
- her customers
- her employees. [9]

6 External influences on business activity

6.1 Government economic objectives and policies

6.1.1 Government intervention

> **TOPIC AIMS**
>
> Students should be able to:
> - state the role of the government in influencing decisions within local, national and international contexts, and explain how businesses may react
> - identify the need for intervention
> - show understanding of the impact of intervention in terms of business decisions (e.g. what is produced and how)
> - give examples of intervention both to support and control the impact of business activity on people, the economy and the environment.

> **DID YOU KNOW?**
>
> Anti-trust legislation consists of laws to break up trusts and limit their power. Since 2000, the US government has used anti-trust laws against the powers of Microsoft.

> **STUDY TIP**
>
> It is important that you understand why governments intervene in an economy by influencing business behaviour. Ask yourself why consumers and employees cannot protect themselves adequately.

Why governments intervene in the economy

A **government** is a body with power to make and enforce laws within a state or over certain groups of people. In some countries, governments are chosen by the votes of citizens. In other countries, governments consist of groups who have established positions of power but have not been elected.

Governments intervene in the day-to-day life of societies. They make laws and carry out activities that affect business. The following paragraphs explain why governments intervene in the economy.

1 To protect individuals and groups from the actions of large powerful organisations. In the United States, the Sherman Act of 1890 was designed to break up the power of huge **monopoly** organisations that were limiting competition. (*Mono* means only: a monopoly is a company that controls a market and is the only supplier in a region or regions.) The act led to the breaking up of huge oil companies (such as Standard Oil) that dominated the US market. Today, most countries in the world have laws against monopolies and price fixing by large organisations. The Sherman Act is still at the heart of anti-trust legislation in the US.

Trusts

In a trust, a number of companies come together to control a market. A board of trustees is set up, with board members exchanging shares in the trust for shares in the individual companies. John D Rockefeller set up the first trust in the US. His board of trustees took control of 40 separate oil companies to create a monopoly that easily undercut prices charged by rivals, so that they were forced out of business.

2 To provide essential industries and services. Some industries, such as transport systems, energy and water supply, post and communications systems, are essential to the smooth running of a country's economy. In many countries, the government owns and runs key industries. In India, the government owns the railways, and in China telecommunications are dominated by three huge state-run companies: China Telecom, China Unicom and China Mobile. These are examples of public sector organisations.

Governments also play a major part in running a substantial part of services such as health and education. In most countries, the police, the legal system and the armed forces are also government-run. The money to pay for government services is obtained largely through taxation.

3 To help the economy to run smoothly and to protect employment. Governments are major employers and spenders. When businesses are laying off workers, the government can take action to protect jobs by increasing its own spending.

Governments should also try to ensure price stability. When prices are steady, business people can make business decisions with confidence because they know how much they will receive for goods sold on credit, or how much they will receive back when they lend money.

The impact of government intervention

Government intervention affects business decision making at local, national and international levels. Consider the following examples:

- Governments create laws about how goods can be produced. For example, health and safety laws determine safe ways of making goods that protect employees. Consumer protection laws aim to protect the end consumer by determining what materials and substances are allowed in goods.
- Government taxes and subsidies (see 6.1.3) encourage certain methods of production, and may discourage others: in recent years, many governments have provided subsidies to farmers for growing crops in particular ways, such as using organic (i.e. not using any artificial fertiliser) farming methods. The Turkish government started subsidising organic farming of raisins, apricots and dried figs in 1985. The subsidies now cover more than 90 agricultural products. This benefits the environment and ensures steady supplies of healthy food.
- Government spending on defence, education and health care provides incentives for companies. Companies producing items such as military aircraft, tanks or school textbooks may supply only to governments.
- Government subsidies and taxes also determine what is produced: taxes and health warnings can discourage spending on tobacco, for example. (Tobacco smoking leads to poor health and high costs of medical care.) In recent years, many governments, including those of Japan, Germany and the United States, have provided subsidies for producers to make more environmentally friendly products, such as unleaded petrol, and electric and hybrid cars.
- Government import tariffs influence what is produced. The Indian government levies an import duty of 40 per cent on most imported electrical goods. These tariffs are designed to protect Indian manufacturers against cheaper imported goods, as well as protecting local jobs.

SUMMARY QUESTIONS

1. Why does government seek to control the power of monopolies?
2. Why does the government subsidise some business activities?
3. How could the national government encourage activities that reduce waste in a domestic economy?

ACTIVITY

What industries does the government run in your country? Do these industries run well? Produce a short newspaper report in which you compare the views of two fictional members of the public:

- a student who is unhappy with services provided (e.g. no one listens to complaints, it provides a poor quality service)
- a manager working in one of these industries who thinks that the public enterprise is being run well (e.g. it meets deadlines, produces a good-quality product).

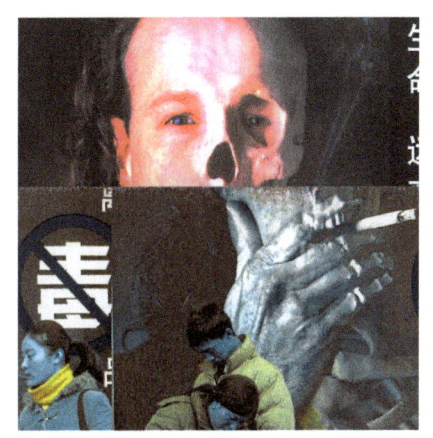

Government health warnings often use graphic images to show the risks and harmful impact of smoking to discourage consumers.

KEY POINTS

1. In every country the government intervenes in economic activity.
2. Reasons for intervention include provision of essential services and protecting weaker members of society.
3. Examples of government intervention include taxes and subsidies and running services such as public transport.

6.1.2 The business cycle

TOPIC AIMS

Students should be able to:
- describe the main stages of the business cycle
- understand the impact of the stages on a business in terms of sales, profits and business costs.

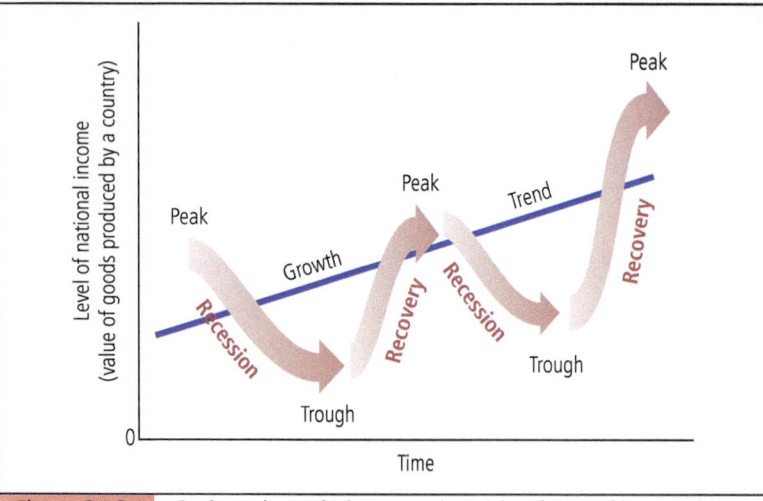

Figure 6.1.2.1 Peaks and troughs in economic activity. The trend is towards growth over time, with a series of recessions and recoveries.

An economic recession such as that of 2008–9 causes many businesses to shut down. As incomes fall, people have less to spend on bicycles and other goods.

STUDY TIP

Do not confuse a business cycle with the flow of money out of and into a business. This is the cycle of spending money to produce goods that generate money to help buy more resources.

The business, or trade, cycle

Unfortunately, economies do not grow in a steady pattern. Instead, there are periods in which the economy grows for a few years, followed by periods in which growth starts to fall. This is known as a **business**, or **trade cycle**.

Recession describes a period in which national income (the total value of goods produced in the economy) falls for at least two quarters of the year – that is, over a 6-month period. When the recession lasts for a much longer period – say, 3 or 4 years or more – this is a slump.

Recovery would be used to describe a period in which national income rises for at least two quarters after a recession or slump. A boom is a period of prolonged increase in national income.

Figure 6.1.2.1 shows that most economies go through a series of recessions and recoveries. When these are maintained over a period of time, they lead to booms and slumps in economic activity.

In a boom:
- output of goods rises
- firms take on more employees
- wages and prices rise
- prosperity rises for many people
- businesses boom.

In a slump:
- output falls
- firms lay off workers
- wages and prices fall
- prosperity falls
- businesses do badly (some cease trading).

Businesses and the business cycle

Businesses favour a boom period in the business cycle. This is the time when order books are most likely to be full and when it is easiest to sell goods.

However, as the boom reaches its peak, costs are likely to rise. At the top of the boom, it will become more difficult to recruit labour, and wages and other costs will rise. Businesses will be far more cautious in the downturn in the cycle and will tend to make cutbacks, such as reducing the size of the labour force and postponing the purchase of new machinery.

Business managers should understand the stages of the cycle and what is likely to happen in the near future. In a period of recession, businesses should be cautious about taking out loans and taking on additional fixed costs. However, in a period of recovery and boom, businesses are prepared to take more risks: they can expand by borrowing more, increasing the number of employees, expanding into new markets or producing a wider range of products.

The downturn of 2008

In 2008–9, the global economy experienced a long-term financial crisis that led to a slump in economic activity. The downturn initially started in the United States and spread across the world's economies. The price of oil, coal, and other minerals collapsed; house prices fell in many countries. The volume of world trade decreased. Millions of people across the world lost their jobs, in industries ranging from construction to car manufacture and banking.

> **STUDY TIP**
>
> Not all cycles are the same! In a business cycle, the economy as a whole goes through phases; a product life cycle refers to changes over time in the level of sales of a particular product for a particular business. Sales of a product may be falling because it is in the decline phase of its cycle, while the economy as a whole is expanding (booming). (See 3.3.2 for more on the product life cycle.)

KEY POINTS

1. The economy rarely grows at a steady rate; it is characterised by periods of recovery and recession.
2. Businesses need to be aware of the current stage and likely future stages of the business cycle.
3. In a recession, businesses cut costs and are cautious about borrowing. In a recovery, they can expand by taking on more finance and increasing their labour force.

SUMMARY QUESTIONS

1. What problems are caused for businesses by recessions? How might businesses react in a period of recession?
2. What is the difference between recession and recovery? How are businesses likely to respond in a period of recovery?
3. State, and explain, the main stages of a business cycle.

DID YOU KNOW?

During the recession of 2008–9, many governments encouraged banks to lend more money, particularly to businesses. They also nationalised a range of industries and businesses that were in danger of collapsing.

6.1.3 Government economic control and business activity

TOPIC AIMS

Students should be able to:
- outline key government economic objectives
- describe the main stages of the business cycle
- show how government control of the economy impacts on business.

DID YOU KNOW?

Greece between 2008 and 2013 was characterised by rising unemployment, negative economic growth, the failure of many large and small businesses. China was characterised by high rates of economic growth and the birth of many small and large businesses.

ACTIVITY

Find out from newspapers and the internet what the current rate of growth of GDP is in your country. Follow stories in national newspapers (in your country) relating to whether more businesses are starting up or closing down.

Key government economic objectives

An essential part of government policy is to grow an economy. Over time an economy needs to be able to provide better living standards, so that people have more goods to consume, more leisure time and better environmental and other living conditions. This is most likely to occur if there is growth in gross domestic product (GDP). GDP measures the total value of goods produced in the economy in a given period – usually one year (or a quarter i.e. a three-month period). It is important for a country's economy that the GDP per head of population is increasing. It is calculated by dividing the country's GDP by the number of people.

Other government objectives are to:

- keep prices stable, i.e. increasing at a relatively slow rate. The overall average rise in prices in a country is called the rate of inflation. With a low and steady rate of inflation business people are able to make well thought out decisions about what prices to charge including charges for supplying goods on credit
- keep the level of employment (percentage of working population in work) high. When people are in work they can contribute to the economy and do not drain government resources in the form of state unemployment benefits
- have high levels of investment in the economy in new research and technological development. Investment leads to the ongoing growth of GDP.

The business cycle

Economic growth does not take place in a steady way. All economies experience periods in which the rate of growth rises, followed by periods in which the rate of growth falls. The business cycle consists of four stages:

1. Growth – in which the rate of growth of GDP increases
2. Boom – period in which GDP is growing rapidly
3. Recession – periods in which for two successive quarters (three-month periods) there is negative growth in GDP
4. Slump – a prolonged period of decline in GDP.

Countries experience different rates of economic growth depending on their relative competitiveness and ability to cope in changing economic circumstances. For example, 2008 was generally a difficult period for the world economy. The illustration below shows that for China this led to a slow down in the rate of economic growth, while for Greece this led to a decline in the overall value of the economy (as measured in GDP). So while the Chinese economy grew, the Greek economy shrank.

Figure 6.1.3.1 GDP in China and Greece, 2008–10

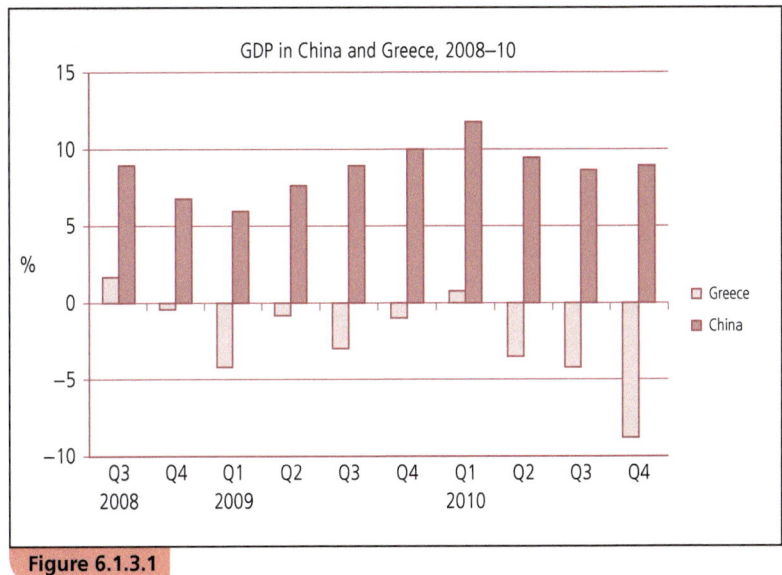

Government will seek to manipulate the trade cycle by encouraging spending when the economy slows down (goes into recession), e.g. by reducing business taxes and spending more money itself. When the economy is growing too quickly (pushing up prices in a boom) the government may raise taxes and reduce its own spending.

Government control of the economy and business

Government seeks to stimulate economic growth and to encourage business in a number of ways, for example by:

- making it easier for business to conduct business, e.g., by lowering taxes
- providing incentives for businesses to set up in growing industries, e.g., solar power energy
- encouraging investment by business, e.g. by lowering interest rates to make it easier for businesses to borrow.

KEY POINTS

1. Government seeks to grow the economy and keep prices stable.
2. The economy goes through cycles of growth and recession.
3. Government will seek to manipulate the trade cycle.
4. Government intervention in the economy (taxing and spending) impacts on business.

SUMMARY QUESTIONS

1. Why does the government place importance on economic growth?
2. How does investment help an economy to grow?
3. What is the impact on business of (a) increased government spending and (b) decreased government spending.

6.1.4 Tax and interest rates

TOPIC AIMS

Students should be able to:
- understand how interest rates affect businesses
- understand how different tax changes affect businesses
- understand how business decisions will be affected by such changes.

STUDY TIP

Remember that interest rates are not a tax levied by the government. They represent the cost of borrowing money. In effect, they are the cost of money to the borrower.

ACTIVITY

Use newspaper reports to find out whether the interest rate is going up or down.

Write a short report explaining the impact of interest rate changes on two separate businesses.

Rising interest rates	Falling interest rates
Raise business costs	Lower business costs
Cut into business profits	Raise business profits
Discourage businesses from borrowing	Encourage businesses to borrow for new projects and to expand

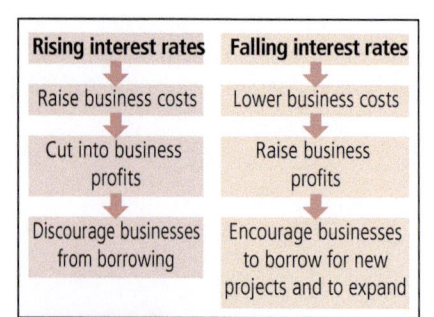

Figure 6.1.4.1 The effects of a rise and fall in interest rates

In August 2008, in an effort to reduce pollution and encourage car manufacturers to produce more small cars, the Chinese government raised its sales tax on large cars to as much as 40 per cent, while drastically reducing taxes on small cars.

Taxes

Changes in tax and interest rates have a direct effect on businesses.

A tax is a compulsory financial charge imposed by a government. Taxes are levied mainly as a way of raising revenue to fund government activity. In addition, taxes are levied to discourage certain types of business behaviour, such as pollution or the creation of waste.

Interest rates

If you borrow money from a bank, you will have to repay what you borrow, as well as interest, a charge made by the bank for lending you the money.

The **interest rate** is the cost of borrowing money. It is charged by lenders to borrowers. It is expressed as a percentage (%). For example, if a business borrows $1000 from a bank for a year at a 5 per cent interest rate, it would expect to pay back $1050, usually in monthly payments.

$1000 (the sum originally borrowed) + **$50** (the interest charge, 5 per cent of $1000) = **$1050**

Nearly all businesses have to borrow money. They hope that when they come to repay the money, the interest rate will be as low as possible. Rising interest rates harm business profits. Sometimes high interest rates can ruin a business. This is because they may have to pay a lot of interest on money they have borrowed and this adds to their costs. Usually the rate of interest is agreed at the start of a loan, except in cases where a 'variable rate' may change.

CASE STUDY: Paying business taxes in Albania

The table below is based on data from the World Bank (Ease of Doing Business Index, December 2011). It shows the main taxes a medium-sized company must pay in Albania, as well as the time spent filling out tax forms and the number of payments that have to be made.

The table shows that an Albanian business will spend 357 hours a year preparing, filing and paying taxes, and that these taxes take 38.7 per cent of profits.

Number of payments per year	44
Hours spent by a business preparing, filing and paying taxes	357
Profit tax	8.6%
Labour tax and other contributions	25.3%
Other taxes	4.8%
Total tax rate (% profit)	38.7%

Questions

1 Why might businesses in Albania have been discouraged by the taxes that they have to pay and the time spent on form filling?

2 How would the taxes that businesses pay affect the costs of running a business and thus the profits that a business can share among the owners?

How tax rates affect business

For businesses, taxes are a cost. They are a deduction from profits and valuable time has to be spent administering them.

Changes in tax rules influence business decisions. For example, if businesses have to pay more in social security contributions, they may decide to employ fewer workers to save on some of these costs. When taxes on profits increase, businesses will be able to retain less profit to invest in new machinery.

The government may tax activities that it sees as harmful – for example, activities that create pollution and waste. Businesses may respond by developing new processes that reduce waste.

The government may also tax imports, goods and services brought in from overseas. These **tariff barriers** may be imposed to protect home businesses from lower-cost overseas competitors.

Subsidies are payments to a business to carry out certain activities. For example, the government subsidises certain types of agricultural production. The government also subsidises certain types of production, such as the production of organic fruit (i.e. fruit that is not sprayed with chemicals). Also subsidies are often given to firms to help them set up business in the first place.

DID YOU KNOW?

'Green' taxes discourage pollution and environmental damage. These might be taxes on the emission of greenhouse gases and pollution into water sources.

KEY POINTS

1 Taxes earn large revenues for governments; they also discourage certain types of activity.

2 A subsidy is a payment made by a government to encourage certain activities.

3 Rises in interest rates can reduce profits; a fall encourages borrowing and can lead to more spending.

SUMMARY QUESTIONS

1 What would be the impact on a small business of a rise in business taxes?

2 A business is considering building a new production line. How would a rise in interest rates affect its decision making?

3 A business is faced by rising labour costs and has large debts built up from the past. How would a fall in interest rates affect this business?

6.2 Environmental and ethical issues

6.2.1 The impact of business activity on the environment

TOPIC AIMS

Students should be able to:

- demonstrate an awareness of the impact that business activity may have on the environment
- use examples to illustrate concepts such as pollution and global warming
- understand some of the issues with regard to 'sustainable development'
- show awareness of the possible impact of business development upon depletion of natural resources.

STUDY TIP

Pollution in its various forms is an example of a social cost. Social costs are costs to the community and society.

ACTIVITY

What are the principal sources of energy used in your domestic economy? Draw a pie chart to represent their use. Which of these energy sources are non-renewable? How dependent is your economy on imported energy resources?

DID YOU KNOW?

Greenhouse gases include methane and carbon dioxide. They are gases in the atmosphere that absorb and emit radiation. They are one of the side effects of increased business activity on a global scale.

Pollution and global warming

Business activity involves the creation of 'goods', such as food and clothing, that benefit people. However, during the last 20 years, scientists, politicians and the wider public have realised that it also creates 'bads' in the form of pollution and industrial wastes. These are substances that harm the environment.

Figure 6.2.1.1 There are different ways of causing pollution.

Water pollution

Businesses such as paper mills and chemical factories are located near the sea and rivers in order to access the water needed for the manufacturing process. They release waste into water sources, which can lead to the depletion of fish stocks, as well as other harmful effects. Businesses need to budget for waste disposal that conforms to correct environmental standards.

Air pollution

Air pollution from business activity such as the generation of coal-fired energy used to heat and power factories, offices and other businesses is one of the most serious threats. Keeping to regulations in this area is a cost for businesses.

Global Warming

During the 20th century an increase in the average temperature of the earth, and the oceans, has been recorded. Although there is yet to be conclusive proof, many scientists believe that this is caused by human activity such as cutting down forests and burning fossil fuels.

People in societies that become more prosperous over time should be able to enjoy consuming more goods and live longer. This progress is 'development'. The challenge facing the planet is to make sure that this growth in prosperity increases over time. A continued growth in well-being is **sustainable development**.

| CASE STUDY | Freshwater prawn farming in Bangladesh |

In Bangladesh, freshwater prawn hatcheries provide one of the most important sectors of the economy. Bangladesh exports about $500m worth of fresh prawns each year. Prawns are hatched from two types of breeding stock – natural prawns that grow in the wild, and prawns that are developed in the new hatcheries. The wild prawns provide by far the superior stock. However, the number of prawns grown naturally in the wild is being rapidly reduced, as farmers increasingly reduce existing supplies to sell them in the market. Catching wild natural prawns in ever-increasing numbers in nets not only reduces their numbers, but also damages the breeding grounds of fish stocks.

Questions

1 Why do you think that farmers are increasingly reducing the supplies of natural prawns?
2 What are the possible long-term effects on the prawn industry in Bangladesh and prawn populations there?

Freshwater prawn farming in Bangladesh: depleting natural stocks of prawns means that the breeding capacity of the prawn population is being reduced.

Sustainable development

Businesses contribute to well-being by providing goods and services for customers. Most businesses, however, create waste and some of this is harmful to the environment. It may be dangerous toxic waste or just discarded packaging. In extreme cases, business activity may lead to floods and famines. Trees that once prevented landslips are cut down for housing; rainforest that absorbed carbon dioxide and other gases is cleared for cattle ranches to provide meat for human consumption. Other damage can be caused by over-using resources: in this case the business will not be sustainable.

The challenge to businesses is to produce 'sustainable' goods that create less waste and pollution. There are now many businesses providing products or services to help protect the environment. These may be companies providing energy sources such as wind farms and solar energy plants, or non-polluting forms of transport such as electric cars. You can also buy items such as energy-saving light bulbs, rechargeable batteries, devices that measure electricity consumption in the home and washing powder that can be used with cold water.

In many countries, recycling is becoming more important. Recycling involves converting 'waste' products for reuse. In some Indian cities, many small enterprises have been set up to recycle waste. Small-scale collectors of rags, paper and metals collect materials from houses, the streets and even from refuse tips. This is then sold on to dealers who collect the materials in bulk. The materials are washed and reprocessed to make new goods such as textiles and newspapers. Many countries now have collection points for consumers to recycle materials such as glass, paper and plastic, and businesses exist that deal with the processing of these wastes.

KEY POINTS

1 As well as creating 'goods', business activity can result in pollution and waste.
2 Sustainable development involves minimising waste and pollution, while producing goods that enable people to enjoy a better life.

SUMMARY QUESTIONS

1 Write down definitions of the following terms: Pollution / greenhouse gases / sustainable development.
2 Explain two of the negative side effects of business activity on the environment.
3 Give three examples of non-renewable resources used by businesses to produce goods.

6.2.2 External costs and benefits

TOPIC AIMS

Students should be able to:

- appreciate the concepts of social costs and benefits
- understand the difference between a social cost and a social benefit, and a financial cost and a financial benefit
- show an understanding of how business activity can create them
- use examples to show how business decisions create social costs and benefits
- apply such concepts to a given business decision
- evaluate the possible consequences to stakeholders of a given business decision.

A new toll road: as well as the financial costs and benefits to the builders, it was necessary to consider wider social benefits, such as the creation of jobs, and also the social costs, such as extra noise and pollution, caused by the new road.

Financial costs and benefits

Businesses need to look at the **financial costs** and **benefits** of carrying out a decision. For example, the decision might be taken to build a new factory in Malaysia. The table shows some of the financial considerations of this decision.

Financial costs of building and operating factory in Malaysia	Financial benefits of building and operating factory in Malaysia
Cost of borrowing necessary finance to build the factory	The revenues earned from the factory
Cost of building the factory and equipping it with machinery	The saving to the business resulting from operating in Malaysia rather than at a higher-cost location
Cost of labour	
Cost of raw materials	

To work out the profit from running the factory, accountants will calculate the net financial return in the following way:

Financial revenues − Financial costs = Net financial return

The net financial return is called profit.

This is a very narrow view of looking at the impact of a business. There are other costs and benefits, which are outlined below.

Social costs and social benefits

Social benefits include the financial benefits to a company and other positive benefits that result from a particular business activity or decision. **Social costs** are the financial costs to the company of building the factory, plus all the other costs resulting from the factory. These external costs might include the traffic noise to people living near the factory. Social costs and benefits might be visualised as follows:

All benefits − All costs = Net benefit

The table illustrates some of the major costs and benefits to a large supermarket chain of setting up a new store in a large city. You can see that different stakeholders are affected in different ways.

Financial costs to the business	Financial revenues to the business
Costs of borrowing finance	Revenues received from the goods sold in the supermarket
Wages paid to supermarket employees	
Costs of buying products to resell in the supermarket	
Additional social costs (external costs)	**Additional social revenues (external benefits)**
Traffic congestion and pollution from shoppers travelling to the supermarket and lorries delivering supplies	Convenience to shoppers of buying a range of goods in one shop
Small shops have to close down because they are unable to compete with the large supermarket	More jobs available for members of the local community

In this example, the owners of a business and its managers are most interested in the financial costs and revenue. Other stakeholders, such as employees, local residents and shoppers, are interested in the social costs and benefits that affect them directly.

CASE STUDY: The Marrakesh–Agadir motorway

In 2006, work began to construct the 233.5 km motorway between Marrakesh and Agadir in Morocco. Costs involved in the project included:

- construction of the road and the interchanges with other roads
- construction of the toll gates
- putting up the signs on the motorway
- paying compensation to people on whose land the motorway was built.

The benefits of constructing the road were to improve the standard of living of communities in Morocco and to create jobs, particularly in the construction and tourist industries. The new motorway was designed to reduce travel time for motorists, reduce accidents and create jobs in constructing and then running and maintaining the motorway.

Questions

1 What were the financial costs and benefits of building the Marrakesh–Agadir motorway?
2 What are the social costs and benefits of the motorway?
3 Which stakeholders will benefit most, and who will experience social costs?

Activities should only be carried out if the social benefits are greater than the social costs. It is not always easy to calculate social costs and benefits and give a monetary value to factors such as noise pollution or the benefit of reduced journey times. Specialists are trained in techniques to attach values to these factors. **Cost-benefit analysis** (CBA) is used as part of the decision-making process, especially for government projects.

Any decision that a business makes affects stakeholders – shareholders, employees, suppliers, customers, the government or the local community. Each of these groups will experience costs and benefits in different ways.

SUMMARY QUESTIONS

1 What is the difference between a financial cost of an activity and the social cost of that activity?
2 Give an example of an activity that involves financial costs and benefits and social costs and benefits. Give examples of these costs and benefits.
3 An independent report has calculated that the social cost of building a new factory in a given location is a lot higher than the financial cost. Should the local planning authority allow the factory to be built there – or should it take into consideration other things?

STUDY TIP

A business making a decision usually only takes into account financial costs and benefits. These are the factors that directly affect the business and influence the profits. Social costs and benefits affect all stakeholders. A decision which is financially profitable might not be in the best interests of the wider community.

ACTIVITY

Imagine that a large retail outlet or factory is to be built close to your school. New access roads will need to be built. Which stakeholder groups will be most affected? In each case, outline one social cost and one social benefit to each of the stakeholder groups of the new outlet.

KEY POINTS

1 Financial costs and benefits are monetary calculations of the effects of a business project.
2 Financial costs and benefits are only one part of wider social costs and benefits.
3 Businesses need to use cost-benefit analysis to take into account social costs and benefits, as well as financial ones.

6.2.3 Ethics in business

TOPIC AIMS

Students should be able to:
- show an awareness of ethical considerations in business activity
- show an awareness of the possible conflict between the profit motive and ethical considerations, such as exploitation of employees (e.g. using child labour).

Many people think that it is unethical business behaviour to use child labour. The children may be prevented from going to school and playing with their peers. Wages may be very low and working conditions dangerous.

STUDY TIP

Make sure that you understand the difference between acting unethically and acting illegally. Acting illegally always means breaking the law; acting unethically means acting in a way that puts profit above morals. The action may not break the law, even if many people disapprove of it.

Ethics

Ethics are the values and principles that influence how individuals, groups and society behave. Business ethics are therefore the values and principles that operate in the world of business. It is possible to carry out many practices that are not strictly ethical, but are still legal.

Ethical decisions

Whether business owners and managers recognise it or not, all business decisions have an ethical dimension. Here are some ethical questions that a business might have to face.

- Should products which might damage the health of consumers (e.g. cigarettes, petrol) be withdrawn from the market?
- Should a firm make sure that its business activities (e.g. making furniture from mahogany and other rare woods) do not harm the environment?
- Should money be spent to create lifts and ramps that allow wheelchair access to workplaces and retail outlets?
- Should a firm refuse to offer money to individuals in a business to help secure an overseas contract?

A firm that answers yes to these questions might be described as operating in an ethical way. Remember, though, that acting in an ethical way may increase business costs, and some customers may be lost. Profits may then decrease.

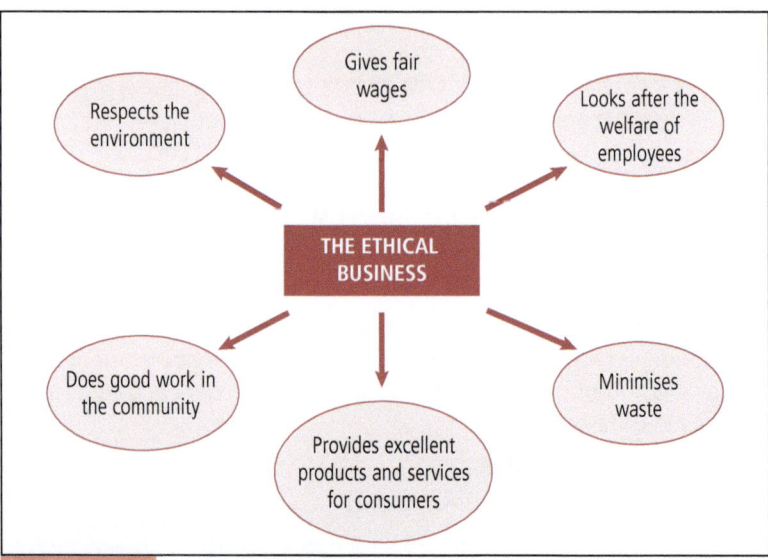

Figure 6.2.3.1 An ethical business

THE ETHICAL BUSINESS:
- Respects the environment
- Gives fair wages
- Looks after the welfare of employees
- Does good work in the community
- Provides excellent products and services for consumers
- Minimises waste

ACTIVITY

Figure 6.2.3.1 outlines some of the most important aspects of an ethical business.

What else can you think of?

CASE STUDY | Low-cost labour

The following illustrations provide examples of business practices that sometimes occur.

- Style Clothing is an international supplier of branded goods which carry the 'S' logo. The international buyer for the company has agreed a deal to buy low-cost T-shirts from a supplier in an overseas country where wages are low.

- Workers in the factory in the country are paid $1 per day to sew the T-shirts. Many are under the age of 13. They work in hot and unpleasant conditions, from 8 in the morning to 6 at night. They do not go to school.

- The shirts that they make are then sold to wealthy consumers, usually in cities like Paris, London, New York, Beijing, Delhi, Moscow and Rio de Janeiro.

- A typical consumer will buy a Style T-shirt at a price which is 10 times the amount that the worker who sewed the shirt together makes in a day.

Questions

1 In what ways does this case study represent unethical behaviour?

2 What could be done to improve this situation? Who should take this action?

Social responsibility

Corporate social responsibility (CSR) describes the way in which an ethical business contributes to society. A firm which behaves ethically towards the local community and society as a whole is socially responsible. Examples of social responsibility include:

- making sure that your business does not use child labour or buy from suppliers that use child labour
- providing fair wages for employees
- giving a fair price to suppliers, particularly in poorer parts of the world – this is sometimes referred to as fair trade
- minimising waste and eliminating or reducing pollution.

ACTIVITY

Choose a big multinational company (e.g. Gap or Coca-Cola). Search the internet for the company's CSR policy. What grounds does the company have for claiming to be socially responsible?

SUMMARY QUESTIONS

1 What is the difference between ethical and unethical business behaviour?

2 Provide two examples of unethical behaviour. What is the relationship between ethical behaviour and business profit?

3 What actions can businesses take to operate in ethical ways?

KEY POINTS

1 Ethics are moral principles or values.

2 Corporate social responsibility involves businesses operating in an ethical way.

3 Examples of unethical behaviour include using child labour, not paying business taxes and the production and supply of harmful and dangerous products.

6.2.4 Legal controls over business activity

TOPIC AIMS

Students should be able to:
- outline the role of legal controls over business activity that affects the environment
- explain how/why business might respond to environmental pressures and opportunities.

The role of legal controls

Governments often take action or make decisions that affect businesses and other members of society. For example they might pass a new law that imposes tighter restrictions on an aspect of business life, such as new regulations about waste management.

In some countries, the government intervenes in nearly every aspect of business life, whereas in other countries it rarely gets involved. Regulation refers to the creation of rules. Deregulation refers to a reduction in the number of rules.

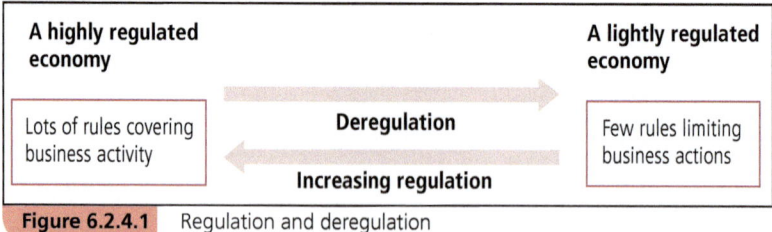

A highly regulated economy		A lightly regulated economy
Lots of rules covering business activity	→ Deregulation → ← Increasing regulation ←	Few rules limiting business actions

Figure 6.2.4.1 Regulation and deregulation

Too much regulation limits the freedom of businesses to make decisions, and businesses become anxious in case they unknowingly break the law. Too little regulation can lead to abuse – for example of the environment.

Environmental regulation

Environmental regulation takes place at international, national and local levels. In recent years there have been a number of inter-governmental agreements relating to the environment.

- The World Commission on Environment and Development (1987) called for global cooperation and supportive actions between countries at different stages of economic development.
- The Earth Summit (1992) took place in Rio de Janeiro. It led to the signing of the Rio Treaty including Agenda 21, an agenda of actions for the 21st century which was signed by 170 countries. A range of regional and industry sectoral plans were developed to reduce the business impact on the environment.
- The Kyoto Treaty (1997) reached an agreement about the creation of greenhouse gases. The agreement focused on countries reducing overall emissions to at least 5 per cent below 1990 levels during the period 2008 to 2012.
- The Earth Summit (Rio + 20) was again held in Rio de Janeiro in 2012 and confirmed a commitment to Agenda 21. A document produced at this meeting – 'The Future We Want' – addressed a range of issues including access to clean energy, food security, water and sustainable transportation.

Inter-governmental agreements feed down into national policies (i.e. national laws relating to issues such as the use of energy, the management of waste, recycling, etc.). National laws are then backed up by local government regulation and laws impacting on businesses in given localities.

ACTIVITY

Identify a pressure group that is active in your own country. What are the objectives of this pressure group? Who do they put pressure on: governments, business or both? What are the results of their actions?

STUDY TIP

Pressure groups often create bad publicity for a business and its activities. The business may stop the activities, because bad publicity usually means lower sales. Lower sales usually mean lower profits. Lower profits mean unhappy shareholders. Businesses change their policy when this happens.

> **CASE STUDY** | The Environment Protection and Pollution Act, Zambia

The Environment Protection and Pollution Act in Zambia sets out overall responsibilities within the country for the management of the environment. This sets out clearly what businesses are required to do in order to protect the environment in the country. The Act sets out the obligation of the Environmental Council with overall responsibility for supervising the management of the environment in the country. The focus is on conserving the environment and/or preventing and controlling pollution. The Environmental Protection and Pollution Act provides for the health and welfare of persons, animals, insects and the environment. It covers areas such as emissions of substances into water and into the air, the management of waste, the use of pesticides and toxic substances as well as noise pollution and other areas. The Act sets out the role of environmental inspectors and the responsibility of the courts to penalise businesses and individuals who break environmental laws.

Questions

1 What is the most important piece of legislation covering environmental protection in your country?

2 Who is responsible for the overall supervision of the environment in your country?

3 What types of penalties can businesses face for violation of regulations governing water and air quality and pollution?

Friends of the Earth campaign against activities that cause oil spills. They can lead to fires which impact on the local, national and international environment.

Intervention by other agencies

As well as government and the courts, other organised bodies intervene to stop social and environmental harm by businesses.

In particular, pressure groups try to influence the government and business. The groups may be a few people complaining about noise from a local factory, or a large environmental group like Greenpeace, campaigning on environmental issues worldwide. Well-known pressure groups like Greenpeace and Friends of the Earth have had a major impact on the activities of governments and multinational companies. They draw attention to actions that threaten the environment and people's general well-being.

Business response

Faced by environmental regulation business response is typically to alter practices to manage waste better, to engage in more recycling activity and to try to reduce the impact of business on the environment. By developing environmental management systems (i.e. developing operations that reduce waste and pollution) a business is able to reduce costs of production, and also to avoid fines and other penalties. Enlightened businesses also see the environmental challenge as an opportunity, e.g. to develop new environmentally friendly products and new processes that cut out waste.

KEY POINTS

1 Government intervention affects businesses through local, national and international laws.

2 Regulation limits how much pollution and environmental harm a business can create.

3 Businesses respond to environmental regulation and pressure groups by altering the way they act.

SUMMARY QUESTIONS

1 What is the impact of international treaties on national government environmental policy?

2 What types of business activity impact negatively on the environment?

3 How do businesses respond to environmental regulation?

6.3 Business and the international economy

6.3.1 Globalisation

TOPIC AIMS

Students should be able to:
- explain the concept of globalisation
- identify opportunities and threats to business
- explain why government might introduce tariffs and quotas.

The nature of globalisation

In a global economy goods can be produced in many different places and transported for sale to destinations on the other side of the world. Globalisation involves the free movement of goods, capital, labour and technology. Globalisation involves intense competition because products and resources can be transferred and brought to market all over the world.

CASE STUDY | Jamaican Blue Mountain Coffee

Blue Mountain Coffee has been grown in Jamaica for over 300 years. It is a variety of coffee that can only be grown in Jamaica. It has a mild flavour, no bitterness and a relatively low caffeine content. As a result it is attractive to coffee connoisseurs across the globe.

As a global product the coffee has an extensive market: it takes a 16-hour flight to transport the coffee from Kingston to Tokyo, but the fact that 80 per cent of the coffee is distributed to Japan shows that distance is no object in a global economy. In Japan, Blue Mountain Coffee competes with other internationally grown coffees from Brazil, Colombia, Kenya and many other countries, but it is carefully branded and marketed to ensure that it is competitive in the global marketplace. Typically Blue Mountain Coffee is bought by consumers in Paris, London and many other cities who are prepared to pay extra for top-quality coffee.

Questions

1 In what ways is Blue Mountain Coffee a global product?

2 In what ways does Blue Mountain Coffee face global competition?

Globalisation involves a number of related concepts. A key feature is that products, people and capital are highly mobile. Shops in the Caribbean stock products sourced from all over the globe, and products from the Caribbean are exported around the world. People travel to and from the Caribbean as students, business managers, technical workers and tourists, etc. Foreigners invest in Caribbean enterprises, and people from the Caribbean invest overseas.

Opportunities and threats

Globalisation provides both challenges and opportunities for Caribbean businesses. A major challenge is the scale of the competition facing Caribbean-based businesses. Multinational companies from the US, Europe, China, Brazil, India and elsewhere have huge domestic markets enabling them to benefit from large-scale production and distribution. Inevitably this drives down their costs. Global companies are able to spread their marketing, advertising and production costs across global sales. Other challenges of globalisation are the cost to a domestic producer in selling their goods overseas – e.g. transporting coffee from Jamaica to Japan, and also the cost of marketing in unfamiliar countries.

However, globalisation also provides real opportunities. Caribbean entrepreneurs can set up joint ventures with overseas partners – that is, new businesses with capital and input both from the owners of existing Caribbean enterprises and the owners of foreign enterprises. The Caribbean entrepreneur brings local knowledge and contacts, while the foreign partner provides additional capital and access to global markets. The internet also provides a channel for accessing global markets particularly for selling niche regional products.

Globalisation offers larger companies the opportunity to exploit vast economies of scale. Large car companies are able to produce vehicles on a huge scale, such as in the car plants in Brazil and Mexico where land and labour are relatively cheap. Marketing costs (including advertising) can be spread over several territories. Large-scale production enables low-cost mass production, advertising and marketing, competitive pricing, global recognition and mass sales.

Tariffs and quotas

Governments may seek to protect domestic markets through tariffs and quotas. A tariff is a tax that has to be paid for trading goods across borders. A quota is a limitation on the number (or weight) of goods that can be traded. Trade restrictions are imposed to:

- allow infant industries to develop in a country. For example, if a Caribbean country was developing new solar power technology, then in its early years it would be beneficial for local businesses if foreign imports of solar products were taxed or the number allowed was limited.
- protect jobs in a local market. For example, many people in the Windward Islands in the Caribbean have small farms growing bananas for export. However, it is very difficult to compete with cheaper imports from mass producers in South America. The government in the Windward Island therefore taxes foreign imports and subsidises banana growers to protect their livelihoods.

DID YOU KNOW?

Services (for example, international banks, insurance companies, hotel chains, casinos) are also part of the globalisation process. There is a globalised market for many services.

KEY POINTS

1 Globalisation involves the free movement of goods, capital, labour and technology around the world.

2 Both large and small niche market players can benefit in a global market.

3 Trying to compete on a global scale can increase some costs such as distribution costs.

SUMMARY QUESTIONS

1 Outline four key features of globalisation.
2 Which businesses benefit most from global production and distribution?

6.3.2 Multinational companies

TOPIC AIMS

Students should be able to:
- identify reasons for the importance and growth of multinational businesses
- explain why multinational companies are created
- understand the potential impact of multinationals on the countries where they are located by looking at the advantages and disadvantages that they create.

Unilever owns 51 per cent of the shares of Hindustan Unilever – India's largest fast-moving consumer goods company, selling toothpaste, shampoo, ice cream and many other products. The company has 40 factories in India, which supply 6.3 million retailers.

A **multinational** is a company with its headquarters in one country but which produces and sells its products in other countries. Many of the goods and services that we consume are produced by multinationals.

You probably use a Unilever product in your home. Unilever is a British-Dutch company employing about a quarter of a million people worldwide. They have 300 local factories and own companies in 88 countries. In 2008, Unilever's top 13 products each had sales of over 1 billion euros. These included Knorr soups, Lipton tea and Omo and Surf washing powders. Some of Unilever's brands, such as Lipton tea or Magnum ice cream, are identical across the globe. Other brands are produced by Unilever specially for a particular country or area – for example, PG Tips in the UK, Home Cup in Nigeria and Ting Hua in China are all Unilever tea products.

Large multinationals

In July 2009, some of the world's largest multinationals in terms of sales were involved in banking and the oil industry. Many of the multinationals had their head offices in North America, Western Europe and Japan. The following table lists some of the largest companies. Their size is measured by the value of their sales.

Company	Sector	Country
Wal-Mart	Retailing	United States
Exxon Mobil	Oil	United States
Royal Dutch Shell	Oil	Netherlands
Toyota	Automobiles	Japan
AXA	Insurance	France
HSBC	Bank	UK
Lukoil	Oil	Russia
Indian Oil	Oil	India
National Australian Bank	Bank	Australia
Bank of China	Bank	China

Multinationals benefit from operating in a range of countries. Benefits include:

- the capacity to make use of natural resources in many countries. Oil companies like Shell and Exxon Mobil drill for oil in almost every continent, as well as on the ocean bed.
- making use of labour in other countries. The sportswear manufacturer Nike has many factories employing thousands of people in countries like Vietnam and Indonesia. These countries provide low-cost labour with the right skills.
- the opportunity to have a global market. In India and China there are over 1 billion potential consumers. Other huge markets include

Brazil, Russia, Nigeria and Indonesia. The French multinational BIC, which produces biros, razors and other widely consumed products, has set up large factories which produce goods that are sold across wide geographical areas.

The impact of multinationals

Multinationals create employment in the countries in which they operate. For example, the Japanese multinationals Toyota and Honda are major providers of employment in the car industry in Britain, India, Thailand and many other countries. Multinationals often help to build up the infrastructure of a country – for example, by building road and railway links. They can also help to spread expertise in new technology to a country – for example, by training their employees.

However, multinationals can also have negative effects. Oil, gas and chemical multinationals often cause pollution and local environments are damaged, through chemical leaks and the destruction of forests. Because of their size, multinationals can often undercut local firms. Huge retailers such as Carrefour (France) and Wal-Mart (USA) do this in the various countries in which they operate. Multinationals also take profits out of the domestic economy and pay them to shareholders, who may live thousands of miles away.

ACTIVITY

Find out which companies are the largest multinationals. Use the keywords World's Biggest Companies to carry out an internet search. One of the top entries you will find is the *Forbes* list of companies. (*Forbes* is an American business magazine.) The homepage gives you the option to get a ranking list of the world's biggest companies. Produce a table, ranking these companies according to the size of their sales, profits and other indicators. Create a chart, showing the companies, the country in which their head office is located, the types of product they make and the number of employees they have. Why is it difficult to say which is the largest company?

STUDY TIP

Many people are concerned at the increase in importance of multinational companies. Multinationals potentially create benefits for the countries where they are situated, but they may also mean losses for smaller businesses and less choice for consumers.

SUMMARY QUESTIONS

1. How many countries does a business need to operate in before it is defined as a multinational? Can you give examples of a multinational company in the following industries: oil and petrol, retailing and clothing sales?
2. What are the advantages of being a multinational?
3. What arguments might be put forward for encouraging multinationals to operate in your country? What arguments might there be against this?

KEY POINTS

1. A multinational is a company that operates in several countries.
2. Companies become multinationals to benefit from wider market opportunities, to access scarce resources, and to take advantage of a new pool of labour.
3. Multinationals create employment and benefits, but they can also cause pollution and the withdrawal of profits from the host country.

DID YOU KNOW?

In rural India, Hindustan Unilever provides 'microcredit' to women – this refers to loans of very small sums of money or the supply of small quantities of goods on credit to set up small businesses. The loans enable women to sell products such as sachets of shampoo and soap to local people. The women benefit from the income; Unilever benefits from extending its sales into rural areas.

6.3.3 Exchange rates

TOPIC AIMS

Students should be able to:

- understand the concept of a rate of exchange of a currency
- understand what is meant by an appreciation or depreciation of a currency
- show awareness of the importance of exchange rate changes to importing and exporting businesses.

The exchange rate

When international trade takes place between businesses in countries that use different currencies, at least one of the businesses will need foreign exchange.

A country's foreign **exchange rate** is the price at which its own currency exchanges for that of others. For example, the Japanese yen can be compared with the US dollar (US$), the European Union's euro, or the Chinese yuan (RMB). (The Chinese currency is called *renminbi*, which means 'the people's money'.)

The importance of the exchange rate to business

There are two main ways in which the exchange rate may influence business activities.

- It may affect the price of goods and services that businesses buy in international markets.
- It may affect the price at which businesses sell goods and services in international markets.

If a business imports good or services, the exchange rate will influence the price of their purchases, and any changes will make pricing more difficult. On the other hand, if they sell goods or services abroad, changes in the exchange rate will affect the amount of foreign currency coming in, and this will change the amount they earn. Changes in exchange rates will therefore affect profit margins. Figure 6.3.3.1 shows how changes in the exchange rate can cause uncertainty in both situations.

The yuan is the national currency of China. The strength of the yuan depends on how many people worldwide want to purchase this currency to trade with China (although Chinese exporters will be quite happy to be paid in dollars and other strong currencies, such as the euro).

BUYS Raw materials, components, finished goods and services in international markets ← **The business** → **SELLS** Raw materials, components, finished goods and services in international markets

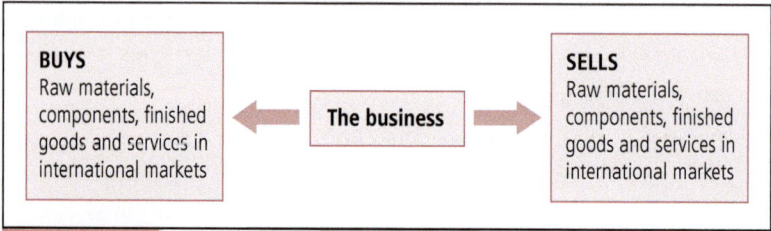

Figure 6.3.3.1 Buying and selling in international markets

The table below shows the effect of rises and falls in the value of a currency.

Home currency appreciates (gets stronger) External value of the currency goes up	Exports from home country become more expensive to customers from other countries, therefore more difficult to sell.	Imports from other countries become cheaper, including raw materials and finished goods.
	Exporters will sell less/make less profit. Value of exports decreases.	Importers will find goods from other countries cheaper to buy, so they can sell more in the home country, enabling them to make more profit. Value of imports increases.
Home currency depreciates (gets weaker) External value of the currency goes down	Exports from home country become less expensive to customers from other countries, therefore easier to sell.	Imports from other countries become more expensive, including raw materials and finished goods.
	Exporters will sell more/make more profit. Value of exports increases.	Importers will find goods from other countries more expensive to buy, so they can sell less in the home country/make less profit. Value of imports decreases.

CASE STUDY — How is the value of the yuan (RMB) determined?

A Chinese importer wishing to buy American goods will usually buy dollars with which to purchase them. In 2009, US $1 was worth about 7 yuan (RMB), the currency of China. So if the Chinese importer wanted to buy a tractor from the United States for a price of $50 000, he or she would have to exchange RMB 350 000 to buy the US dollars. However, exchange rates change over time. A currency can become stronger (appreciate) or weaker (depreciate). If, for example, the yuan appreciated against the dollar to US$1 = 5 yuan, the American tractor would become much cheaper for the Chinese importer. Instead of having to give RMB 350 000 for it, the importer would only have to give 250 000.

The result of this would mean that the importer can show an improved profit margin or invest the money saved in other parts of the business.

Questions

1 Find out the most recent exchange rate – how has it changed since 2009?

2 Has the yuan appreciated or depreciated against the dollar since 2009? What will be the effect on Chinese exports to the United States?

ACTIVITY

Look in a newspaper or on the internet to find out the most recent exchange rate between the yuan (RMB) and the US$. Has the yuan been rising or falling in value against the dollar? What are the implications for Chinese importers and exporters?

CASE STUDY

Some countries are grouped into an area that uses a single currency. The European Union consists of 28 countries, including Germany, Ireland, Italy, Spain and Greece. The single common currency is the euro. A small number of countries in the Union are not members of the eurozone. This includes the UK, which still uses the pound sterling (£). There are other trading zones that use a common currency, such as countries in the eastern Caribbean.

When businesses import and export within a common currency zone, they do not have to worry about fluctuations in exchange rates.

Questions

1 What is the advantage of many countries using a single currency?

2 What other EU countries apart from the UK are not part of the eurozone? Try to find out why they have decided to retain their existing currency.

STUDY TIP

When answering a question on the effects of a change in exchange rate, keep your analysis in the context of the home country, or where the business is based. This way you are less likely to become confused.

KEY POINTS

1 The exchange rate is the price at which one currency exchanges for that of other currencies.

2 An appreciation in the currency involves an increase in the price against other named currencies; a depreciation involves a fall against other currencies.

3 Businesses need to be aware of any changes in their currency level.

SUMMARY QUESTIONS

1 What is the difference between the appreciation and the depreciation of a currency?

2 How does the appreciation or depreciation of a currency affect a business that exports goods overseas? Use the example of a business that exports from your own country.

Unit 6 — Practice questions

SECTION 1: Short-answer questions

1. Identify and explain TWO objectives that a government may try to achieve by regulating business activity. [4]

2. Explain the difference between private costs and social costs in the context of business activity. [3]

3. Explain the difference between private benefits and social benefits in the context of business activity. [3]

4. Identify and explain ONE social cost and ONE social benefit that might result from a new shopping centre on the outskirts of town. [4]

5. Explain, with examples, the part that organisations such as Greenpeace may play in cutting down external costs caused by large business organisations. [4]

6. Explain how the following organisations may give rise to external benefits:
   - a government recycling scheme
   - a new school in a rural area
   - a vaccination programme against malaria. [6]

7. Analyse, with examples, why working towards an economic objective may help the government of your country meet a social objective. [6]

8. Explain why governments in many countries undertake the provision of public transport services. [4]

9. Analyse why many governments around the world impose high taxation on the sale of cigarettes. [4]

10. Explain the difference between a grant and a subsidy in the context of business activity. [3]

11. Identify and explain ONE social cost and ONE social benefit that may result from moving a steel factory to a rural location. [4]

12. Explain, with examples, what is meant by ethical behaviour. [4]

13. Explain how the following organisations may behave in an ethical manner:
    - a fast-food company that causes street litter
    - a company offering tourist boat tours on a lake
    - an individual who is awarding government contracts to business. [6]

14. Analyse, with examples, why an ethical business, working in a socially responsible manner, may suffer from higher costs, but gain customers. [6]

15. Identify and explain how sales and profits of a company that exports goods from your country may be affected by:
    - home currency strengthening
    - home currency weakening. [4]

16. What are the likely effects of a recession on a company producing the following?
    - Essential food
    - Cars [4]

SECTION 2: Longer-answer questions

The textiles factory

Jing runs a fabric-dying factory by a river, close to Jakarta, Indonesia. Cotton cloth arrives in bulk and is then dyed in batches to a selection of traditional patterns. The work is unpleasant and hours are very long. Jing sometimes has difficulty finding staff, so she often employs young workers without checking if they are old enough to be employed. The factory is unpopular locally due to several incidents where dye has spilled into the river, making the water undrinkable for cattle and killing the fish.

Jing has recently received a letter from the local government inspector, saying that he will be visiting in the near future to check that the business is complying with regulations about employment, pollution, and health and safety. Jing is worried and thinks the factory may have to close.

1. Identify and explain TWO reasons why production processes in a business such as Jing's factory may be regulated by the government. [4]

2 Analyse why many governments legislate to prevent young children gaining employment in factories. [4]

3 Analyse ONE advantage and ONE disadvantage to Jing's employees of regulations about maximum working hours permitted. [6]

4 Jing has said: 'All these regulations will add to my costs and we will not gain any benefits'. To what extent do you agree? [6]

5 Evaluate the extent to which regulation against pollution can be used successfully against businesses such as Jing's. [6]

The new metro system

Bangalore residents are looking forward to the completion of their new metro system, which is due to revolutionise public transport in the city. The metro, which has cost millions of rupees of public money, should cut down road traffic and reduce journey times in the city. As a result, pollution caused by traffic congestion should also reduce, making the city a much more pleasant place in which to live and work.

However, the disruption to traffic while the building project is going on has been huge, and many residents are complaining about what they see as the slow progress of the work.

1 Identify and explain TWO objectives that the metro project may help the Bangalore government to achieve. [4]

2 Identify and explain TWO reasons why governments often fund public transport provision. [4]

3 Identify and explain ONE private cost and ONE private benefit that may arise from the metro project. [4]

4 Evaluate the extent to which the fares to be charged on the metro should reflect the construction costs. [6]

5 Analyse TWO other ways that traffic congestion and pollution may be reduced in big cities. [4]

The fair-trade souvenir shop

Ethical Gifts is a business selling African souvenirs in Livingstone, Zambia. Customers are mainly foreign tourists who are visiting the Victoria Falls, who come to buy jewellery, ceramics, wood carvings and textiles. Ethical Gifts' unique selling point is that all of its products are sourced from suppliers who pay fair prices to the makers of the products. Non-renewable hardwood objects are not sold and nor are animal skin products. Ethical Gifts' prices are higher than the competition, but customers, mainly from developed Western countries, are happy to pay them, secure in the knowledge that they are buying ethically produced goods.

1 Explain what is meant by 'ethically produced goods' in this context. [4]

2 Analyse how Ethical Gifts' unique selling point helps the company to add value to the souvenirs. [4]

3 Analyse TWO difficulties Ethical Gifts may have in ensuring that the goods it sells are 'ethically produced'. [6]

4 Analyse TWO social benefits that may arise from the trade in ethical products. [6]

5 To what extent is the willingness to pay more for ethically produced products 'a luxury which only benefits rich tourists'? [6]

The Shop 'n' Save supermarket

The Shop 'n' Save supermarket is having a hard time due to the economic recession. A major business has closed down in the town and there are very few employment opportunities for those made redundant. Customers therefore have little money to spend and are looking for basic necessities at bargain prices. Many of the company's competitors have ceased trading, but Abdul, the owner of Shop 'n' Save, is determined to try to weather the storm.

1 Identify and explain TWO ways in which consumers may be affected in a recession. [4]

2 Analyse, with an example, why some businesses may cease trading in a recession. [4]

3 Explain why Abdul may believe it is worth weathering the storm during the recession. [4]

4 Identify and explain THREE types of product that Abdul should stock to help him increase sales during a recession. [6]

5 Do you agree that the local government in Abdul's town should offer him some support during the recession? Explain your answer. [6]

Glossary

A

Acid test ratio sometimes referred to as the **Quick Ratio**. It is a ratio of the trade receivables and cash to current liabilities. It compares the size of the assets that can most quickly be turned to cash compared with debts the business may have to pay out in the very short period.

Adding value increasing the value of the product for the final consumer, through manufacturing processes, advertising, distribution, etc.

Annual General Meeting (AGM) yearly meeting of shareholders at which the Company Report is presented by Directors.

Appraisal formal evaluation of an employee's performance over a particular period.

Assets what a business owns, or is owed by others.

Automation operations controlled by machinery rather than people.

B

B2B business-to-business dealing through the internet.

B2C direct links between businesses and consumers through the internet.

Balance sheet statement that shows a firm's assets, liabilities and sources of capital at a moment in time.

Batch production manufacturing items in sets for a particular length of time, before switching the manufacturing line to produce a different type of set.

Behavioural segmentation identifying segments of potential customers with similar behaviour patterns (e.g. those who like to be the first to try out new fashion clothes).

Benefits advantages, tangible or intangible, gained by customers from the product or service that they buy.

Board of Directors a body representing shareholders in a company, with the responsibility for looking after their interests.

Brand a product with a unique, consistent and well-recognised character. The uniqueness can come from a factual product detail or from its image.

Break-even analysis comparison of a firm's revenue with its fixed and variable costs to identify the minimum sales level needed to make a profit. The comparison can be shown on a graph known as a **break-even chart**.

Budget a plan, usually set out in table form, indicating how financial targets will be reached.

Business cycle up and down swings in the economy as indicated by movements in Gross Domestic Product.

C

CAD (computer-aided design) using a computer to design new products and processes.

CAM (computer-aided manufacturing) using computers in the control and management of machinery and processes.

Capital money or resources invested by the owner/s of an organisation; a source of finance used by the business to acquire assets.

Cash money in the tills and bank account of a business.

Cash flow forecast prediction of the flow of money into and out of a business.

Charity organisation whose purposes are to do good rather than to make a profit.

Closed question a question with a choice of prepared answers (e.g. in a market research questionnaire).

Communication the process by which information is exchanged between one group or individual and another.

Company a business that is registered as being owned by a group of shareholders and managed in their common interest.

Contract of employment legal document setting out terms and conditions of employment.

Corporate social responsibility (CSR) responsibility of a business to society.

Cost-benefit analysis to determine the net benefit of an activity, all the benefits are added up and all the costs deducted.

Cost of sales the cost of making the products and services sold to customers.

Cost-plus pricing working out how much each unit of production costs to produce and then adding a fixed percentage for profit.

Costs the expenses incurred by a firm in producing and selling its products. They include expenditure on wages and raw materials.

Current assets shorter-term items such inventories, trade receivables money in the bank and cash in hand.

Current liabilities debts that a business needs to pay in the short term (usually less than 1 year).

D

Delegation passing power and authority down the hierarchy in an organisation so that decision making can take place at lower levels.

Demand consumers' wishes to purchase products, backed up by their willingness to spend money on them.

Discrimination favouring or showing preferential treatment to one group or individual over others.

Diseconomies of scale the result of a firm becoming too large, when inefficiencies occur, leading to rising costs.

Distribution channels the route through which a good or service is moved to the market.

Glossary

Dividends the share of profits earned by an organisation that is paid to its shareholders.

E

Economies of scale the advantages of a larger firm over a smaller one, enabling it to produce larger outputs at lower costs per individual unit.

Economy the system in a particular country for creating goods and distributing incomes to those involved in production.

Entrepreneur risk taker in a business (e.g. the shareholders, a single owner or a partner).

Ethics sets of moral principles that guide behaviour.

Exchange rate the rate of exchange between one country's currency and that of another (e.g. the South African rand against the Ghanaian cedi).

Export sale of goods or service to another country.

Externality the spillover effect resulting from a particular activity, such as pollution caused by a production process. Externalities can generate benefits and costs for stakeholders outside the business.

F

Fair dismissal when a worker is sacked for reasons that are acceptable in law.

Fixed costs any costs that do not vary with the level of output (e.g. rent and rates).

Flow production continuous production of goods which 'flow' down a production line.

Forecast an estimate of what is likely to happen in the future.

Franchise permission to use a business's name and to sell using that name in a particular locality.

G

Gearing ratio ratio of capital used to finance a business that is raised from shareholders, compared with funds that are borrowed from outside the business.

Global warming rise in air and sea temperatures which may be caused by increasing industrial activity.

Globalisation the ability to produce anywhere, sell anywhere and place profits anywhere in the world.

Gross profit the profit that a firm earns from trading or selling goods before the overheads and expenses have been deducted. It is calculated by: Revenue – Costs of sales = Gross profit.

H

Hierarchy layers of decision making within an organisation. A hierarchical organisation has several layers and decision making is made in a downwards direction.

I

Import to bring in foreign goods to a country or use foreign services.

Income money received in return for providing a product or service, including labour time.

Income statement an accounting statement showing a firm's revenue over a trading period and all the relevant costs generated to earn that revenue.

Incorporation establishing a business as a separate legal entity from its owners, and therefore allowing it to have limited liability.

Interest rate the price charged for borrowing money.

Internal communications communications that take place within an organisation.

International trade the process of buying and selling goods on international markets.

Internet a means of connecting to other computers anywhere in the world so that information of all kinds can be sent and received.

Intranet electronic communications system set up for and accessed by members of an organisation. The system is not accessible for those outside the organisation.

J

Job description a written document relating to a particular role, indicating, for example, job title, hours of work.

Job production a single piece of work produced for a particular customer.

Job specification the mental and physical requirements needed to carry out a role effectively.

Joint venture an organisation jointly set up by two organisations; frequently set up when one international company wants to enter a new market.

Just in time (JIT) production and distribution system which involves providing raw materials, components and supplies at the time when they are required by a customer rather than being produced earlier and stocked.

K

Kaizen system of making regular small-step improvements to production processes. *Kaizen* is Japanese for 'continuous improvement'.

L

Leadership the process of driving through change by persuading others to do what you want.

Leadership style the predominant manner in which a manager acts. For example, a laissez-faire manager tends to stand back and let others make decisions themselves; an **autocratic** manager is much more controlling.

179

Glossary

Lean production eliminating all forms of waste.
Liabilities what an organisation owes at a particular moment in time.
Lifestyle pattern of behaviour associated with particular groups of people.
Limited company one whose shareholders have a liability only to the extent of their investment.
Limited liability the greatest amount that a company's owners might have to pay out to meet debts, the top being the sum that they invested in the business.
Line production producing goods in a set of sequenced steps along a production line.
Liquidity the ease with which an asset can be converted into cash.
Location of business where a firm is set up, and exists.

M

Manager someone with responsibility for resources and people within an organisation.
Market any situation where buyers and sellers come into contact.
Market economy economy in which decisions about what is produced and what is bought for consumption is strongly influenced by market prices rather than decided by the government.
Market research systematically gathering, recording and analysing data on the possibility of sales of a good or service.
Market segmentation grouping consumers into sections with similar characteristics, such as age, preferences, tastes, etc.
Marketing identifying and anticipating what the customer requires and then providing what they want.
Marketing mix a particular blend of price, product, promotion and place, designed to attract customers.
Maslow's hierarchy of needs a graded list of human needs. At the bottom are **basic** needs such as food and shelter. At the top are **self-actualisation** needs of individuals to be totally fulfilled in their lives. Most jobs meet lower level needs; only a few jobs enable people to have their higher needs fulfilled.
Mass marketing activities designed to appeal to the whole of a particular market rather than a smaller segment.
Mass production producing a standard product in very large quantities.
Mixed economy economies in which decisions are made through a combination of buyers and sellers deciding what to buy, produce and sell, coupled with some government interference such as taxing or subsidising the production of some goods.
Monopoly a single seller in the market.
Mortgage a loan that is made and secured on property.
Motivation the desire to achieve a particular goal, backed up by the drive to perform.
Multinational a company with its head office in one country, but operating in at least two countries.

N

Nationalisation the taking over of a business by the government.
Newly industrialised country (NIC) countries such as Brazil, Russia, India and China that are currently experiencing rapid industrial progress.
Niche marketing activities designed to reach and appeal to a particular segment of a larger market.
Non-current assets that stay within a business rather than being sold. Examples include building and machinery.
Non-current liabilities debts that have to be paid, usually after 1 year.

O

Objectives clearly defined ends towards which an organisation works.
Off-the-job training training not specifically related to carrying out a work-based task.
On-the-job training instructing employees at their place of work while they carry out their normal work-based activities.
Open question in a market research questionnaire, a question that allows respondents to answer in their own words.
Operations the processes involved in producing goods and services.
Opportunity cost the next-best alternative that is given up when a decision is made.
Organisation chart a diagram setting out the relationships between people in an organisation.
Overheads costs incurred in the daily running of a business that do not vary with the quantity of production.
Owner's capital finance provided by the owner of a business.

P

Partnership a business owned by two or more people, often carrying out professional work or a business service on a local scale.
Penetration pricing charging a low initial price to win market share.
Piece rate payment according to the number of units or pieces produced.
Pressure group a group or association formed to promote a particular interest or cause by influencing businesses and public policy.

Glossary

Price fixing groups of producers or sellers collaborating together to set prices rather than competing with each other.

Primary industry the first stage in a production process that uses natural resources (e.g. land for farming).

Primary data use of first-hand sources (e.g. asking questions directly of respondents).

Private company a company whose shares are not up for sale on a stock exchange. Buying and selling shares may only be done with permission from the Board of Directors.

Private benefit the benefit to an individual or firm of engaging in a particular activity.

Private costs the costs to an individual or firm of carrying out a particular activity.

Private sector the part of the economy that is owned by private individuals and organisations rather than the government.

Privatisation the switching of businesses from government ownership to private ownership.

Product life cycle the key stages in the life of a product, and how long the cycle lasts.

Productivity a measure of the output of a firm in relation to the inputs.

Profit the surplus left after all relevant costs have been deducted from income

Promotion money and effort dedicated to increasing the sales of a product.

Public limited company (plc) a company that is allowed to sell shares through the stock exchange.

Public sector part of the economy run and managed by a government.

Q

Quality fitness for purpose, when a good, service or process does exactly what the customer expects.

Quality assurance checking at the end of the line that the product meets a required standard.

Quality circle small groups of people who meet regularly to discuss work problems, usually with a leader.

Quota limitation on the numbers of items that can be exchanged between countries.

R

Ratio the relationship between one business variable and another (e.g. profit: revenue).

Recession two or more consecutive quarters (three-month periods) in which GDP is falling.

Regulation supervision of the way in which a business or organisation can run; setting limits and rules relating to its activities.

Retail the final link in the chain of distribution from manufacturer to end-user. A retailer holds inventories at a location convenient to the customer and provides a choice of products. Retail outlets include supermarkets, small shops and street-corner sellers.

Revenue the value of total sales made by a business within a period, usually 1 year.

Risk the possibility of not reaching a desired outcome. For example, in setting up a business there is a risk that the expected profits do not result from business activity.

ROCE (Return On Capital Employed) Businesses invest capital in new projects. ROCE measures the return on these investments as a percentage on the capital invested.

S

Secondary industry the stage in the production of goods concerned with making or using raw materials from primary industries.

Secondary research using existing information sources to find out something for your own research.

Security Offered by borrowers when money is loaned, for example allowing the lender to take possession of some of their property if they fail to repay the loan.

Selling seeking to persuade potential customers that the business has the appropriate solutions to meet their needs.

Share a unit of ownership of a company, held by a **shareholder**, who can own one or many shares in a company. Shareholders receive a share certificate showing how many shares they own.

Shareholders part-owners of a company, with shares in the company.

Skimming creaming off successive layers of the market by charging an initial high price and then lowering it.

SMART the qualities of well written objectives: Specific, Measurable, Achievable, Realistic and Time-related.

Social benefit the advantages of a particular activity to members of a society.

Social enterprise a business with mostly social objectives that reinvests profits to achieve its social aims.

Sole trader a business owned by one person.

Stakeholders people who have an interest in how an organisation or group is run.

Strategic decisions plans that have a major impact on the whole organisation.

Subsidy money granted by the state to keep down the price of goods.

Supply the availability to customers of goods and services

Sustainable development growth of society in terms of what is produced and consumed. The nature of this growth is that it can be maintained over a period of time and that it does not take place at the expense of people and the environment.

T

Tariff a sum of money that an importer or exporter has to pay to trade goods across borders.

Tariff barriers a tax on imports designed to protect producers in a particular country from foreign competitors.

Team people working together with a shared sense of purpose and commitment to achieve shared results.

Technology techniques involving the application of scientific principles to production processes.

Tertiary sector service industries concerned with providing value for people (e.g. postal services, insurance and banking services).

Total quality management (TQM) building quality into production at every stage in the production process, rather than checking for it only at the end of the line.

Trade union body recognised in law consisting of employees with common work interests who seek to further their collective interests through bargaining with employers.

Training enabling employees to develop the knowledge, skills and attitudes required to carry out the work needed to meet an organisation's objectives.

U

Uncompetitive practice carrying out activities designed to reduce the ability of competitors to compete, for example business agreeing with a buyer not to buy goods from a competitor.

Unfair dismissal loss of a job for reasons that are not acceptable in law.

V

Value added the increase in value of a product at each stage in production.

Variable costs costs which vary with the level of output (e.g. fuel costs, raw material costs).

Video conference a meeting that uses electronic connections so that participants in different locations can see each other and converse.

W

Website internet location providing information, advertising and details of an individual, organisation or topic, etc.

Index

A
accounts 144–51
acid test ratio 149
acquisitions 17
adding value 2, 3, 106, 110
advertising 12, 71, 94, 95, 100
   of jobs 56, 59
age and market segmentation 78
agriculture 7, 17, 112
aims (goals) 8, 9, 30–1, 34–5
annual general meeting (AGM) 22
annual reports 150, 151
appraisals 52, 60, **69**
appreciation of currency 174–5
apprenticeships 61
assets 130, **142**–3, 146–7
   and working capital 148, **149**
autocratic management 52, 53
automation 107, 113
average cost 115

B
B2B/B2C 96
balance sheets 142–3, 146–7, 148–9
   users of 150, 151
bar charts 84, 85
basic biological needs 40, 180
batch production 108–9
behavioural segmentation 79
benefits 46–7, **88**, 164–5
board of directors 22
bonus payments 44, 45, 107
boom, economic 156, 157, 158
brands 3, 34, **88**
break-even analysis 118–19
break-even charts 118
BSI standards 120–1
budget 178
business cycle 156–7, 158–9
business plans 12–13

C
CAD 112
CADCAM 112
CAM 178
capital 4, 24, 128–9
   and business type 20, 21, 25
     companies 22, 23, 25
   risking 26, 27
   start-up costs 126
   working capital 128, 148–9
   see also owner's funds
cash 134–5, 142, 148, 149
   and profit compared 138–9
cash flow 13, 18
cash flow forecasts 134–5
charities 178
charts and graphs 84–5
child labour 166, 167
CIM 113
closed questions 82
commission payments 44, 45
communication 66–71, 117
   and business location 123
communities 32–3, 162, 164–5
   and ethics 166, 167
   and objectives 11, 30, 35
companies 21, **22**–3, 24–7
   multinationals 172–3
competition 4, 29, 76–7, 170–1
   and business failure 18, 19
competitive pricing 91
computers 107, 112–13, 178
construction industries 6
consumer panels 83
consumers 18, 76, 94–5
   internet buying 96–7
   legal protections 100–1
   see also customers
contract of employment 64
corporate social responsibility (CSR) 167
cost of sales 136, 137, 140–1
cost-benefit analysis (CBA) 165
cost-plus pricing 91
costs 114–15, 118–19, 164–5
   of borrowing 132, 160
   and business ethics 166, 167
   and the internet 96, 97
   and location 122–3
   and pollution 162, 164
   and pricing 90, 91
   in production 110–17, 120, 157
   and profit 136–7, 139, 145
   of recruitment 56, 59
   start-up costs 77, 126–7
   of transport 92, 93, 122
   see also opportunity cost
credit cards 129, 133
creditors 146
currency and exchange rates 174–5
current assets 142–3, 146–7, 148–9
current liabilities 143, 146–7, **148**–9
customers 18, 33, 70, 98, 122
   B2C buying and selling **96**–7
   loyalty of 34, 89
   market segmentation of 78–9
   needs of 2, 74–5, 82–3
   see also consumers

D
data 82–3
debtors 146
debts 21, 26, 27, 134, 135
   on balance sheets 142, 143
   see also loans
decision-making 22, 118–19, 134–5
   ethics in **166**–7
   social costs/benefits 164–5
deindustrialisation 6
delegation 49, 51
demand 90
democratic management **52**, 53
denationalisation 8
depreciation of currency 174–5
deregulation 168
disciplinary procedures 55
discrimination 65
diseconomies of scale 117
dismissal 62, 63, 64–5
distribution 89, 92, 94
distribution channels 92
dividends 137, 140
division of labour 4–5

E
e-commerce 92, 93, 96–7
e-mails 67, 68, 70–1
e-tailers 92, 93
economies of scale 116–17, 171
economy 154–9
efficiency 112–13, 117, 136
elasticity of demand 90
electronic communications 67, 68, 69, 70–1, 123
electronic data interchange (EDI) 71
employees/labour 4–5, 62–5, 116
   and ethical business 166, 167
   legislation 62, 63, 64–5
   and location 122–3, 172
   and productivity 107
   recruitment 56–9
   as stakeholders 33, 151
   trade unions 33, 54–5
   training for **60**–1
employment/jobs 14, 40–1, 112
   classification of 7
   protection 29, 155, 158
   multinationals create 173
entrepreneurs 4, **8**, 10–11, 12
environment 162–3, 168–9, 173
   and stakeholders 32, 33
EPOS 113
equal opportunities 56, 57
esteem needs 40, 41, 46

Index

ethics 166–7
exchange rates 123, **174**–5
expansion 13, 127, 137, 157
exports 174–5
external communication 70–1
externality 179

F
factors of production 4–5
fair dismissal 62, **64**–5
fair trade 167
faxes 68
final accounts 146
finance 126–7, 132–3
   accounts 144–51
   balance sheets 142–3, 146–9
      users of 150, 151
   cash flow 13, 18, 134–5
   and economies of scale 116–17
   and the economy 154–9
   exchange rates 123, 174–5
   and sole traders 20–1
   sources of 25, 128–33
      government 14–15, 123
   see also costs; debts; ownership
financial benefits **164**–5
financial costs **164**–5
financial rewards see pay and benefits
financial statements 144–51
fixed assets 146
fixed costs 114–15, 118–19
   in start-ups 126
flat organisations 49
flat rate of pay 44, 45
flow production 109, 110
focus groups 83
forecasts 12, 134–5, 140
formal communications 68–9, 70
franchises 22–3, 25
fringe benefits 46–7

G
gearing ratio 131, 146
gender and market segmentation 78
global markets 76, 77, 170–1
   multinationals use 172–3
   see also overseas markets
global products 170–1
global warming 162
globalisation 77, 170–1
goals see aims (goals)
goods 2, 6, 120–1, 170–3, 174
   see also products; services
governments 154–5, 158–9, 168
   and business location 123
   grants and loans by 14–15, 131
   own public corporations 28, 77
   as stakeholders 33
   subsidies from 155, 161
   see also public sector; taxes
grants, government 14–15, 131
graphs and charts 84–5
greenhouse gases 162, 168
gross profit 136, 137, 140, 141
gross profit margins 144
growth, business 17, 19, 30, 127
growth, economic 156, 158, 159

H
health and safety laws 65, 102, 155
Herzberg's motivational theory 43
hierarchy of an organisation **48**–9
hierarchy of needs 38, **40**–1
hire purchase 130, 131
human resource management 52

I
imports 174–5
   see also tariffs
income 135
   of consumers 40, 76, 79
income statements 140–1, 144–5, 146, 150
incorporated businesses **22**, 24, 25
   and limited liability 26–7
incorporation 22
induction 60
inelastic demand 90
inflation 158
inputs 106–7, 112
   see also resources
interest 132, 133, 146
interest rates 132, 159, **160**
internal communications 68–9
international trade 174
   see also global markets
internet 67, 96–7, 123, 171
   see also technology
intranet 67, **68**, 69
inventory 110, 142–3, 146, 147
   computer control of 113
   and liquidity 148, 149

J
job descriptions 56, 57, **58**
job enrichment 39, 52, 107
job production 108
job rotation 39, 52, 107
job satisfaction 38–9, 52
job specifications 58, **59**

jobs see employment
joint ventures 23, 25, **103**, 133, 171
   and distribution 93
just in time (JIT) 111

K
kaizen 111

L
labour see employees/labour
laissez-faire management **52**, 53
language 67, 102
laws and regulations 154, 168–9
   and business location 123
   employment 62, 63, 64–5
   health and safety 65, 102, 155
   and marketing 100–1
   in new markets 102
   for start-ups 14, 15
leadership 50, 52–3
leadership styles 52–3
   see also managers/management
lean production 110–11
leasing 130, 131
legislation see laws and regulations
letters 70
liabilities 142, 143, 146–7
   and working capital 148, **149**
lifestyles 76
limited companies 22, 26–7
limited liability 21, 22, 26–7
line graphs 85
line production 109, 110, 111
liquid assets 148
liquidity 146, 148, 149, 150
liquidity ratios 148–9
loans 127, 129, 130, 131
   choice of finance 132, 133
   government-provided 14–15
   and interest rates **160**
   see also debts
location of business 78, **122**–3
long-term finance 128, 131
long-term liabilities 146
love and social needs 40, 41, 46

M
managers/management 48–53
   and accounts 150
   and the business cycle 157
   and economies of scale 116
   training for 61
   see also leadership style
managing directors 22, 48
manufacturers 92–3

Index

manufacturing 6, 7, 17, 122
   see also production
market economy 180
market orientation 82
market research 74–5, **82**–5
   and marketing strategy 98, 99
market segmentation 78–9
market share 16, 30–1, 145
marketing 74–5, 80–1, 100–1
marketing mix 86–99
marketing strategy 98–103
markets 12, 19, 76–7, 80–1
   distance to 122
   entering new markets 102–3
   global 76, 77, 170–1, 172–3
   overseas see overseas markets
Maslow's hierarchy of needs 38, **40**–1, 42, 46
mass customisation 108
mass marketing 80
mass production 42–3, **108**, 171
maturity phase 89
meetings 69
memos 68–9
mergers of businesses 17
microcredit/finance 128–9, 173
minimum wage 64
mixed economies 8
mobile phones 67, 68, 69
monopolies 100, **154**
mortgages 129, 131, 132, 142
motivation 38–9, 42–3
   and fringe benefits 46–7
   and leadership styles 52–3
   and productivity 107
multinationals 172–3

N

narrow span of control 49
nationalisation 8, **29**
needs
   of customer 2, 74–5, 82–3
   Maslow's hierarchy 38, **40**–1, 42, 46
   social enterprises address 31
net assets 143, 146, 147
net profit 146
newly industrialised country (NIC) 7, 14, 76
niche marketing 80–1
non-current assets 142, 143, 146–7
non-current liabilities 142, 143, 146–7
not-for-profit organisations 31

O

objectives 8, 24–5, 30–1
   of governments 158
   private sector 8, 34
   public sector 9, 28–9, 35
   of stakeholders 33
observation 83
occupation 79
off-the-job training 60
on-the-job training 60
open questions 82
operating cycle 148
operating profit 140
operations 106
operations management 106
opportunity cost 3, 5
ordinary shares 139
organisation charts 48
organisation types 20–9
outputs 16, 106–7, 112
overdrafts 129, 130, 131, 133
overheads 136–7, 145
   on income statements 140, 141
overseas markets 25, 76, 102–3
   joint ventures 23, 93, 133
   see also global markets
overtime rate of pay 44
owners 12, 19, 33, 150
   and profit 136, 138, 140
owner's funds (capital) 129, 130, 131
   on balance sheets 146, 147
   and growth 17
   see also capital
ownership 20–3, 25, 26
   of public corporations 28–9

P

packaging 88
partners 130, 150
partnerships 21, 24, 25, 27
pay and benefits 44–7, 54, 64
   and motivation 42, 43
penetration pricing 91
performance rates of pay 45
person specifications 56, 57, 58
personal selling 95
physiological needs 40, 41, 46
pictograms 84
pie charts 84
piece rate 44, 45
place 74, 86–7, 92–3, 98
place of sale, controls on 101
planning/plans 12–13, 19, 50
pollution 161, 162, 163

   legal controls 168–9
   as a social cost 164, 165
   and stakeholders 32, 33
preference shares 139
pressure groups 33, 168, 169
price elasticity of demand (PED) 90
price fixing 154
prices 74, 86–7, 90–1
   and competition 77
   controls on 101, 154
   and exchange rates 174
   extend product lifecycle 89
   in marketing strategy 98
   and profit margin 144
   reducing, in promotion 95
primary data 82–3
primary industry 6, 7
private benefits 181
private businesses 20–3
private companies (ltd) 22
private costs 181
private sector 8–9, 20, **34**, 136
   privatisation 29
privatisation 8, 28, **29**, 77
product life cycle 88–9, 99, 157
production 2, 3, 106–21
   costs of 114–19
   factors of 4–5
   lean production 110–11
   methods of 108–9, 112–13
   quality in 120–1
   scale of 116–17
productivity 106–7, 112
products 86–9, 98, 157
   global 170–1
   legal controls on 100
   market research for 74–5
   in new markets 102
   see also goods; services
profit 17, 25, 130, **136**–9, 138
   as an objective 24, 30, 34, 35
   on balance sheets 146, 147
   in decision-making 118–19, 164–5
   ethics may decrease 166
   and exchange rates 174–5
   on income statements 140–141, 150
   and interest rates **160**
   in the product life cycle 89
profit margins 18, 144–5
profit sharing 45
promotion 74, 86–7, 94–5
   extending lifecycle with 89
   in marketing strategy 98
   misleading 100
   and technology 97

Index

promotion of employees 43, 56
promotional pricing 91
public corporations **28**–9
public limited companies (plc) 22, 26
public relations 70, 95
public sector 8–9, 20, **34**
   aims and objectives 9, 28–9, 35

Q

quality 77, 90, **120**–1
quality assurance 120
quality circles 120
questionnaires 82–3
quick ratio 149
quotas 171

R

ratios 131, 144–5, 146, **148**–9
raw materials see resources
recession 156, 157, 158, 159
recruitment 56–9
redundancy 62–3
regional factors 5, 9, 123
regulation 168
   see also laws and regulations
relocation of businesses 122, 123
resources 2, 106–7, 112, 122
   over-use of 163
retail 92–3, 94
revenue 136, 140–1, 144–5
   see also sales
risk 26, 132, 138, 139
   and the business cycle 157
   and high gearing ratio **131**
risk-bearing economies of scale 117
ROCE (Return On Capital Employed) 145, 146
roles 48, 50–1

S

safety and security needs 40, 41, 46
salaries see pay and benefits
sales/sales revenue 134, 157
   in break-even analysis 118–19
   and pricing 90–1
   in the product life cycle 88–9
   and promotion 95
   see also revenue
scale of production 116–17
scientific management 42–3
secondary industry 6, 7
secondary research/data 82, **83**
security for loans **127**
segmentation 78–9

self-actualisation 40, 41, 46, 180
selling 18, **74**, 116–17
services 2, 6, 7, 107, 122
   in global markets 171, 172
   and lean production 111
   legal controls 100
   public sector 29, 35, 154
   quality standards for 120–1
shareholders 8, **17**, 22, 150
   finance from 17, 130, 133
   and liability 26–7
   profit for 33, 137, 139
shares 16, **17**, 130, 133, 139
short-term finance 128, 129
   sources of 130, 131
short-term liabilities 142, 143
size of business 16–17
skimming 91
slump, economic 156, 157, 158
small businesses 14, 16, 19
SMART objectives 30
social benefits 164–5
social class 79
social costs 162, **164**–5
social enterprises 31
social media and networks 97
social responsibility 167
sole traders 20–1, 25, 130, 150
span of control 48–9
specialisation 4–5
spending patterns 76
stakeholders 32–3, 164–5
   and accounts 142, 150–1
standards 101, 120–1
start-ups, business 14–15
   costs of 77, 126–7
   failure of 18, 19
stock 146
stock exchanges 23
strategic decisions 22
subsidiaries 16
subsidies 155, **161**
suppliers 33, 142, 150, 151
supply 92
surveys 38–9, 82, 83
sustainable development 162–3

T

takeovers 16, 17
tall organisations 49
target market 82, 83, 86, 98
targets, employee 45, 52, 60
tariff barriers 23, 102, **161**
tariffs 155, 171

taxes 155, 159, 160, 161
   for essential services 154
   and public enterprise 9
   for start-ups 14, 15
   see also tariff barriers; tariffs
teams 41, **69**
technology 67, 68, 69, 70–1
   and location 123
   and production 112–113
   e-commerce 92, 93, 96–7
   and overseas markets 103, 171
telephones 67, 68, 69, 71
tertiary sector 6, 7
time rate of pay 44, 45
total costs 114–15, 118–19
total quality management (TQM) 113, **120**
trade credit 129, 130, 131, 133
trade cycle 156
trade payables 18, 138, 146
trade receivables 18, 146
   on balance sheets 142, 143, 147
   as current assets 148, 149
trade unions 33, **54**–5
trading and profit and loss account 146
training 60–1
transport costs 92, 93, 122
trusts 154

U

uncompetitive practice 101
unfair dismissal 64
unlimited liability 20–1

V

value adding 2, 3, 106, 110
variable costs 114–15, 118–19
   wages as 126
venture capital 131, 132
verbal communication 69
video conferencing 68, **69**, 71

W

wages see pay and benefits
waste 161, 168, 169
   in lean production 110, 120
   and pollution 162, 163
websites 71, 92, 93, **96**–7, 103
wholesalers 92–3, 94
work see employment/jobs
workforce see employees/labour
working capital 128, 148–9
written communication 68–9, 70